The Gospel and the Greeks

About the Author

RONALD H. NASH   Dr. Ronald H. Nash is professor of philosophy and theology at Reformed Theological Seminary in Orlando, Florida. He joined the RTS faculty in 1991 after retiring from Western Kentucky University, where he served as professor of philosophy and department head for some twenty-seven years. Dr. Nash is a graduate of Brown University and received his Ph.D. from Syracuse University. He is the author or editor of more than twenty books, including *Beyond Liberation Theology, Winning the Battle in the World of Ideas, Poverty and Wealth, The Closing of the American Heart, Faith and Reason,* and *Choosing a College.* Dr. Nash has lectured at more than fifty colleges and universities in the United States, Great Britain, and the Soviet Union. He has served two terms as an advisor to the U.S. Civil Rights Commission and also serves as a fellow of the Christianity Today Institute.

The Gospel and the Greeks

Did the New Testament Borrow from Pagan Thought?

Ronald H. Nash

PROBE
Books

RICHARDSON, TEXAS

DISTRIBUTED BY WORD PUBLISHING
DALLAS   LONDON   SYDNEY   SINGAPORE

Copyright   © 1992 by Probe Ministries International

Library of
Congress
Cataloging-in-
Publication Data

Nash, Ronald H.
    [Christianity and the Hellenistic world]
    The gospel and the Greeks : did the New Testament
borrow from pagan thought? / Ronald H. Nash.
      p.   cm.
    Originally published under title: Christianity
and the Hellenistic world.
    Includes bibliographical references and indexes.
    1. Christianity and other religions. 2. Christianity
—Origin. 3. Rome—Religion. 4. Church history—
Primitive and early church, ca. 30–600. 5. Judaism
—History—Post-exilic period, 586 B.C.–210 A.D.
6. Philosophy, Ancient. 7. Gnosticism. I. Title.
[BR128.A2N36 1992]
230'.12—dc20   91-40299
                                      CIP

ISBN   0-945241-09-7

Place of Printing   *Printed in the United States of America*

Design   Book design by Louise Bauer
Cover design by John M. Henderson/JMH III
    Designs

92 93 94 95 96 97 98 99 / 10 9 8 7 6 5 4 3 2 1

What Is Probe?

Probe Ministries is a nonprofit corporation whose mission is to reclaim the primacy of Christian thought and values in Western culture through media, education, and literature. In seeking to accomplish this mission, Probe provides perspective on the integration of the academic disciplines and historic Christianity. The members and associates of the Probe team are actively engaged in research as well as lecturing and interacting with students and faculty in thousands of university classrooms throughout the United States and Canada on topics and issues vital to the university student.

In addition, Probe acts as a clearing house, communicating the results of its research to the church and society.

Further information about Probe's materials and ministries may be obtained by writing to Probe Ministries International, P.O. Box 801046, Dallas, Texas 75204.

Contents

Book Abstract

Many scholars still claim that early Christianity (first century A.D.) borrowed some of its essential beliefs and practices from the pagan religions and philosophical systems of that time.

Scholars in the fields of biblical and classical studies regard this claim as highly improbable; yet, the claim persists in fields (such as philosophy and history) outside those disciplines which are most familiar with the problem.

In this work, the author carefully examines the contemporary claims for Christian dependence on Hellenistic philosophy, the Greco-Roman mystery religions, and Gnosticism. He carefully discusses the historical-cultural milieu in which Christianity arose and during which its essential belief system gained ascendance. He finds the case for Christian dependence in the strong sense tenuous, demonstrating this by a philosophical and historical evaluation of the claims and evidence.

chapter one

Introduction

The author introduces the main issues dealt with in this book, including the claims of several modern scholars that early Christian beliefs were dependent on the pagan philosophical and religious belief systems prominent in the first century A.D.

This book offers an answer to one basic and extremely important question: Did early Christianity (the Christianity of the first century A.D.) borrow any of its essential beliefs and practices from the pagan religious and philosophical systems of the time? In other words, was first-century Christianity, the Christianity reflected in the New Testament, a syncretistic religion? During a period of time running roughly from about 1890 to 1940, scholars often alleged that primitive Christianity had been heavily influenced by Platonism, Stoicism, the pagan mystery religions, or other movements in the

Hellenistic world. Largely as a result of a series of scholarly books and articles written in rebuttal, allegations of early Christianity's dependence on its Hellenistic environment began to appear much less frequently in the publications of Bible scholars and classical scholars. Today, in the mid-1980s, most Bible scholars regard the question as a dead issue.[1] Since this is true, why should another book on the subject be necessary?

THE RATIONALE FOR THIS BOOK

I can think of at least three good reasons why this book is needed:

1. Even though specialists in biblical and classical studies know how weak the old case for Christian dependence was, these old arguments continue to circulate in the publications of scholars in such other fields as history and philosophy. For example, in a philosophy text that is still consulted, the late E. A. Burtt argued that the theology of Paul was dependent on ideas borrowed from the Hellenistic world.* Burtt claimed that Paul blended basic ideas from his Jewish background with various Hellenistic concepts. In his words, "Paul also absorbed from his Hellenistic environment, at Tarsus and elsewhere in the east Mediterranean region, religious ideas which dominated the non-Hebraic world of his day, and for which he felt a deep personal need. Greco-Roman culture at this time was swept by a host of so-called 'mystery cults,' promising personal immortality to their converts through mystic identification with a savior-god who had died and then triumphed over death by resurrection to a renewed divine life."†[2] The result of Paul's mature reflection about his own religious experience, Burtt concluded, "may be

---

*Burtt was, for many years, a professor of philosophy at Cornell University.

†As I will point out later, Burtt's paragraph can serve as a paradigm of most of the errors and oversimplifications to which theories of this type are prone.

briefly described as a remolding of the moralized cult of Yahweh, developed by the Hebrew prophets, into a mystery religion of personal salvation, in which the crucified Jesus of Nazareth appears not merely as the promised Messiah but also as a savior-god."[3]

Similar claims can be found in a widely used history of philosophy textbook by W. T. Jones, a professor of philosophy at California Institute of Technology. In *The Medieval Mind,* the second of a multivolumed set, Jones spends the first two chapters (about 70 pages) reiterating many of the old arguments about Christian dependence on the pagan mystery religions or on Hellenistic philosophy.[4] It is hardly to his credit that his one-sided discussion fails to inform the students who use his book of the weighty scholarly opinion opposed to his conclusions. In fact, Jones seems unaware of the extent to which his conclusions are disputed in scholarly circles.

The circulation of such one-sided and misinformed arguments is not limited to philosophers, however. In history books about the Hellenistic age, one occasionally encounters restatements of the old arguments about Christian syncretism. One example of such is *The Ancient World,* a textbook by Thomas W. Africa, a historian at the State University of New York at Binghamton.[5] In discussing the origins of early Christianity, Africa makes repeated assertions about its dependence on pagan systems in the Hellenistic world.[6]

These few examples of contemporary textbooks that persist in repeating claims and arguments that should have been laid to rest decades ago make it clear that there is still work to be done. The contemporary student needs to be reminded of this older debate and to be shown the errors of these claims and arguments.

2. But there is another reason for writing this book, namely, a renewed interest in the phenomenon of ancient Gnosticism. This interest grows

out of the remarkable discoveries of long-lost documents like the Dead Sea Scrolls and the Gnostic writings found in Egypt. It has taken years for this material to be translated and studied. Advocates of an early Christian syncretism, after going into hibernation when the weakness of their claims became generally known, have felt new life as they sense the possibility that some of these new discoveries may finally provide some of the evidence that their theories, to this point, have lacked. Consequently it is important that this book make available to nonspecialists the best up-to-date conclusions regarding these new discoveries.

3. My third and final reason for writing this book is the lack of a recent book for nonspecialists that provides an overview and summary of the entire debate over the alleged syncretism of early Christianity. Even if the old errors were not being circulated in recent textbooks and even if there were not renewed interest in the Gnostic movement, there is a need for one book that will review deliberations over this question since 1900 and bring the discussion up to date.

THE PLAN OF THE BOOK

Consideration of the one basic question—*Did early Christianity borrow its essential beliefs and practices from the Hellenistic world?*—will necessitate my addressing three subsidiary matters. These concern three proposed sources of the alleged syncretistic faith of first-century Christians. Each source will be examined in a separate part of this book. Part 1 will investigate possible influences of Hellenistic philosophy on the New Testament. Part 2 will discuss the relationship of early Christianity to the pagan mystery religions. And part 3 will explore the complex issues involved in the relationship between early Christianity and Gnosticism.

Each of the three major areas of alleged Christian dependence (that is, pagan philosophy, the mystery religions, and Gnosticism) gives rise to many additional questions. To consider only those associated with the problem of the mystery religions, these additional questions include:

1. What is a mystery religion?
2. What were the major types of mystery religion?
3. What were they like?
4. In what ways were the mystery religions supposed to have influenced early Christianity?
5. What scholars made allegations of dependence?
6. What reasons did they give?
7. And finally, do claims of Christian dependence on the mystery religions hold up under careful examination?

I mention these questions here at the beginning so the reader will have a clear idea of the difficult ground we have to cover. The importance of this study should be obvious. Many of the claims about early Christian syncretism imply that New Testament Christianity is false. Unless those charges are answered, Christianity must be either rejected or else totally recast.

PRELIMINARY DISTINCTIONS AND QUALIFICATIONS

1. I do not plan to say much about Christians who wrote in the years after the close of the New Testament canon—that is, after the end of the first century A.D. Traditional Christians regard the books of the New Testament as divinely revealed truth, truth that is therefore normative for Christian belief and practice.[7] The conviction that the New Testament was inspired by God and thus authoritative would be weakened considerably by evidence that the New Testament writers had derived any essential beliefs from their pagan milieu. But one's commitment to defend the New Testament writers against charges of essential accommodation to pagan ideas does not necessitate defending Christian

thinkers who wrote following the close of the New Testament canon. Prior to his conversion to Christianity, Justin Martyr (about A.D. 100–163) was a Platonist. After he became a Christian, a number of sub-Christian ideas could still be found in his thought. Origen (A.D. 185–254) believed in the preexistence of the soul, an obvious residue of Platonism, even after his conversion to Christianity. Even Augustine (A.D. 354–430), the greatest of the church fathers, continued to believe in the preexistence of the soul for several years after his conversion. The discovery of unbiblical or pagan convictions in postbiblical writers should not be surprising. As Gordon Clark cautions:

> While Christianity and the Greek philosophies, as systems, have no element in common, the Christians, as people, often held pagan ideas. They had been converted from paganism and could not divest themselves of familiar modes of thought all at once. Therefore when they came to expound and defend Christianity, they inconsistently made use of Platonism or Stoicism. By a long and arduous struggle these inconsistent elements were gradually removed from a few fundamental areas, and thus a purely Christian Nicene Creed came into being. But on other topics, and especially in cases of individual authorship, the struggle was not so successful. Then, too, as time went on, the attempts to escape pagan ideas and to preserve the purity of New Testament thought grew weaker, and, one might say, almost ceased.[8]

My major concern is with problems that appear to undermine the fundamental Christian conviction that the New Testament is a divinely inspired book.

2. I am also attentive to those Christian beliefs and practices that are essential. A belief is essential to Christianity if its truth is a necessary condition for the truth of Christianity. Such essential beliefs include the conviction that Jesus Christ was God incarnate, that He came to earth to die vicariously for the sins of the human

race, that His death was accepted by God the
Father as an atonement for human sin, and that
the efficacy of His sacrifice was attested by His
victorious resurrection from the dead. While it is
a bit more difficult to provide a formal definition
of an essential Christian practice, the obvious
examples are baptism and the Lord's Supper. If
someone could prove that early Christianity
borrowed essential elements of its Christology
from paganism, it is difficult to see how the truth
of traditional Christianity could be maintained.
If it should turn out that Christian baptism or the
Lord's Supper was borrowed from earlier pagan
rites, the consequences would be only slightly
less serious. In addition to these essential beliefs
and practices, the New Testament alludes frequently to nonessential beliefs and practices of
the early church that, not surprisingly, reflect
the fact that Christians belonged to a particular
culture. They often used terms reflecting a pagan
heritage. But as Gordon Clark points out,
"Since the New Testament was written in
Greek, it uses words found in pagan writings. . . . But the point in question is not the use
of words but the occurrence of *ideas*. . . . One
cannot forbid Christian writers to use common
words on pain of becoming pagans [emphasis
mine]."[9] We should avoid jumping to the conclusion that simply because a New Testament
writer used terminology prominent in some
pagan philosophy or religion, he used it in the
same sense or that his use proves his dependence on the pagan usage.

3. Even the presence of real parallels between
the New Testament and pagan literature does
not necessarily prove dependence.* Nor do
undeniable instances where a New Testament
writer is aware of pagan ideas and terminology
prove that he actually derived his concepts from
his pagan milieu. Informed and responsible

---

*I word my point in this way because, as my later
discussion will reveal, many alleged parallels turn out on
careful analysis to be spurious.

Christians do not believe that God dictated His revelation to human authors. They recognize that divine inspiration came to human writers whose writings reflect their distinctive backgrounds and education. It is one thing to discover that a New Testament writer like the anonymous author of the Epistle to the Hebrews was familiar with Hellenistic philosophy. But this interesting bit of biographical information does not necessarily prove that the writer was actually influenced by some alien system or terminology.

4. It is important to recognize different senses of the words *influence* and *dependence*. A casual disregard of these distinctions is responsible for much of the misinformation and faulty reasoning present in many discussions of the alleged Christian dependence on pagan sources. While I want to avoid getting too technical, there will be times when the need for clarity will force me to state my point in a technical way. This will be one of those times.

In regard to the subject of dependence, there are at least two varieties of what can be called strong dependence. One takes "B is dependent on A" to mean that A is a necessary condition for B. Translated into more ordinary language, this means that if a writer had not first known or believed A, he would never have come to know or believe B. This theory of dependence is operative when scholars argue that Paul's view of Jesus as a dying and rising savior-god *would never have occurred to him* if he had not first become aware of similar notions in the pagan mystery religions of his day.

The other way to view strong dependence takes the statement "B is dependent on A" to mean that A is a sufficient condition for B. Thus someone's knowledge of A or belief in A is the cause of his coming to know or believe B. If this second kind of dependence had been operative in Paul's work, then Paul actually came to believe Jesus was the dying and rising savior-god *because of* the pagan ideas he absorbed. To consider a nonbiblical example, it is sometimes argued that Charles Darwin did not "discover" his theory of evolution but actually plagiarized it from the work of earlier thinkers. If this were true, these earlier writings functioned as a sufficient condition for Darwin's own theory.

In contrast with these strong senses of dependence and influence, there are several weaker senses of the terms that need pose no problem for someone holding a high view of Scripture. To continue my use of Darwin as an example, suppose we assume that Darwin's theory was original with him, that he did not plagiarize the theory of evolution from the work of earlier thinkers. If this was the case, Darwin's claims about the importance of his discovery would not be diminished in any way by recognizing his extensive background of information, including all of his observations during the voyage of *The Beagle*. Anyone can absorb from his culture a terminology and background of ideas that may consciously or unconsciously form only the backdrop for significantly new theories. Or one might recognize that if he is going to communicate effectively with his contemporaries, he must use language and examples that will be understood by his audience. Many twentieth-century missionaries involved in translating the Bible for hitherto unevangelized people have found it necessary to accommodate their translations to the culture of their audience to facilitate better communication.* There is no question but that terminology and concepts from Hellenistic philosophy and religion appear in the New Testament Epistle to the Hebrews.† But simply to note this and, without any further analysis, conclude that Hebrews is therefore a

---

Accommodate is another word that can be used in either a strong or a weak sense. Accommodation may also occur either in essential or nonessential matters.

†Later in this book, I devote an entire chapter to the questions raised by this observation.

syncretistic work would be shoddy and simplistic scholarship. After all, Hebrews is at the same time the most Jewish and the most Greek book in the New Testament. We must ask about the author's intentions in using such language and concepts. Was he actually borrowing from his non-Christian surroundings? Or was he using concepts and language familiar to him before his conversion, because they could help him communicate better with an audience also familiar with these ideas and terminology?* Once again, the mere presence of parallels in thought and language does not prove any dependence in the strong sense. This is especially true in cases where the author appears to have used such concepts and language to communicate more effectively with a particular audience. While evidence of an early Christian dependence (in the strong senses noted above) on pagan writings or practices would create a serious problem for anyone holding a high view of Scripture, recognition of dependence or influence in one of the weak senses might only enhance our understanding of Scripture.

To repeat, the basic question examined by this book is this: Was first-century Christianity a syncretistic religion? Was early Christianity a synthesis of ideas and practices borrowed from different sources, some of them pagan? To the extent that key words like *dependence, influence, accommodation,* and *borrowed* are understood in a strong sense, my answer to this question will be an unequivocal *no*.

THE HELLENISTIC WORLD

The word *hellenistic* was coined early in the nineteenth century as a name for the period of history that began with the death of Alexander the Great in 323 B.C. and ended with the Roman conquest of the last major vestige of Alexander's

---

*This would be influence in the weak sense.

empire, the Egypt of Cleopatra, in 30 B.C.

Obviously if this were the exclusive use of the term, it would make little sense to talk about "Christianity and the Hellenistic world." But the fact is that the phrase "the Hellenistic world" is used to refer to the whole culture of the Roman Empire. While Rome achieved military and political supremacy throughout the Mediterranean world, it adopted the culture of the Hellenistic world that preceded its rise to power. Thus, while political control of the Mediterranean belonged to Rome, the culture continued to be Hellenistic.

One of the major characteristics of the Hellenistic world was a new kind of *cosmopolitanism*. More than ever before, the peoples and nations of the Mediterranean world were united. In an even more important sense than mere political union (as under the one government of Rome), they were united by a common law, a common language (Koine Greek) and an increasingly common culture. People could trade and travel more widely; people of different races and nations could converse in a common language; intellectual exchange was easier.

But along with the growing cosmopolitanism of the age was a new *individualism*. There was little room for individualism in the Greek city states prior to Alexander. This is evident in Plato's and Aristotle's political writings, which illustrate the subordination of the individual to the larger community that was the norm for their times. Even though Rome represented the greatest consolidation of political power to date, it also left more room for a growth of individualism. There was less emphasis on patriotism, for the simple reason that nationalism was less important. People tended to think of themselves less as some local group, whether national or racial, and more as Romans. Because of the difficulties involved in any individual man or woman identifying with such a massive empire, the very size and power of Rome added impetus to the rise of individualism. Individualism in religion was encouraged by the general inclusivism of the Roman religion. Even the insistence on the worship of the emperor was not regarded as inconsistent with other religious beliefs and practices. One major cause of the Roman persecution of Christians was the exclusive nature of Christian belief. Christianity simply did not tolerate the worship of any other God, including the emperor.

A third general trait of the Hellenistic world was *syncretism*. In fact, theologian J. Gresham Machen has described the Hellenistic age as "the age of syncretism *par excellence*."[10] The Hellenistic world contained an almost endless variety of combinations of religion and philosophy. Christianity began in a world in which the spirit of syncretism was king. Students of the history of philosophy know that gradually, during the Hellenistic age, most of the walls between the major philosophical systems began to break down. This is especially true in the case of Platonism and Stoicism from about 100 B.C. to A.D. 100. There was little to prevent an especially religious person from worshiping any number of gods that belonged to an equally large number of religions. As we will see, some have uncritically advanced the general eclecticism of the age as an important part of their argument that early Christianity was a syncretistic faith. One major flaw in this line of reasoning is early Christianity's uncompromising exclusiveness. There is only one God, it taught; those who worship any but the true God are lost. There is only one Mediator between God and man: Jesus Christ. Any who seek to approach the Father in any other way are lost. There is only one ground of human salvation, the death and resurrection of Jesus Christ. Those who seek redemption in any other way will perish. Thus evidence furnished by the New Testament suggests that early Christianity was an exception to the syncretism and inclusiveness of the Hellenistic age.

The Hellenistic world also spawned a revived interest in religion. Many writers have referred to the "Hellenistic quest for salvation." The Christian message did not come at first to an irreligious and spiritually unconcerned world. On the contrary, it came to a world that was yearning for salvation and a relationship with the divine.

> Christ appeared at the time when all the striving and hopes of all peoples were converging to a focus, when the vast majority of mankind were hungering for religious support, when East and West had been wedded, when men were expecting a new era, when the philosophy of Greece and the religious consciousness of the Hebrew were pointing toward a new revelation. Christ came at the one time in history when all civilised nations lived, as it were, under one roof, when the happiness of mankind depended on the will of one, when all were able to communicate in one language, when men were unanimous as to the perils and needs of the world, when there was peace on earth . . .[11]

MacGregor and Purdy note both negative and positive aspects of the Hellenistic quest for salvation:

> On the one hand there is the negative aspect — escape from those forces which hold man a helpless prisoner, whether it be from the mere weight of material existence, or from that fear of Chance's whim and Fate's inexorable decree which with its denial of free will was perhaps the chief root of ancient pessimism, or, to put the same thought otherwise, from the wheel of cosmic necessity to which man imagined himself to be bound, controlled by starry influences and subject to those demonic . . . "world-rulers of this darkness" . . . which loom so large in Apostolic polemic.[12]

As for the positive side to the Hellenistic search for salvation, "it is the achievement by the individual of his quest for eternal life, wherein the soul, akin by nature to the divine, lays hold of its true birthright. And here we touch the core of Hellenistic theology; the way to such salvation is through the knowledge of God."[13] Because of this widespread interest in salvation, there may never have been a more opportune time for the proclamation of the Christian gospel. As MacGregor and Purdy explain, "men everywhere were keenly awake to every new message of hope and eagerly prospecting for a 'saviour'."[14] Many students of the Bible regard this as the message of Galatians 4:4. Christ came just when the stage was set, when the time was ripe.

Once again, I warn, it is irresponsible for proponents of an early Christian syncretism to make too much of the Hellenistic concern for salvation. Early Christian writers welcomed this similarity as part of God's providential preparation of the world for the gospel. The Christian answer for the world's spiritual hunger was unique in the sense that it offered one exclusive way of salvation not amenable to accommodation to other religious systems. This exclusiveness gave the Christian way of salvation a measure of difficulty missing in all of the competitors of Christianity.

THE ROLE OF PRESUPPOSITIONS IN THE DEBATE

Human beings do not think in a vacuum. Their conclusions frequently reflect ultimate commitments to basic presuppositions that are often unstated and unexamined. While the traditional Christian readily acknowledges his fundamental commitment to the inspiration, truth, and authority of the New Testament, this should not lead him to deny or ignore evidence that appears to contradict his understanding of Scripture and the Christian faith. Rather, he should forthrightly test the alleged evidence. We will discover that the alleged evidence falls far short of proving the claim of early Christian syncretism. It is the proponent's own naturalistic presuppositions that bridge the gap between what the evidence actually supports and what the proponent of syncretism believes it supports.

The reader should be constantly on the watch for ways in which the skeptic's faulty evidence and reasoning are buttressed by his one controlling presupposition, that is, that orthodox Christianity is not true. For those with a skeptical approach to the facts, it is a simple matter to see dependence and influence where, in fact, none exists. For example, one frequently encounters in the literature a tendency to dismiss any disliked portion of the Gospels on the ground that it results from a Hellenistic influence on the Gospel writer. Thus, if one approaches the New Testament convinced of the impossibility of miracles, the presence of a miracle in the text can easily be disposed of as Hellenistic. If one is repelled by the New Testament doctrine of the atonement, charge it off as another intrusion of Hellenistic influence into the biblical text. A similar motivation can easily support the search for parallels for the virgin birth and the resurrection of Jesus. Many of the claims that we will encounter are by no means inferences that objective scholars have been logically compelled to draw from indisputable evidence. We will find many instances where scholars "found" exactly what they were seeking. Their research and their reasoning were controlled by a prior commitment to what could and could not be true.

We are seeking a more exact understanding of the relation between early Christian belief and the historical-cultural milieu in which that belief arose. The first area that we will examine is the prevailing philosophy of that time. Following that, we will turn our attention to the Hellenistic mystery religions and then to Gnosticism.

Part One:

Hellenistic Philosophy

chapter two

Philosophy From Plato to Middle Platonism

This chapter introduces the major systems of Hellenistic philosophy popular just prior to and during the establishment of early Christianity. Further, the author reviews the tenets of these systems, focusing on Plato, Aristotle, and Middle Platonism.

This chapter is the foundation of much that follows. It provides an introduction to the more important features of the major philosophical systems of the Hellenistic age. While many of the views to be examined are relevant to claims about an alleged Christian dependence on Hellenistic philosophy, to attain the necessary overview requires some consideration of theories that usually do not appear in discussions of early Christian syncretism.

If any Hellenistic philosophies influenced early Christianity, the place to look for them is the period of time between 100 B.C. and A.D. 100. If   27 the apostle Paul, for example, studied any philosophy as a young man, he would probably have read philosophers like the Stoic Posidonius (130–46 B.C.), whose writings have been lost and whose views are seldom discussed except in the most specialized courses on Hellenistic thought. It would be a mistake to think that Paul could have visited a corner bookstore and picked up a copy of Plato's *Dialogues* or Aristotle's *Metaphysics*.*

Philosophy during these two centuries (100 B.C.–A.D. 100) is, for the most part, characterized by its lack of originality, by its eclecticism, and by the transitional role it played in the overall development of philosophical systems. When German scholars in the nineteenth century began to write histories of philosophy, they coined names that make clear the transitional status of some of the Hellenistic systems. For example, they called some of the Platonists of this period Middle Platonists. As concerns the time from Plato (d. 347 or 348 B.C.) to Plotinus (A.D. 205–270, the most important representative of what is now known as Neo-Platonism), the relatively unnoticed Middle Platonists (100 B.C.–A.D. 100) are seen as representing only a transition from an important past to an important future (Neo-Platonism).

Stoicism between 150 B.C. and approximately A.D. 50 is also characterized by its transitional role between what is now called the Early Stoa (approximately 300 to 200 B.C.) and the Later Stoa, which includes the three best known Stoic authors—Seneca (A.D. 1–65), Epictetus (A.D. 50–138), and Marcus Aurelius (A.D. 121–180). While some aspects of Aristotle's philosophy (such as his view of God) played a minor role during the

---

*What we know today as the works of Aristotle are a result of editing and possible rearrangement some 250 years after his death. Aristotle's writings were effectively lost for several generations until published in imperfect form in 86 B.C. A much more accurate edition was published between 43 and 20 B.C.

two centuries we will examine, it took some time before Aristotelianism as a system gained much of a following.

The fourth major philosophical system of the Hellenistic age, Epicureanism, also lacked much of a following and can safely be ignored as a possible source for any New Testament ideas.* The final system that will be mentioned here is now called Neo-Pythagoreanism, a revival of certain ideas first circulated by a movement in Italy a century or two before Plato.

When I mentioned earlier the eclectic nature of Hellenistic philosophy during the centuries that interest us, I was referring to the fact that the sharp distinctions between the major schools of philosophy began to disappear during this period. This is especially true of Platonism and Stoicism. So-called Stoic philosophers evidence the influence of Platonism, while Platonists borrow from early Stoics.

The purpose of this part of the book is to examine the possibility that some of the New Testament writers borrowed essential concepts from Hellenistic philosophy. As already explained, if this did occur, the influence could have come either from representatives of first-century Platonism or from members of the Middle Stoa. Other possibilities include the Stoic philosopher Seneca, who was a contemporary of Paul, and the Jewish Platonist Philo, who lived from about 25 B.C. to about A.D. 50.

To assess more accurately the claims of an early Christian dependence on these philosophers of the day, it will be necessary first to go back to the original sources of these Hellenistic ideas. Before one can fully understand and appreciate later Platonism, for example, it is important to have an overview of not only which elements of Plato's thought were most important to members of the movement but also which

---

*The other three, of course, were Platonism, Aristotelianism, and Stoicism.

elements they modified. These major changes that took place in Platonism came to affect the Stoic philosophers as Stoicism and Platonism moved closer to each other. This is not the place to provide anything approaching a complete exposition of Plato or Aristotle or the early Stoics.[15] In its stead, I will offer only a brief overview of those aspects of the work of Plato, Aristotle, and the early Stoics that have relevance to our investigation of the relationship between early Christianity and Hellenistic philosophy.

THE PHILOSOPHY OF PLATO

During the centuries following Plato's death in 347/348 B.C., his system underwent a number of significant developments. While it is important for us to know what Plato himself taught, it is equally important that we know what happened to his system in the centuries between his death and the origin of Christianity. To whatever extent Paul knew of Plato's philosophy (and we have no direct evidence that he did), he would have known it through the mediation of thinkers like the Stoic Posidonius. To whatever extent the writer of the New Testament book of Hebrews knew Platonism (on this point, the evidence is more substantial), he knew it most likely through the mediation of Alexandrian Jews like Philo.

An Overview   While Plato's writings raise many difficult problems of interpretation, it is clear that he opposed seven prevalent beliefs of his day: atheism, empiricism, relativism, hedonism, materialism, naturalism, and mechanism. Plato's view of God is anything but clear. While some passages in his dialogues refer to "the gods," other texts support a possible movement of his thought toward an ambiguous monotheism. What is clear, however, is Plato's rejection of *atheism. Empiricism* is the belief that human knowledge can be derived exclusively through the bodily senses. Plato opposed empiricism throughout all of his writings, maintaining that it is impossible for the human senses ever to bring a human being to knowledge. Plato's own theory of knowledge is a form of *rationalism:* human knowledge is attainable only by reason. *Relativism,* both in the areas of knowledge and human conduct, was propagated in ancient Athens by philosophers known as Sophists. Plato believed in the existence of absolute and unchanging standards that preclude moral or epistemological relativism. Neither truth nor goodness nor beauty is relative. *Hedonism* is the belief that goodness and pleasure are identical. Plato objected to hedonism on the ground that since all men recognize the existence of bad pleasures, pleasure and the good cannot be identical.

The *materialistic* strain of Greek philosophy is seen most clearly in the work of Democritus (460–371 B.C.), a contemporary of Socrates and Plato, who is one of the founders of Atomism. According to Democritus, everything in the universe (including the human soul) is composed of different combinations of solid, eternal bits of matter called atoms. In contrast, Plato opposed all forms of materialism by arguing for the existence of an immaterial or ideal world that exists independently of the physical world we inhabit through our bodies. *Naturalism* and *mechanism* are also typified by the atomist system of Democritus. Naturalism in this sense is the belief that the natural, material universe is self-sufficient and self-explanatory. Everything that happens within the natural universe happens according to laws and principles that operate mechanically, without any presence of purpose or design. In contrast with the mechanism of the atomists, Plato's view of the universe was teleological in the sense that he believed that a divine intelligence and purpose is at work in the universe.

A. H. Armstrong not only summarizes Plato's

most important contributions to Western thought but also points out his relevance for later Christian thought:

> Everyone who believes in an objective and unchanging standard of morality governing public as well as private life, in the soul as immaterial and immortal and the most important part of man, in the governance of the world by Divine Reason and in the existence of eternal archetypes or patterns of all things that come to be and pass away, with which our behaviour and thought must conform, everyone who believes all this or an important part of it can claim to be in the tradition which goes back unbroken to Plato and Socrates: though the later development of the Platonic school and, much more, the transforming influence of Christianity have very much altered the content of these beliefs, yet the tradition of their development has been continuous. However much we may find ourselves in disagreement with Plato on really serious and vitally important subjects, the nature of God, the eternity of the cosmos, the uncreatedness of matter, the value to be attached to the body and to sense-experience . . . yet in other vital matters we are still of his school. As against the host of materialists, relativists, pragmatists, positivists, deniers of any eternal universal and objective truths or standards, who dominate so much of our thinking today and whose feebler predecessors were dealt with by Plato in his time, we who still hold to the older tradition are on Plato's side and he and Socrates are on ours, and we should reverence them as of the greatest among the founders and fathers of our thought.[16]

Plato's Theory of Forms

The heart of Plato's philosophy is his theory of Ideas, or Forms. Plato believed that human beings participate in two different worlds. One of these is the physical world that we experience through our bodily senses. The particular things (e.g., trees, rocks, and animals) that are part of this world exist in space and time. The other world in which we participate is more difficult to describe, a fact that helps explain why so many people doubt its existence. It is a world of immaterial and eternal essences that we contact through our minds. Plato's ideal world (sometimes called the world of the Forms) is actually more real than the physical world, inasmuch as the particular things that exist in the world of bodies are copies, or imitations, of their archetypes, the Forms.

For Plato, a Form is an eternal, unchangeable, and universal essence. Some of Plato's Forms are relatively easy to grasp. He believed that what we encounter in the physical world are imperfect examples of unchanging absolutes— including Goodness, Justice, Truth, and Beauty—that exist in an ideal, nonspatial world. Plato also believed that the world of the Forms contained exemplars of such mathematical and geometrical entities as numbers, circles, and squares. The imperfect circles that we encounter in the physical world are copies of one perfect and eternal circle that we know through our minds. It would be a mistake to think that Plato viewed these Forms as existing only in people's minds. The whole point to his theory is that these strange essences have an objective, or extramental, existence. They would exist even if no human being were thinking of them. In fact, it is only when human minds focus on the Forms that genuine human knowledge becomes possible. Truth, Beauty, Goodness, and the other Forms existed before there were any human minds.

Sometimes Plato wrote as though there were a Form, or archetype, for every class of object in the physical world. If so, this would mean that the world of the Forms contains a perfect dog, a perfect horse, and a perfect man, along with the other Forms already noted. This last group of Forms raised some difficult questions for Plato, and some interpreters think he wavered on this matter late in life.[17]

**Plato's Form of the
Good**

In books 6 and 7 of his *Republic*, Plato appears to teach that the world of the Forms contains one Form that is higher, or more important, than the others. The language Plato uses to describe this Form—the Form of the Good—has led some interpreters to conclude that he is talking about his God. Plato's first reference to the subject occurs in a discussion where Socrates points out that even though Justice and the other virtues are great, there is something still higher. "For you have often been told that the highest object of knowledge is the essential nature of the Good, from which everything that is good and right derives its value for us."[18] Plato has Socrates go on to make three points about the Good.

First, the Good is the ultimate end of human life. The highest goal of which man is capable is knowledge of the Good. Without knowledge of the Good, the knowledge of everything else would have no value. In comparison, all else pales in significance.

Second, the Good is the necessary condition of human knowledge. Without the Good, the world could not be intelligible and the human mind could not be intelligent. Just as light from the sun is necessary to turn potential color into actual color, so the light from the Good is necessary in order to make knowledge of the other Forms possible. If it were not for the Form of the Good, no human being could attain knowledge of any of the other Forms.

Third, the Good is also the creative and sustaining cause of the intelligible world, the world of the Forms. Plato actually suggests that if the Form of the Good did not exist in some prior capacity, nothing else would exist, including the rest of the Forms.[19]

It is impossible to say if Plato himself thought of this highest Form, the Good, as his God. But we do know that this is how Xenocrates (396–315 B.C.), one of his important early followers, understood the passage. Much later, the identification of God with the Good would become one of the more important innovations in Middle Platonism. Whatever Plato actually meant, his language conveys a meaning compatible with Christian truth. The Christian regards God as the creative and sustaining cause of everything else that exists. Unless God existed, nothing else would exist. The Christian also recognizes that God is the necessary condition of human knowledge. Unless human beings possessed the image of God,[20] they would be mere brutes, incapable of knowledge. And finally, the Christian views God as the supreme absolute and ultimate end of human life.

Plato's God

What was Plato's view of God? In spite of the interesting way in which Plato in his *Republic* seems to approach the notion of one supreme God, his assorted comments on the subject make it quite impossible to answer the question with certainty. For one thing, he never completely disavowed the gods of the Olympian religion, though this may have been due to fear of persecution as much as anything else.* Even so, his attitude toward the Olympian gods was very noncommittal, and it seems likely that he himself did not believe in them. What complicates our understanding of Plato's God is not the case of the Olympian deities; it is the presence of at least two other candidates for divinity that appear prominently in his writings.

In the *Timaeus,* one of his most important writings, Plato presents a myth about the creation of the world. He has Socrates ask if the world is eternal or if it had a beginning. He concludes that the world was indeed created.[21] But how, then, did the world come to be, and who or what created it? Socrates explains that "the maker and father of the universe" is

---

*One of the official charges for which Socrates was tried and executed was impiety towards the Olympian gods.

difficult to know and even more difficult to explain to others.[22] Plato goes on to describe the creation of the world as the work of a divine Craftsman, or Demiurge, who fashions the world out of a preexisting matter after the patterns he finds in the world of the Forms. Interpreters of Plato have puzzled over the relationship between the divine Craftsman of the *Timaeus* and the supreme Good of the *Republic*. No effort to combine these two figures into one being has succeeded. Does this mean that Plato leaves his readers with two candidates for God?

Complicating the situation even more are some statements Plato makes in his *Symposium,* where he mentions intermediary beings (which may be viewed as gods) between God and the world.[23]

Plato's Theory of Knowledge

The usual name for the branch of philosophy that studies human knowledge is *epistemology*. The first thing to note about Plato's epistemology is the intrinsic connection that exists between being (what is real) and knowing. How humans *know* is related to *what is*. We have already seen that for Plato there are two distinct kinds of reality: the world of particular things and the world of the Forms. Corresponding to these two kinds of reality are two distinct epistemological states: opinion and knowledge.

In order for a human being to have genuine knowledge (as opposed to some other epistemological state, such as a belief or hypothesis), the object of that knowledge must be unchanging. One can only have knowledge of that which is unchanging. But Plato believed that immutability is an exclusive property of the Forms. Every particular thing existing in the physical world is constantly undergoing change. Since our bodily senses afford us only an awareness of the changing particular things in the physical world, it follows then, for Plato, that our senses can never give us knowledge. If the only possible objects of knowledge are the unchanging Forms, and if the only way to apprehend the Forms is through our reason, it follows that knowledge must be a function of our minds. The most that we can attain through our senses is opinion, not knowledge. Given Plato's analysis of the meaning of knowledge, sense experience fails the test.

Plato's View of Body and Soul

Given Plato's denigration of the bodily senses, it is not surprising to find that he often suggests that the human body is less important than the soul. Plato advanced one of the most rigorous separations of the human soul and body to be found in philosophical literature. Not only do the soul and body differ with respect to corporeality (the soul is immaterial, while the body is material) and mortality (the body dies, while the soul is immortal); Plato's philosophy also retained the older idea—taught by the Orphic religion and continued by the philosophical movement known as Pythagoreanism—that the body is the prison house of the soul. In this view, the body is not simply inferior to the soul; it is a real hindrance as the soul attempts to progress toward truth and virtue. The attainment of both truth and virtue depends on achieving a degree of freedom from the influence of the body. The human body, for Plato, is really secondary and incidental to humanness. The real person is the soul, which can exist whole and immortal in total isolation from its corruptible body. The philosopher should not fear death, because dying only delivers the soul completely from the hindrances of the body and makes it possible for the philosopher to achieve his ultimate goal of truth and virtue.

Plato's Dualism

One way to get a handle on the essence of Plato's philosophy is to see it in terms of its basic *dualism*. Taking the points already discussed, Plato's system is marked by three kinds of dualism: *metaphysical, epistemological,* and *anthropological.*

1. The *metaphysical dualism* of Plato's philosophy is seen in his distinction between two worlds, or two levels of reality—the imperfect, changing, temporal, material world of particular things over against the perfect, unchanging, nontemporal, nonmaterial world of the Forms.

2. The *epistemological dualism* of Plato is evident not only in his radical distinction between sense experience and reason but also in his claim that sense experience always falls short of producing knowledge. True knowledge is attainable only by reason and, even then, only as human reason apprehends the Forms.

3. Plato's *anthropological dualism* is apparent in his radical distinction between body and soul. Just as there are two worlds (particulars and Forms) and two ways of apprehending these two worlds (sensation and reason), so man is a composite of two parts (body and soul). For Plato, the attainment both of knowledge and of virtue depends on lessening the power of the body over the soul.

**Unresolved
Tensions in Plato's
Philosophy**

Plato never completed his system. Like a fussy and temperamental artist, he continued to tinker with it until his death. Unfortunately, this meant that Plato never resolved a number of important questions that arise in his writings. He left his followers a number of loose ends. Many of the more important later developments in Platonism can be viewed as attempts to tie those loose ends together. Four of these unresolved questions have special relevance to developments within Platonism during the early Christian era.

1. The first loose end resulted from Plato's failure to remove the ambiguities in his view of God. We have already noted the two major candidates for Plato's God: (1) the supreme principle, which in the *Republic* he calls the

Form of the Good, and (2) the Craftsman, or Demiurge, who brings the material world into existence, as described in the *Timaeus*. Since he also applied the word *god* to intermediary beings who exist between the physical world and the supreme being, it is difficult to produce from his writings any systematic and coherent theory of God. Several attempts to produce such a theory have been made, of course. According to one of these, both the Good and the Craftsman may be considered to be God, because they are different ways of looking at the same being: the Good is God as He is in Himself, whereas the Craftsman is God in relation to the world. The demons, or intermediary beings, would then be forces, or powers, by which God deals with the world. A different interpretation sees the Craftsman, while still a divine being in some sense, as subordinate to the supreme being, the Good. The intermediary gods, on this view, would be lesser beings brought into existence either by the Good or by the Craftsman to serve as channels through which divine power might reach the world. Accordingly, these intermediary beings would be creatures with superhuman, not divine, properties and powers.

One of the more important features of Middle Platonism was its adoption of the view that there is only one God who should be identified with Plato's Good. Middle Platonism is often credited with originating the idea of intermediary beings between God and the world. But it should be remembered that the inspiration for the idea undoubtedly came from Plato's writings. The identification of God with the Good became quite common in Hellenistic philosophy. It appears in Philo, in most of the Platonists of the Christian era, and also (as discussed in part 3 of this book) in the Hermetic literature.[24]

It is interesting to speculate to what extent confusion over the relationship between Plato's two "gods" contributed to certain developments in Gnosticism. In some of its forms, Gnosticism taught the existence of two gods: (1) a good God analogous to Plato's Good and (2) a second God that it identified with the Demiurge of Plato's *Timaeus* as well as with the Jehovah of the Old Testament. The creator-god described in the first verse of Genesis was not the Gnostic's supreme good God but an inferior subordinate being who was, to put it as politely as possible, rather stupid. The Gnostics were radical dualists who believed that matter is evil. Thus, they concluded, any being who would bring a material world into existence could not be the supreme good God who will have nothing to do with matter. Whatever contact the good God has with the evil and material world takes place through intermediary beings.

2. A second unanswered question in Plato's system concerns the relation between God and Plato's world of the Forms. If the Craftsman of the *Timaeus* was Plato's God, then there is a sense in which the Forms are "above" God. At the very least, they exist independent of the Craftsman, whose creative power is limited by them. On the other hand, if Plato's God is the Good, then the other Forms are subordinate in some sense to God. Plato certainly teaches that the other Forms depend on the Good for their very existence. The importance of this question becomes evident when we consider the systems of Philo (who died about A.D. 50) and the Middle Platonists (who can be dated after Philo). Both systems contain the exciting suggestion that the eternal Forms are really ideas that subsist eternally in the mind of God. Centuries later, the greatest of the church fathers, Augustine, made this theory a cornerstone of his theory of knowledge.[25]

3. The third unresolved problem in Plato's system—noted here because of its role in the development of Hellenistic thought—is Plato's failure to bridge the great gap he established between his two worlds. How is the eternal, unchanging, immaterial, and ideal world of the

Forms related to the temporal, changing, corporeal, and imperfect world of particular things?
Given the radical separation between them in
Plato's system, how could any Platonist hope to
bring them together? This problem became
especially acute in the dualistic systems of the
Hellenistic age: Philonism, Middle Platonism,
and Gnosticism. Once we assume two radically
distinct types of reality—one immaterial and
good, the other material and evil—and once this
dualism is coupled with the belief that the good
God belongs to the spiritual world of light, how
can we explain the origin of the temporal world
and subsequent interactions between them? The
Hellenistic dualists bridged this gulf with a host
of intermediary beings that make it possible for
the good God to maintain indirect contact with
the material world.

4. Plato's system has one other loose end that
I will mention, namely, the lack of an adequate
answer to the question, how do human beings
actually attain knowledge of the ideal world and
of the good God who exists in that world?
Plato's claim that humans apprehend the ideal
world through reason does not really answer the
question; it only tells us where to look for an
answer. Throughout his life, Plato sought an
answer in several different myths and metaphors. One of these is his famous allegory of the
cave (*Republic* book 7), but, like most of his
efforts, it ends up using unanalyzed metaphors
like "seeing with the eyes of the mind." In some
of his middle dialogues, such as the *Meno* and
Phaedo, he suggested an answer based on the
myth of reincarnation. If reincarnation were
true, then presumably the immortal human soul
would have to dwell somewhere between incar-
nations (between the death of one bodily existence and rebirth in the next). If we assume that
during these intervals the soul rises to the world
of the Forms, it would be possible for the soul,
unencumbered by its bodily prison, to see or
view the Forms as they really are. Of course,

once the soul descended into another body, it would forget its vision of the Forms. But assorted experiences in life could bring some people to the point where a dim memory or recollection of the Forms could make knowledge possible. Many scholars doubt that the mature Plato meant this story to be understood literally. This doubt is supported by Plato's failure to utilize the doctrine of recollection in his later writings.

A clue to Plato's possible dissatisfaction with all of his earlier attempts to answer this problem may appear in the complicated argument of one of his dialogues, the *Parmenides*. In this, his most puzzling work, Plato describes an imaginary conversation between a very young Socrates and Parmenides, the greatest of the pre-Socratic philosophers. Parmenides challenges Socrates' belief in the theory of the Forms by using a series of arguments that Socrates apparently is unable to answer.* Our present question arises out of one of these arguments. Parmenides tries to get the young Socrates to see that once he admits a radical disparity between the world of the Forms and the world of bodies, he is faced with a whole series of problems. For one thing, Socrates admits that human beings are bound, by their bodies, to the lower world. But the only objects of true knowledge exist in the higher, nonmaterial world. If humans are stuck "down here" and the only possible objects of knowledge are "up there," how can any human being ever know anything? Moreover, God is "up there," in the world of the Forms. Consequently, Socrates' doctrine (which is really Plato's) also implies the impossibility of any human knowledge about God. And, as if this were not bad enough, God, who dwells in the world of the Forms and who has perfect knowledge of all the

---

*Plato often used Socrates as a spokesman for his own ideas, especially in his later writings. It is quite clear that the historical Socrates did not hold to the theory of the Forms; the concept was Plato's.

Forms, is precluded from knowing anything that exists in the physical world. And since human beings exist in the physical world, this means that God cannot possibly have knowledge about any human being! While Socrates agrees that depriving God of any knowledge at all would be a monstrous thing, he offers no escape from the skeptical trap laid by Parmenides.[26]

In the work of later Platonists, this aspect of Plato's system evolved into a kind of general agnosticism with regard to the nature of God. As Philo, the Middle Platonists, and the Gnostics saw it, the good God is completely transcendent and is thus essentially unknowable. The earliest Christians, however, had a far different view. "In the past," they believed, "God spoke to our forefathers through the prophets at many times and in various ways, but in these last days he has spoken to us by his Son, whom he appointed heir of all things, and through whom he made the universe."[27]

Obviously, this chapter has provided only the sketchiest account of Plato's philosophy. It necessarily ignores many important aspects of Plato's philosophy, such as his ethics and his political theory. Once again, our concern is not simply to understand the Plato of the fourth century B.C. but to grasp the essential elements of that system that achieved prominence in Hellenistic philosophy between 100 B.C. and A.D. 100.

THE MODIFICATION BY ARISTOTLE

The fact that my discussion of Aristotle is so brief and appears as merely a section of a long chapter on Plato and Platonism is a sign neither of a negative bias nor of disrespect for Aristotle's unquestioned significance in the history of philosophy. It is instead a reflection of this book's primary concern with those ideas and movements that are alleged to have had a formative influence on the writers of the New Testament. As important as Aristotle is for the history of philosophy in particular and the history of Western civilization in general, I know of no one who has found any evidence that he had a direct influence on the New Testament. He did come to have an influence on early Christian thinkers after the first century because of elements of his thought that became a part of Middle Platonism. For several centuries after his death in 322 B.C. , his influence was spotty. This resulted largely from the fact that his writings became so inaccessible as to be almost forgotten until they were rediscovered, edited, and published in the late first century B.C. The school of Aristotle (the Peripatetic school) was less interested in philosophical speculation than in more specialized scientific studies. My brief discussion of Aristotle will concentrate on some of his more important disagreements with Plato (as they pertain to the interests of this book) and the doctrines that later Platonists of the Hellenistic Age attempted to make a part of their theology.

One way to approach Aristotle's philosophy is to view it as a development of what Plato began. In a sense, the essence of Aristotle's philosophy was a rejection of Plato's more radical dualism. Aristotle rejected Plato's metaphysical dualism, namely, Plato's separation of the Forms from the material world. Aristotle objected to Plato's epistemological dualism, which had set reason in oppostion to experience as an avenue to knowledge. And Aristotle replaced Plato's anthropological dualism with a holistic, or unitary, view of human beings. I will comment briefly on each of these three points before concluding my treatment of Aristotle with an examination of his view of God.

Aristotle's Rejection of Plato's Metaphysical Dualism

As we saw, Plato's primary reality was the unchanging world of Forms that exists separate, or apart from, the world of particular things. For Plato, the most important things that exist belong, not to the earthly world of bodies, but to the strange, spaceless, timeless world of the

Forms. As Plato himself recognized in his

Parmenides, the most serious problems with his theory result from the extreme separation between his two worlds. Aristotle repeated many arguments found in the *Parmenides** against the separate existence of the Forms. To these he added the new charge that the world of the Forms is a useless duplication of the physical world. Aristotle believed he could avoid introducing this unnecessary duplication of the one and only world that exists and still explain everything Plato tried to explain with his separate Forms. The central issue in Aristotle's disagreement with Plato's theory of the Forms was Plato's insistence on their separate existence. As things turned out, Aristotle continued to believe that Forms or universals exist. He also believed that the Forms were the only proper objects of human knowledge. What Aristotle did—to describe his move in the rather crude way some professors adopt—was to bring Plato's Forms down to earth. Aristotle brought Plato's two worlds together. Although Forms exist, they exist in this earthly world as part of the particular things that constitute the world.

Whereas Plato's primary reality was the separate world of the Forms, the primary reality for Aristotle was this world of particular things. Plato's thinking was always directed upward and outward toward the ideal world. Because Aristotle's attention was directed toward this world, one residual benefit of his approach is the extent to which it encourages the development of scientific thinking. Within this world, the primary reality is what Aristotle called a substance. By substance, Aristotle meant any given thing that exists or has being. Hence, the chair I am sitting on, my typewriter, and the paper on

*It is interesting to speculate whether Plato, the teacher, first heard some of those objections from Aristotle, the student. Aristotle's arguments against Plato's theory appear in his *Metaphysics,* Book I.

which these words are written are all substances. Anything that has being is a substance.

Aristotle believed that every being, with the exception of God and some other god-like beings, is a composite of two factors that he called Form and Matter. To put this distinction in its simplest possible terms, the Matter of any given substance is whatever it happens to be made of. The Matter of the chair on which I am presently seated happens to be wood, but it could just as easily have been metal or plastic. The Form of any given substance is the set of essential properties that makes it the kind of thing it is. Like Plato's Form, Aristotle's Form is an unchanging essence. But unlike Plato's, Aristotle's Form is an essential part of the substance it composes. For our purposes in this book, there is no reason to pursue the intricacies of Aristotle's theory any further. His doctrine of substance, as constituted by Form and Matter, gains relevance for our study of Hellenistic philosophy because of its contribution to his peculiar theory of God.

**Aristotle's Rejection
of Plato's
Epistemological
Dualism**

Aristotle certainly recognized the difference between reason and sense experience; who doesn't? But whereas Plato denigrated the human senses and argued that they could never supply human beings with knowledge, Aristotle's account of human knowledge is more complex. For one thing, once Aristotle rejected Plato's doctrine of two separate worlds, he was released from Plato's major reason for grounding human knowledge on reason alone. According to Plato, the bodily senses bring humans into contact only with the things that exist in this world of particulars, and no particular can ever be a sufficient object of true knowledge; thus it is obvious why Plato was the kind of rationalist he was.[28] But in Aristotle's system, the Forms (which for Aristotle continue to be the only proper objects of knowledge) are not in some other world where they can only be apprehended by reason. The Forms exist as essential parts of the particular things that we apprehend through our senses. Thus, Aristotle rejected Plato's extreme disjunction between reason and sensation, regarding them instead as integral parts of the knowing process. The way in which Aristotle explained what experience and reason contribute to human knowledge turned out to be extremely significant in Hellenistic philosophy.

For one thing, Aristotle distinguished between "soul" (*psychē* in Greek)* and "mind" (*nous*). He then drew a distinction between two aspects of the human mind, calling them the passive intellect and the active intellect.[29] There is a part of the mind, Aristotle taught, that is *passive* in the sense that it *receives* information from the senses. Another part of the mind is *active* in the sense that it *acts* upon that which is received by the passive intellect. Aristotle explained our knowledge of the world as a product of the interaction of these two aspects of *nous*. The physical world, as we have seen, is the only world that exists for Aristotle. Obviously our knowledge of chairs and mountains and trees and humans is mediated by sensations that we have of those objects. The sensed object (a tree, for example) produces an image (phantasm) within the mind of the perceiver. This image of a sensed object is received by the passive intellect. But this sensible image of a particular thing is not yet knowledge; it is only potential knowledge. What is needed to turn this potential knowledge into actual knowledge is some additional process that is performed by the active intellect. The active intellect abstracts from the particular sensible image the Form, or universal element, that alone can be the object of knowledge. Human knowledge, therefore, has two necessary components: the passive intellect,

*The difference between Plato's and Aristotle's use of "soul" will be examined in the next section of this chapter.

which receives information from the senses, and the active intellect, which alone performs the crucial function of abstraction that isolates the Form of the particular thing that has been sensed.

Aristotle went on to say some very mysterious things about the active intellect, things that gave later interpreters much difficulty. For instance, he declared that the active intellect is "separable and immortal." Coming from Plato, such words would not have raised so much as an eyebrow. But, scholars were convinced, the entire drift of Aristotle's psychology was away from a Platonic soul that could exist forever in separation from the body. What then did Aristotle mean when he referred to an active intellect present in every human soul that is both separable and immortal? There have been three major attempts to interpret Aristotle's doctrine of the active intellect in a way that would avoid any contradiction in his system.

1. About A.D. 200, Alexander of Aphrodisias, greatest of the Aristotelian commentators, identified Aristotle's idea of the active intellect with God. According to this interpretation, the active intellect, or light within the soul that makes knowledge possible, would not be a part of the individual human soul but a presence of God within the soul. As an interpretation of Aristotle, Alexander's view must be rejected because of its obvious inconsistency with Aristotle's clear emphasis on the transcendence (otherness) of God.

2. During the Hellenistic Age, Plotinus interpreted the active intellect as a cosmic principle of intelligence to which every human intellect is related. At death, the intellects of individual human beings are absorbed back into the cosmic mind (*nous*), which is eternal and impersonal. Later, Plotinus's view appeared in the thought of such medieval Arabic Aristotelians as Averroes and the Christian Averroists whom Thomas Aquinas (1225–1274) debated. As Aquinas would go on to show, this doctrine is incompati-

ble with Christianity because it leads to a denial of personal immortality.

3. The third major interpretation of Aristotle's doctrine of the active intellect was proposed by Aquinas himself as an alternative to the heretical teachings of certain Christian disciples of Averroes at the University of Paris. Aquinas identified the active intellect with something individual and particular in each human being. If Aquinas was right and the active intellect is a separate part of each human mind, then Aristotle's claim that the active intellect is both separable and immortal could only mean that the great Aristotle believed there is something within human beings that is immortal. The major difficulty with Aquinas's interpretation—which should be kept distinct from its merit as a separate theory—is its obvious conflict with the picture of humankind presented in Aristotle's work on psychology, *De Anima*.

For this reason, I concur with those who argue that the second interpretation of the active intellect, the one associated with Neo-Platonism and medieval Averroism, is most likely correct.[30] As we shall see, later Platonists will put Aristotle's notion of a cosmic intelligence to good use as they gradually merge elements of Aristotelianism and Stoicism with Platonism.

Aristotle's Rejection of Plato's Anthropological Dualism

Aristotle also rejected Plato's radical separation between soul and body. Aristotle's understanding of human nature (which includes his view of the relationship between body and soul) is one of the more complex parts of his system. But this much is clear: Aristotle stressed a holistic, or unified, view of human beings. Humans are not a composite of two radically different substances—soul and body. They are instead a holistic unit; both body and soul are essential aspects of a human being.

Aristotle's use of the word *soul* is quite different from Plato's. When Plato talked about the soul, he meant the essential and immaterial part of a human being—the seat of intelligence and the cause of motion. Aristotle used *soul* as a synonym for *life*. Once this is grasped, it becomes easier to understand what Aristotle meant when he said there are three levels of soul, or life: the vegetative, the sensitive (or animal), and the rational. Plants possess life, or soul, but they lack the higher powers of life that we find in animals and in humans. Animals manifest the basic life functions that go with the vegetative soul, but they are also capable of the higher functions of life that Aristotle associates with the sensitive soul. For one thing, they are capable of sense perception. But humans possess all three levels of soul. Like plants and animals, humans carry on basic life processes, such as digestion and respiration. Like animals, humans are capable of sense perception. But unique to human beings is the capacity for knowledge that is the function of the rational soul. Hence, unlike Plato, Aristotle drew an important distinction between soul and mind.

What is Aristotle's view of the relationship between the human soul and body? This is not an easy question to answer. It is clear that Aristotle thought the relation was much closer than did Plato. But interpretations of precisely what Aristotle meant have ranged from positions that see him as a precursor of behaviorism to views that present his position as an anticipation of the New Testament's holistic view of human beings. I myself lean to the latter view.[31]

Aristotle's View of God

Aristotle was not an especially religious man. His God did not fulfill any particularly religious function; in other words, Aristotle did not worship or pray to his God. Aristotle believed in a supreme being because he thought there were certain things about the world that could not be explained without the existence of a God. His God was a metaphysical necessity, a concept required lest the rest of his system contain some huge holes. His system forced him to questions that he could not answer without postulating the existence of a perfect being who is the Unmoved Mover of the universe. Aristotle believed that there had to exist an uncaused and unchanging being who is the ultimate cause of everything else that exists. If this ultimate cause itself moved or changed in any way, it could not then be the *ultimate* cause, since we would be forced to ask why it changed and what changed it. Because of Aristotle's earlier discussion of Form and Matter, he was forced to conclude that the ultimate cause of the universe had to be Pure Form unmixed with any Matter. Matter, Aristotle thought, is synonymous with potentiality. But potentiality implies the possibility of change and hence imperfection. Therefore, Aristotle's God would have to be Pure Actuality, in other words, Form without Matter.

Now this doctrine of God as Pure Form has raised all kinds of problems in the histories of philosophy and theology. For one thing, what can a God who is Pure Form—the Unmoved Mover of the universe—*do?* He cannot go for a walk or preach a sermon, because He does not have a body (He lacks any Matter). He cannot do anything that entails change in His own being or knowledge, because He is perfect and incapable of change.[32] To shorten and simplify a rather long and complex argument, it turns out that the only thing Aristotle's perfect and unchanging God can do is think. But since He is immutable perfection, it follows that all He can think about must also be perfect and unchanging. But this means that He can think only about Himself! We noticed how Plato's reflections about God led many of his followers to a concept of an unknowable, transcendent God. Aristotle's reflections have brought us to the same spot. Once again, we are back to the concept of a radically transcendent, wholly other, God who, it appears, can have no direct, personal, and essential relationship with people or the world.

FURTHER DEVELOPMENTS IN PHILOSOPHY

What is the significance of all this? While one must look very hard to find much of an Aristotelian influence in Hellenistic philosophy between 100 B.C. and A.D. 100, some elements of Aristotle's system gradually entered the mainstream of Hellenistic thought through the back door. One sign of this influence is the radical transcendence of God in the writings of Philo, of the Middle Platonists, and of many of the Gnostics. By the third century A.D., Plotinus and other Neo-Platonists effected a more complete synthesis of Platonism and Aristotelianism. Although the dominant philosophical movements of the centuries we are studying were Platonism, Stoicism, and mixtures of the two, an understanding of Aristotle's system is necessary to complete the picture.

Middle Platonism

The philosophers who are usually mentioned in discussions of Middle Platonism include Plutarch (A.D. 45–125), Albinus (second century A.D.), Apuleius (born around A.D. 125), and Atticus (active around A.D. 176). Two pre-Christian thinkers—Antiochus (130–68 B.C.) and Eudorus of Alexandria (active around 25 B.C.)—are sometimes included in treatments of Middle Platonism, though they are usually regarded as precursors of the movement. The name Middle Platonism is a modern invention that, among other things, reflects a common prejudice that members of the movement were less important, transitional thinkers who helped prepare the way for the great Plotinus (died in A.D. 270) and the much more important movement called "Neo-Platonism." Since the Middle Platonists from Plutarch on did their writing after the close of the New Testament canon, there can be no question that they had any influence on it. But since their work reflects what was going on a generation or two before them, and since some of their themes reappear in other movements of the time (Philo, the Christian Gnostics, the Hermetic literature), they deserve at least a brief mention.

Middle Platonism is terribly difficult to reconstruct. Only the writings of popular thinkers have survived.* Our earlier discussion of Plato contained several suggestions of how the Middle Platonists sought to resolve unanswered questions in Plato's philosophy. For one thing, they identified the Supreme Mind, or God, of their system with Plato's Form of the Good. A. H. Armstrong explains how their view of God was central to their position:

> The first and in many ways the most important of [Middle Platonism's] distinctive theological doctrines is the placing of a supreme Mind or God at the head of the hierarchy of being, as the first principle of reality. Of this Supreme Mind the Platonic Forms are represented as thoughts; they are not only its content and the object of its thinking, but it is actually their cause.[33]

A second major innovation of Middle Platonism was its interpretation of Plato's Forms as ideas in God's mind. Albinus went further, identifying Plato's Good both with Plato's Craftsman and with Aristotle's Pure Form. From Aristotle, the Middle Platonists appear to have borrowed a rather extreme emphasis on the transcendence of God.[34] This led to a belief in God's essential ineffability, or unknowability.

Middle Platonism was primarily not an abstract philosophical system but a system of theology and a religion. "The religion of a Middle Platonist consisted of a remote intellectual devotion to the remote Supreme, to the vision of whom he hoped to attain in the next life and perhaps for a few rare moments in this,

---

*Plutarch wrote in Greek, whereas Apuleius wrote in Latin.

combined with a vigorous practice of the normal pagan piety towards the inferior gods, the star-gods and the other deities of mythology and public cult, who administered the affairs of the visible universe and with whom in this life we were most closely concerned."[35] They developed a theology that attempted to synthesize what Plato and Aristotle had taught about God and the universe. Locating the Forms in the mind of God, they merged Plato's Forms, Plato's Good, and Aristotle's divine Mind into one system. As imperfect as the product of their efforts may have been, it laid an important foundation for significant developments that would be made by such later thinkers as the pagan Plotinus and the Christian Augustine. But these influences obviously do not imply any influence on New Testament writers.

Neo-Pythagoreanism

Other currents present in the Hellenistic world contributed to the development of the ideas we are tracing. Therefore, a few brief comments about Neo-Pythagoreanism are in order. As its name implies, this was a revival of an older movement that appears to have died out in the fourth century B.C. The old Pythagoreans were a strange group of people who combined a keen interest in, and mystical reverence for, mathematics with a scientific curiosity about the role of number in the universe. They lived together in religious brotherhoods that believed in the transmigration of the soul and followed a strange set of moral rules that often provide a few laughs for students of ancient philosophy. Pythagoreanism had a definite influence on Plato.

Neo-Pythagoreanism was equally strange, but in rather different ways. A. H. Armstrong explains:

> Neo-Pythagoreanism might mean nothing more than astrology, occultism, and twaddle about the mysterious properties of numbers. But it might also

be quite a serious philosophy, and from Eudorus the eclectic Platonist of Alexandria down to Numenius at the end of the second and beginning of the third century A.D. we meet philosophers, sometimes calling themselves Platonists, sometimes (like Numenius) Pythagoreans who emphasize certain doctrines which can be regarded as characteristic of this revived Pythagoreanism.[36]

The metaphysical beliefs of Neo-Pythagoreanism are often indistinguishable from Middle Platonism, and this has resulted in some thinkers being placed in both schools. Apparently beginning in Alexandria, Neo-Pythagoreanism maintained the extreme body-soul dualism that Plato had borrowed from the older Pythagoreanism. Neo-Pythagoreans borrowed heavily from Platonism, Aristotelianism, and Stoicism. This is not to say that the school produced one official synthesis from these various sources. Rather, individual Neo-Pythagoreans borrowed different elements or emphasized different points in producing their own particular synthesis. The major historical significance of this movement appears to lie in its development of a divine hierarchy composed of an unknowable first God at the top, then a second God (the Demiurge), and finally the world. This view exerted an important influence on later Neo-Platonism. Neo-Pythagoreanism also had some connection with the Hermetic literature that we will examine in part 3.

CONCLUSION

This completes our survey of the philosophical background required to evaluate claims that early Christianity was a syncretistic religion. The rest of part 1 will deal with the alleged influence of Hellenistic philosophy on the early development of Christianity. Thus, in chapter 3 I will examine the most frequently encountered charges that Paul was influenced (in the strong sense) by aspects of Platonism. Chapter 4 will consider allegations of the presence of a Stoic influence in the New Testament. In chapter 5 the focus will be on the important New Testament use of the term *logos,* which functioned as a technical term in Stoicism and in the system of Philo. And finally, chapter 6 will conclude part 1 by investigating claims about the presence of philosophical concepts and terminology in the Epistle to the Hebrews.

chapter three

Paul and Platonism

It is frequently claimed that the writings of the apostle Paul in the New Testament exhibit Platonic dualism. This chapter examines those allegations in light of the available evidence.

Claims about a Platonic influence on the New Testament used to be common. William Fairweather's book *Jesus and the Greeks* typifies the form these allegations took during the 1920s.[37] While the number of publications making such claims began to drop after the 1920s, they were still widespread during the 1930s.[38] By the 1960s, however, many New Testament scholars, such as Frederick C. Grant, were conceding a philosophic influence "only in certain rare passages" of the New Testament.[39] But apparently news of the growing skepticism about any philosophical influence (in the strong sense) on the New

57

Testament was slow in reaching scholars in other fields. American philosopher W. T. Jones, already mentioned in chapter 1, continued to advocate a strong Platonic influence in the writings of Paul.[40]

ALLEGATIONS OF PLATONISM IN PAUL

This chapter will examine the arguments for the view that Paul borrowed from Platonism or was influenced by it. By the time we are finished we will not only understand better why such claims are seldom made any more; we will also have cause to marvel at why any careful student of the New Testament ever thought the charges had merit. The publications that assert a Pauline dependence on Platonism all tend to center on a similar cluster of charges. For instance, Paul's writings supposedly evidence a dualistic view of the world, a view that is said to be especially clear in his radical distinction between the human soul and body. Moreover, it is alleged, Paul manifests the typical Platonic aversion to the body, the body being evil, a prison house of the soul, from which the Christian longs to be delivered. Until this deliverance actually comes by means of death, the Pauline Christian is supposed to denigrate his body through various ascetic practices. Such are the charges that appear in almost every publication alleging Paul's dependence on Platonism.

These claims are typically supported by references to passages in Paul's writings. Occasionally, portions of the texts that seem to support the allegation are quoted. More frequently, the author simply gives the location of the text in parentheses, safe in the knowledge that few readers will actually go to the trouble of checking to see if the verse says what he claims it does. And it is precisely at this point that the claims about Pauline dependence on Platonism fall apart. When the alleged proof texts are studied by anyone trained in theology and biblical studies, it is seen that the verses suppos-

edly proving Pauline dependence do nothing of
the kind. Moreover, anyone without such training who properly utilizes good commentaries
will be able to reach the same conclusion.

A Study of Major Claims About Paul

A good place to begin our examination of
these claims and the relevant proof texts is a
1928 book by George Holley Gilbert entitled
Greek Thought in the New Testament.[41] Gilbert
writes:

> In his view of man's constitution, the apostle
> [Paul] stands with the Greek philosophers rather
> than with the Hebrew Scriptures. With Plato he
> [Paul] thinks of a human being as consisting of an
> outer man and an inner man (2 Cor. 4:16), and with
> Greek philosophy in general he thinks of the body
> as the prison of the spirit (Rom. 7:24; 8:23). With
> the Orphic faith he holds the doctrine of original sin
> and locates the evil principle in the "flesh," where
> it has been enthroned since the hour of Adam's
> transgression (Rom. 5:12). The dual aspect of his
> thought comes to its classic expression in Rom.
> 7:15–18.[42]

When an author makes so many mistakes in
such a short space, the real challenge is knowing
where to begin one's rebuttal. But I should
remind the reader that there was a time in many
universities and seminaries when errors like this
held the status of an official doctrine. Suppose
we begin with Gilbert's claim that the distinction
in 2 Corinthians 4:16 between an outer and inner
man proves Paul's dependence on Platonism.
The verse actually reads as follows: "Therefore
we do not lose heart. Though outwardly we are
wasting away, yet inwardly we are being renewed day by day." Quite frankly, this hardly
sounds like Platonism. Paul is using a very
common form of speech, popular in his day (and
now), to describe what could be obvious to
many people totally uninformed about Platonism. Many people have felt their physical
strength and health waning at the very time that

they felt themselves growing stronger mentally or spiritually. Where is the Platonism in all this? Ironically, the terminology "inner and outer man" does not even appear in Plato's writings. This significant slip on Gilbert's part suggests that he was just as willing to read Paul into Plato as the reverse.

What about Gilbert's second claim, that Paul thinks of the human body as a prison house of the spirit? Once again, it is important to see what Gilbert's alleged proof texts actually say. Romans 7:24 reads: "What a wretched man I am! Who will rescue me from this body of death?" It is obvious that in this verse Paul uses neither the word *prison* (*phylakē*) nor the idea that the body is a prison of the soul. As a matter of fact, nowhere in Scripture does Paul write of the body in terms of a prison. In all likelihood, Paul in this verse used the word *body* metaphorically. Gilbert's other proof text is equally useless in establishing his case. Romans 8:23 reads, "Not only so, but we ourselves, who have the firstfruits of the Spirit, groan inwardly as we wait eagerly for our adoption as sons, the redemption of our bodies." If anything, this verse *disproves* Gilbert's thesis, since the redemption that Paul awaits is the glory that will follow his bodily resurrection, a most un-Platonic hope.

The next of Gilbert's claims is probably central to the entire question of Paul's alleged dependence on Platonism. Practically every author who claims such dependence refers to Paul's repeated use of the word *flesh* in contexts that associate it with evil. What could be more natural for any writer who approaches Paul's writings already convinced that Paul is a Platonist than to conclude that his view of the flesh is a reflection of the Hellenistic belief that matter and the body are evil?[43] To be sure, Paul repeatedly describes a moral conflict. Plato described a similar struggle between reason and desire. Later dualists saw the struggle in terms of a conflict between body and spirit. Paul identifies the antagonists as flesh and spirit. Philosopher Gordon Clark warns against a careless reading of Paul that would make Paul's term "flesh" mean body. Instead, Clark avers, "a little attention to Paul's remarks makes it clear that he means, not body, but the sinful human nature inherited from Adam."[44] Theologian J. Gresham Machen elaborates on the real significance of Paul's use of the term *flesh*.

> The Pauline use of the term "flesh" to denote that in which evil resides can apparently find no real parallel whatever in pagan usage. And the divergence appears not only in terminology but also in thought. At first sight there might seem to be a parallel between the Pauline doctrine of the flesh and the Greek doctrine of the evil of matter, which appears in the Orphic sects, then in Plato and in his successors. But the parallel breaks down upon closer examination. According to Plato, the body is evil because it is material; it is the prison-house of the soul. Nothing could really be more remote from the thought of Paul. According to Paul, the connection of soul and body is entirely normal, and the soul apart from the body is in a condition of nakedness. It is true, the body will be changed at the resurrection or at the coming of Christ; it will be made more adequate for the Kingdom of God. But at any rate, there is in Paul no doctrine of the inherent evil of matter.[45]

Paul's condemnation of "flesh" as evil has absolutely no reference to the human body. It does not refer to the physical stuff of body but rather to a psychological and spiritual defect that leads every human being to place self or the creature ahead of the Creator. As Machen explains:

> The "flesh" in Paul, when it is used in its developed, ethical sense, does not mean the material nature of man; it includes rather all that man receives by ordinary generation. The contrast between "flesh" and "Spirit" therefore is not the contrast between matter and spirit; it is a contrast

between human nature, of which sin has taken possession, and the spirit of God.[46]

The New International Version makes this clear by translating *sarx* ("flesh") by the phrase "sinful nature." For instance, Romans 7:5, a verse often used as a proof text for the claim that Paul believed matter was evil, reads: "For when we were controlled by the sinful nature, the sinful passions aroused by the law were at work in our bodies, so that we bore fruit for death." Once what Paul meant by *flesh* is understood, none of the texts in which he uses the term in its ethical sense can support the allegation that he was a Platonic dualist. Consider the well-known passage of Romans 7:15–18, where he describes the moral battle he felt within him:

> I do not understand what I do. For what I want to do I do not do, but what I hate I do. And if I do what I do not want to do, I agree that the law is good. As it is, it is no longer I myself who do it, but it is sin living in me. I know that nothing good lives in me, that is, in my sinful nature.

Paul, then, never taught that his body was evil or the source of his sinning. Human beings commit acts of sin because they are born with a sinful nature. Paul's use of *flesh* in this way has no parallel in pagan usage. Paul's teaching was undoubtedly derived from the Old Testament, though he develops it beyond its Old Testament usage.

The claim that Paul believed that matter is evil is also refuted by his belief that the ultimate destiny of redeemed human beings is an endless life in a resurrected *body,* not the disembodied existence of an immortal soul (as held by the Orphics, the Pythagoreans, and Plato). Paul's doctrine of the resurrection of the body (1 Cor. 15:12–58) is clearly incompatible with a belief in the inherent wickedness of matter. Attempts to attribute an evil matter–good spirit dualism to Paul also stumble over the fact that Paul believed in the existence of evil spirits (Eph. 6:12), a belief that obviously implies that not all spirit is good. The additional fact that God pronounced His creation good (Gen. 1:31) also demonstrates how far removed dualism is from the teaching of the Old and New Testaments.[47]

It is an equally serious mistake to read a Platonic dualism into the biblical teaching of human nature. As British classicists A. H. Armstrong and R. A. Markus explain:

> In Jewish-Christian tradition man is a single whole of which body is just as much a part as soul; and for this way of thinking the resurrection of the body is a natural and inevitable part of any doctrine of the future life. And the evils and impediments to the spiritual life which our present life in the body brings are explained not as natural and inevitable consequences of earthly embodiment but as the result of the Fall of Man, which leaves open the possibility that our Redemption from that fall may bring us to a perfect and glorious life in a spiritualized earthly . . . body and not require our transference to a body actually placed in the heavens and made of celestial material.[48]

Armstrong and Markus go on to point out that "Christian theologians insist that the resurrection bodies will be real human bodies, however spiritualized and transformed, and not properly astral or celestial bodies, thus remaining faithful to the Jewish-Christian tradition and avoiding a complete slipping back into the spatial otherworldliness of the cosmic religion."[49] At this point, then, it would be difficult to imagine two views in sharper contrast than the Christian and Hellenistic views of man.

OTHER CHARGES AGAINST PAUL

The last points left to those seeking clear evidence of Platonism in Paul's writings consist of appeals to various texts in which Paul allegedly denigrates the body, advocates asceticism, or actually mentions harming his own body. Gilbert appeals to 2 Corinthians 5:4 in order to support his claim that Paul denigrated the human body.

He considers Paul in this verse to be presenting the material body as "a house in which the spirit is burdened and groans—this is the imagery that had long been familiar to Greek thinkers."[50] While that may be, it is also an imagery familiar to millions of human beings who never heard of Plato but who have suffered from headaches, arthritis, or birth pangs. All Paul is doing is referring to something that every human being who has experienced illness or the advent of old age knows personally. But Gilbert is not yet finished with Paul. From what he calls Paul's "fundamentally sad view of the body it is but a step to the 'bruising' it, of which Paul speaks (1 Cor. 9:27), and subjecting it to 'bondage'. . . . Paul takes pleasure in persecutions and distresses, in injuries and necessities, for he feels that they contribute to his inward strength (2 Cor. 12:10)."[51] The charge that Paul was an ascetic is false, a fact that is clear to anyone familiar with the whole of his writings. Paul knew how to be abased and how to abound (Phil. 4:12). He wrote the New Testament's strongest attacks against asceticism (e.g., Col. 2:16–23). Clark correctly observes that Paul's teaching "is not motivated by a desire to free a divine soul from a bodily tomb, much less by the idea that pain is good and pleasure evil. Rather, Paul was engaged in a race, to win which required him to lay aside every weight as well as the sin which so easily besets. Willing to suffer stonings and stripes for the name of Christ, he never practiced self-flagellation."[52]

Paul's views about sex and marriage have also been greatly distorted.[53] Once one accepts the assumption that Paul was a typical Hellenistic dualist who denigrated the human body, it is a simple matter to conclude that such a person must also have despised sex and marriage and advocated celibacy. However, the texts that are offered in support of this conclusion are isolated either from their immediate context or from qualifying statements in other Pauline writings, or else they once again illustrate the tendency of people to read their prejudices into the text. The truth is that Paul spoke in support of marriage (e.g., 1 Tim. 3). He used the marriage relationship as an illustration of the close bond between Christ and His church (Eph. 5). He warned against ascetic heretics who prohibit marriage (1 Tim. 4:1–5). Most of the confusion about Paul's views regarding sex and marriage is based on a misreading of what he says in 1 Corinthians 7. But—as contemporary biblical scholar Robert Gundry succinctly points out—nothing in that chapter supports the dualist's thesis.

> According to chapter 7 [of 1 Corinthians], voluntary celibacy is good; but because of the sexual impulse God has provided marriage for the avoidance of illicit relationships. Within marriage, then, there should be a complete giving of the partners to each other. Paul wishes all might be free from marital responsibilities, as he is, not because asceticism is spiritually superior, but because the single person can devote full energy to preaching the gospel. He realizes, however, that in this respect God's will varies for different Christians.[54]

After an intensive investigation of Paul's views on sex and marriage, Herman Ridderbos concludes that "there is no basis for the opinion that on ascetic-dualistic grounds Paul considered sexual intercourse itself sinful, or would have judged marriage on the basis of ascetic-dualistic motives. The contrary is rather the case. Paul values marriage as an institution of God, protected by the express commandment of Christ, to be accepted and experienced in Christian liberty. Even in 1 Corinthians 7, the chapter to which appeal is made for an opposite opinion, in our view no ascetic-dualistic motives are to be discovered with reference to marriage."[55]

Part 3 of this book will investigate Paul's relation to another type of Hellenistic dualism, Gnosticism. For now, at least, it is safe to say that the case for a Pauline dependence on Platonic dualism is extremely weak.

chapter four

Stoicism and the New Testament

An overview of the doctrines of Stoic philosophy important to the debate about Christian dependence is presented. Questions of alleged Stoic influence on Pauline and Petrine writings are raised and discussed.

The other Hellenistic philosophy besides Platonism that is said to have had a major influence on the New Testament is Stoicism. On the whole, cultured people during the first century A.D. were influenced more by Stoicism than by any other philosophical movement.

SURVEY OF STOICISM

The history of Stoicism is customarily divided into three periods: the Early Stoa, the Middle Stoa, and the Later Stoa. The Early Stoa, which can be dated roughly from 300 to 200 B.C., includes the major thinkers active during the 67 beginning of the movement: Zeno of Citium (336–264 B.C., the founder of the school), Cleanthes (331–232 B.C.), and Chrysippus (280–204 B.C.). The two major representatives of the Middle Stoa—approximately 150 B.C. to the beginning of the Christian era—were Panaetius of Rhodes (185–110 B.C.) and Posidonius (130–46 B.C.). The Later Stoa is represented by philosophers whose names are more familiar, including Seneca (A.D. 1–65), who served in Nero's government; the Roman slave Epictetus (A.D. 50–138); and the Roman Emperor Marcus Aurelius (A.D. 121–180).* The only complete Stoic writings that have survived come from the Late Stoa.[56] The thought of earlier Stoics must be carefully reconstructed from references and quotations in other books.† My treatment of Stoic thought will of necessity be selective. For the most part, I will focus on those theories that have relevance for our interest—the possible influence of Stoicism on the New Testament. Rather than say anything about the Stoics' logic and epistemology, I will focus on their ethics and cosmology, especially their views about God, the Logos, and the conflagration of the world. I will also draw attention to some of the more important ways in which later Stoics modified the views of their predecessors.

The Early Stoa   The early Stoics were materialists; they believed that everything that exists, including God and the soul, is corporeal. They were also monists, seeing all reality as composed of one ultimate type of being. The Stoics followed Heraclitus of Ephesus (a pre-Socratic philosopher who flourished about 500 B.C.) in identifying fire as the basic *arche* of the universe—that is, the ultimate cosmic stuff of which everything

---

*Marcus Aurelius reigned as emperor from A.D. 161 to 180.

†The brief account below of the cosmology and ethics of the Early Stoa will be drawn largely from what we know of the work of Chrysippus.

else is made. The Stoics were also pantheists, believing that the ultimate stuff of the universe is divine and that God has no personality. They thought that God and the world were related like soul and body: God is the soul of the world, and the world is the body of God. Unlike the Judeo-Christian God, who is an eternal, almighty, all-knowing, loving, spiritual *Person*, the Stoic God is impersonal and hence incapable of knowledge, love, or providential acts.

The Stoics related their cosmic fire and impersonal God to a cosmic Reason that they called the Logos.* A divine but impersonal Reason is immanent throughout all of reality. What we know as human reason is but a part of, a divine spark of, the cosmic Reason. The Stoics even spoke of *rationes seminales*, rational seeds, which have been implanted throughout all nature and guide nature's development. An important corollary of the Stoic confidence in a cosmic rationality was their belief in natural law. A. H. Armstrong ties these notions together and explains their significance:

> The most important expression of Stoic cosmopolitanism was their doctrine of "natural law," the universal decrees of the Divine Reason which are the same for all men and with which all positive law should correspond. The idea of unwritten divine laws superior to human law goes far back in the Greek tradition. We can find it in the fifth century [B.C.] most notably expressed in the "Antigone" of Sophocles, and as we have seen, the idea of an absolute moral law discoverable by reason is the foundation of the ethics of Socrates and Plato. But it was the Stoics . . . who presented it first as a universal law, the law of the City of the Cosmos, the same everywhere and superior to merely local custom and tradition.[57]

*Although *logos* was a common Greek word with a number of meanings (rule, law, reason, reasoning, measure, proportion, explanation, hypothesis), its first use as a technical term in philosophy occurred in the thought of Heraclitus.

The last element of the Stoic cosmology to be noted here is its *determinism*. The Stoics denied any possibility of free will or chance. Everything that happens occurs by necessity. Human free will is an illusion. Hence, there is nothing a human being can do to alter his or her future; there is no way to alter or avoid our fate. The Stoic ethic is an elaboration of the best life available to anyone who accepts the Stoic picture of the world.

The Stoics taught that only one thing is intrinsically good: virtue. Conversely, only one thing is inherently evil: vice. Once we understand that by virtue and vice the Stoics are referring to traits or dispositions within a human being, the paradox of their claim becomes obvious. Most of us believe that all kinds of things that go on in the world beyond our mind are good or evil. Are not earthquakes and tornados evil? Is not war? Are not heart disease and cancer evil? They were not for a Stoic. After all, things like storms and earthquakes and disease are part of the determined course of nature (God). There is nothing we could have done to avoid them. It is best, then, not to think of them as evil but as morally neutral or indifferent. Similarly, neither money nor success nor good health is intrinsically good. They too are part of the inevitable plan of nature. Therefore, the Stoic says, to find good and evil, we must turn away from whatever happens of necessity and look within. The wise man will distinguish between the few things that are in his power (primarily his attitude) and the many things over which he has no control. Personal virtue or vice resides in our attitudes, in the way we react to the things that happen to us.

The key word in the Stoic ethic is *apathy*. The good person will recognize that there is nothing he or she could have done to avoid what fate has sent. There is nothing he can do to avoid the inevitable that is yet to come. Hence, the good man or woman will acquiesce to his or her fate, will accept whatever happens as "the will of God."* One of the early Stoics illustrated this in terms of a dog tied by a rope to a horse-drawn wagon. The poor dog is going to go wherever the cart goes, whether he knows it or likes it. That is his destiny. Thus, *where* the dog goes is not under his control. What is within the dog's power is *how* he goes. The dog can fight, resist, and pull on the rope; or else he can put his head down and follow obediently wherever the cart goes. Either way, he will end up at the same place. The only difference is how he gets there. This is a picture of life, for the Stoics. Everything that happens to a human being is fixed by that person's fate. But most humans resist their destiny. Like the dog, they struggle and complain. But none of their resistance or pain changes anything. Others, enlightened by Stoicism, become resigned to their fate and go along obediently.

The Stoic believed, therefore, that our duty in life is to live according to nature, to accept the will of the Stoic's impersonal God. As Epictetus was to put it centuries later, all of us are actors in a play. But the role we play and how long we play it is determined by Another. Our task is to play as best we can whatever role God (Nature) gives us. Central to the Stoic notion of happiness (the good life) is the notion of apathy. The truly virtuous person will eliminate all passion and emotion from his life until he reaches the point that nothing troubles or bothers him.

The Stoic, then, is a person who lives in a materialistic universe controlled by an impersonal Reason. A slave to his fate, the Stoic learns the secret of the only good life open to him: eliminate emotion from your life and accept whatever fate sends your way.

One other element of the early Stoics must be noted here—their doctrine of the universal

---

*It is important to remember that the phrase "the will of God" meant something quite different to a pantheistic Stoic than it does in the context of New Testament theism.

conflagration. The early Stoics taught that the world would eventually be entirely destroyed by a universal conflagration. But then the world would begin anew and duplicate exactly the same course of events of the previous cycle. Each event would happen again in exactly the same order; each person would live again and go through precisely the same history until once again the world would be destroyed by fire. The Stoics coupled this with a doctrine of eternal recurrence: the history of the world will repeat itself an infinite number of times. As we shall see, this doctrine of the conflagration has been suggested as the source of the New Testament teaching that the world will be destroyed by fire (2 Peter 3).

The Middle Stoa

During the Middle and Late Stoa, Stoicism became more humane, gentle, and reasonable. During these periods of its development, Stoic writers adopted a number of elements from Platonism. One of the major changes introduced during the Middle Stoa was a rejection of the older Stoic belief in a universal conflagration. This view was probably totally abandoned by the beginning of the Christian era.*

Any serious study of philosophy during the lifetime of Paul would have included the work of Posidonius, a middle Stoic who died about 46 B.C. Armstrong refers to Posidonius as "by far the most notable figure in the intellectual life of his age, a distinguished geographer and historian as well as a philosopher, and a voluminous writer."[58] Unfortunately, none of his writings have survived. Because the accounts of his views that appear in the writings of others are fragmentary and often unclear, it is difficult to reconstruct his thought. He is believed by some to have been the first Hellenistic philosopher to

*The Middle Stoa replaced the doctrine of universal conflagration with a belief in the eternity of the world.

suggest explicitly that human beings are a kind of intermediary being, occupying a rank between the divine and the animal. He also appears to have been the first to suggest that the knowledge of God transcends the human mind. Like the early Stoics, Posidonius was both a materialist and a pantheist. He regarded the human soul as a part of the being of God.

The Late Stoa

Cosmological speculations, though found often during the period of the Early Stoa, are almost completely missing from the writings of the Late Stoa. By this time, Stoic authors had become preoccupied almost exclusively with reflections on the moral life. Seneca, tutor of the young Nero and later minister in his government, is the most superficial of the later Stoics. Armstrong describes his essays as little more than "lay sermons on practical moral topics."[59] The most important of the late Stoics are Epictetus and Marcus Aurelius, a Roman slave and emperor respectively. The writings of Epictetus are full of the joy that accompanies a willing acceptance of the divine will. He appears to have abandoned the impersonal God of earlier Stoic pantheism in favor of a personal and transcendent deity. Marcus Aurelius was another in a long line of Hellenistic eclectics. His thought included both Epictetus and Plato among its sources. Since the writings of Epictetus and Marcus Aurelius postdate the close of the New Testament canon, claims about a possible Stoic influence on the New Testament usually center on Seneca, especially Seneca's possible relationship with Paul.[60]

STOICISM AND SCRIPTURE

We turn our attention, therefore, to a consideration of the connection between Stoicism and Scripture, specifically the New Testament. We will discuss first the relation between Stoicism and Paul, then that between Stoicism and Peter.

**Paul's Alleged
Dependence on
Stoicism**

That Paul actually quoted from Stoic writers is clear. His famous sermon on Mars Hill in Athens (Acts 17) contains a quotation from a Stoic poet.* American philosopher John Herman Randall, Jr., attributed the strong social emphasis of Paul's moral philosophy to Stoicism.[61] Others have claimed to find parallels to Stoicism in Paul's ideal of human brotherhood. William Fairweather found a parallel in the fact that both Paul and Stoicism "attach importance . . . [not to] the outward act, but [to] the animating motive."[62] In other words, both stressed the importance of the inward motive in determining the morality of an action. About one hundred years ago it was fashionable in some circles to maintain that Paul used terminology that he obviously borrowed from Seneca. Wild flights of fancy accompanied speculation about Paul's alleged relationship with Seneca. These theories ranged from suggestions that Paul was influenced by Seneca to claims that Seneca had become a Christian, perhaps under the influence of Paul. Theories at both extremes of the continuum have been rejected for years.[63]

Does Paul's quoting a Stoic writer in Acts 17:28 demonstrate anything more than a passing acquaintance with Stoicism? It must be remembered that Paul was an educated man who was speaking to Stoics. What better way to gain their attention than to show that he had some acquaintance with their writers and could quote them with appreciation? But it would be exaggerating the importance of Paul's quotation to read more than that into it. One quote hardly proves that Paul had much familiarity with Stoic writings. Many modern men and women can quote two or three lines from Shakespeare without being especially familiar with the Bard's writings.

---

*The actual wording of Paul's quote in Acts 17:28 could have come either from a hymn by Cleanthes or from a poem by Aratus. J. B. Lightfoot thinks Paul had both sources in mind. See n. 60.

Many writers have examined and discredited the alleged parallels of expression in Paul and Seneca. Albert Schweitzer concluded that they "have only an external resemblance. They are not really analogous."[64] Schweitzer explained the pessimism of Stoics like Seneca as

> purely a result of reflection on the conditions of the present life. Existence appears to Seneca a burden which one may at any time cast off—by suicide. For Paul the present world is evil because it is sinful, lies under the dominion of the angel powers, and is subject to corruption. He judges it, not in itself, but with reference to a new and perfect world which is soon to appear. The idea of suicide does not enter into his thoughts, indeed he dreads that he might be released from the present earthly existence before the parousia occurs.[65]

Although Seneca's language may, on occasion, sound Christian, its meaning is quite different.[66] When properly understood, Seneca's ethic is repulsive to Pauline Christianity. It is totally devoid of genuine human emotion and compassion; there is no place for love or pity or contrition. It lacks any intrinsic tie to repentance, conversion, and faith in God.

To be sure, there are coincidences of language and imagery between Paul and Stoics like Seneca. But even though Paul used such images and language, he transformed and purified the ideas. If Paul did actually use Stoic language, he gave the words a new and higher meaning and significance. "But for the Stoic and the Christian the same language did not necessarily convey the same meaning. To the Christian, God, as a personal Being and as a Father, is more than the world; sin is more than mere error; and regulating the passions differs from merely crushing them. In Stoicism as represented by Seneca 'God is nature, is Fate, is Fortune, is the Universe, is the all-pervading mind.' "[67]

When a Stoic writer used a phrase like "imitation of God," he did not have in mind anything resembling its New Testament meaning. As New Testament scholar J. B. Lightfoot explains, the Stoic meant "nothing deeper than a due recognition of physical laws on the part of man, and a conformity thereto in his own actions. The phrase ['imitation of God'] is merely a synonym for the favourite Stoic formula of 'accordance with nature.' This may be a useful precept; but so interpreted the expression is emptied of its religious significance. In fact to follow the world and to follow God are equivalent phrases with Seneca."[68] Seneca's equating "following the world" with "following God" directly contradicts New Testament teaching.

Stoics like Seneca also lacked any real consciousness of sin, which, of necessity, presupposes an awareness of a personal and holy God.

> With Seneca error or sin is nothing more than the failure in attaining to the ideal of the perfect man which he sets before him, the running counter to the law of the universe in which he finds himself placed. He [Seneca] does not view it [sin] as an offense done to the will of an all-holy all-righteous Being, an unfilial act of defiance towards a loving and gracious Father. The Stoic's conception of error or sin is not referred at all to the idea of God. His pantheism had so obscured the personality of the Divine Being, that such reference was, if not impossible, at least unnatural.[69]

Attempts to trace Paul's attack on distinctions between Jew and Gentile back to Stoicism's ideal of human brotherhood can only persuade those who are uninformed about the significant differences between Stoicism and Pauline Christianity. As Machen explains, Christianity

> enunciated with an unheard-of seriousness the doctrine that all classes of men, wise and unwise, bond and free, are of equal worth. But the equality was not found in the common possession of human nature. It was found, instead, in a common connection with Jesus Christ. "There can be neither Jew nor Greek, there can be neither bond nor free, there can be no male and female"—so far the words of

Paul can find analogies (faith analogies, it is true) in the Stoic writers. But the Pauline grounding of the unity here enunciated is the very antithesis of all mere humanitarianism both ancient and modern—"for ye are all one person," says Paul, "in Christ Jesus." Christianity did not reveal the fact that all men were brothers. Indeed it revealed the contrary. But it offered to make all men brothers by bringing them into saving connection with Christ.[70]

Even if some coincidences between Paul and Seneca exist, they can be explained either as a "natural and independent development of religious thought"[71] or as one educated man's use of contemporary language and imagery to communicate an essentially different message. Only a serious misreading of the New Testament could give rise to claims of a Stoic influence (in the strong sense) on the New Testament.

Stoicism and 2 Peter 3

Students of the New Testament are familiar with the teaching in 2 Peter 3 that at the end time, God will destroy the world by fire. The key verses of this chapter (verses 7, 10, 12) read as follows:

> By the same word the present heavens and earth are reserved for fire, being kept for the day of judgment and destruction of ungodly men. . . . But the day of the Lord will come like a thief. The heavens will disappear with a roar; the elements will be destroyed by fire, and the earth and everything in it will be laid bare. . . . That day will bring about the destruction of the heavens by fire, and the elements will melt in the heat.

Many writers have claimed to see in this passage echoes of the Stoic doctrine of a universal conflagration. For example, American theologian George Holley Gilbert wrote:

> The conception of a conflagration that burns up not only the adversaries of God but all men and the solid earth and the host of heavens is not Jewish but Greek. The Stoic philosophers taught that the

cosmos will sometime be consumed by fire, and that after an interval the formation of a new universe will begin, which will be in all particulars like the old. . . . Thus it appears that the universal conflagration taught in Second Peter is adapted from Greek speculation.[72]

But writers who allege the dependence of 2 Peter 3 on the Stoic doctrine of a universal conflagration fail to mention one extremely important detail, namely, that major Stoic writers had completely abandoned this doctrine by the middle of the first century B.C. Since the Stoic writers of the first century A.D. repudiated the doctrine, claims that the writer of 2 Peter borrowed from the prevailing Stoic teaching lose much of their credibility.

Moreover, claims that 2 Peter 3 draws on the Stoic doctrine also ignore major differences between the long-since repudiated Stoic belief and the New Testament teaching. For example, the Stoic conflagration was an eternally repeated event that had nothing to do with the conscious purposes of a personal God who had created the world. American philosopher Gordon Clark, himself a specialist in Hellenistic philosophy, explains how the radical differences in the two views undercut the alleged dependence: "the conflagration in II Peter is a sudden catastrophe like the flood. But the Stoic conflagration is a slow process that is going on now: it takes a long time, during which the elements change into fire bit by bit. The Stoic process is a natural process in the most ordinary sense of the word; but Peter speaks of it as the result of the word or fiat of the Lord."[73] Furthermore, Clark explains, while the Stoic conflagration is part of a process in which all of reality is deified (is, in other words, part of a pantheistic system), the conflagration described in 2 Peter is the divine judgment of a holy and personal God upon sin. Finally, Clark argues, "the Stoic conflagration occurs an infinite number of times in the infinite universal cycles. Peter's occurs just once, like the flood.

The new heavens and new earth are not a repetition of past history point by point as in Stoicism, but the final state of everlasting felicity with our Creator and Redeemer."[74] The parallel between 2 Peter 3 and the Stoic doctrine of universal conflagration turns out, on careful analysis, to be superficial. The two doctrines are different.

Other, but considerably less significant, evidences of Stoicism are sometimes claimed to exist in the New Testament.[75] But at most, all that any of them would show is that Christian writers utilized language and imagery of their time in a new and qualitatively different way. They do not prove that the New Testament appropriated any Stoic ideas.[76]

chapter five

The Christian Logos

A number of scholars have claimed that the New Testament concept of Logos, prominent in the Fourth Gospel and other Johannine literature, was borrowed from either Philo or Alexandrian Judaism. This chapter examines not only those claims but also two alternative sources for the Logos concept.

As we have noticed, the Greek word *logos* was a technical term used prominently in several philosophical systems that antedate Christianity. Its philosophic use goes back to Heraclitus (about 500 B.C.). It was then used by the Stoics, some of whom influenced Philo, the Jewish philosopher of Alexandria. It was probably inevitable that some writers would conclude that the important appearance of *logos* in the prologue to John's Gospel evidences the influence of these earlier uses.[77] Fifty years ago, the view that the writer of the Fourth Gospel was influenced by Philo's use of *logos* was something of an official doctrine in certain circles.[78] With very few exceptions, however, the drift of contemporary scholarship has been away from a Philonic source of the Johannine Logos doctrine. But as we have already seen on several prior occasions, news of this change in scholarly opinion was slow in reaching some philosophers. And so, John Herman Randall, Jr., for many years a professor of philosophy at Columbia University, declared in 1970: "In his Prologue about the Word, the *Logos*, he [John] is adopting Philo Judaeus' earlier Platonization of the Hebraic tradition."[79] And in his history of philosophy text, W. T. Jones continues his search for Hellenistic sources of early Christian belief by claiming that the "mysticism" of the Fourth Gospel was grounded in the Platonism of Hellenistic Alexandria:

> John . . . was more philosophically oriented than the apostle of the Gentiles [Paul] and brought to the developing Jesus movement his understanding of current philosophical concepts. For him [John], Christ Jesus was not Paul's resurrected God; he was at once more exalted and more abstract—the logos of Hellenistic philosophy.[80]

The purpose of this chapter and the one that follows is to evaluate such claims of an early Christian dependence on the Logos teaching of the Hellenistic world.

HELLENISTIC JUDAISM AND PHILO OF ALEXANDRIA

Hellenistic Judaism was distinct both from its predecessor—the religion of the Old Testament—and from its successor—Rabbinic Judaism. By the beginning of the Christian era, Alexandria, Egypt—an important center of the Jewish Dispersion—had become the chief center of Hellenistic thought. The large colony of Jews who claimed Alexandria as their home became hellenized in both language and culture.

While still observing the Jewish religion, they translated their Scriptures into the Greek language (the Septuagint). This tended to increase their cultural isolation from their Hebrew roots because they now had even less incentive to remain fluent in the Hebrew language. Given the intellectual interests of the Alexandrian Jews, it was only natural that the importation of philosophical systems to Alexandria would eventually affect them. And so they came to know about Platonism and Stoicism. An influential and typical writing that came out of Alexandrian Judaism is The Wisdom of Solomon. Written by an anonymous Hellenistic Jew in Egypt and usually dated between 100 and 50 B.C., the work is a synthesis of Old Testament religion (primarily Moses and the Prophets) and the pagan Hellenistic philosophy of the day. Some commentators see signs that the writer was familiar with some of Plato's writings (e.g., *Phaedo* and *The Republic*), with Heraclitus, and with Stoicism. The Wisdom of Solomon appears to synthesize notions borrowed from Platonism and Stoicism with the personification of Wisdom found in Proverbs 8. The author's view of creation is similar to Plato's teaching in the *Timaeus* that the world was created out of a formless matter. He believes in the immortality, immateriality, and preexistence of the soul and writes of a Wisdom (the Greek word is *sophia*) that is immanent in the world. However, The Wisdom of Solomon does not use the word *logos*.

The greatest of the Alexandrian Jewish intellectuals was Philo Judaeus, who lived from about 25 B.C. to about A.D. 50. Philo's work illustrates many of the most important elements of the synthesis of Platonism and Stoicism that came to dominate Hellenistic philosophy during and after his lifetime. He is the best example of how intellectual Jews of the Dispersion, isolated from Palestine and their native culture, allowed Hellenistic influences to shape their theology and philosophy.

Like Plato, Philo distinguished between the physical world and the ideal world of the eternal forms. But whereas Plato had left the relationship between God and the ideal world indeterminate, Philo took the important step of interpreting Plato's forms as eternal thoughts in the mind of God. Philo also taught an exaggerated view of the divine transcendence, but this left him with the problem of explaining how his transcendent and unknowable God has any dealings with the physical universe. Philo explained this in terms of intermediary beings through whom God acts upon the world. The most important of these intermediaries, for Philo, was the Logos.

Philo has become famous for his use of the term *logos*. Ironically, it is impossible to find any clear or consistent use of the word in his many writings. For example, he used *logos* to refer to Plato's ideal world, to the mind of God, and to a principle subordinate to God. At other times, he applies *logos* to any of several mediators between God and man (e.g., angels, Moses, Abraham, and the Jewish high priest). But his lack of clarity and consistency aside, his use of the term has raised questions about the interrelationship between Alexandrian Judaism and such New Testament writings as John's Gospel.

ALTERNATIVE SOURCES FOR THE JOHANNINE LOGOS

In the rest of this chapter we will review the two most commonly offered alternatives to a Philonic source of the Johannine Logos. In chapter 6 we will examine the most important reasons given by scholars for discounting a Philonic source for the New Testament Logos. Also in chapter 6 we will examine the presence of an implicit Logos doctrine in the Epistle to the Hebrews, offer a theory that explains that presence, and suggest a new theory regarding the source of John's use of the term *logos*.

Most contemporary New Testament scholars see no need to postulate a conscious relationship between Alexandrian Judaism and the New Testament use of *logos*. They point out that alongside of the philosophical or Alexandrian views of *logos,* there were two similar but independent notions in the Judaism of the time. One of these was a pre-Christian Jewish speculation about a personified Wisdom. This personification of Wisdom appears in Proverbs 8:22– 26, where Wisdom speaks as follows:

> The LORD possessed me at the beginning of his work, before his deeds of old;
> I was appointed from eternity, from the beginning, before the world began.
> When there were no oceans, I was given birth, when there were no springs abounding with water;
> Before the mountains were settled in place, before the hills, I was given birth,
> Before he made the earth or its fields or any of the dust of the world.

As British scholar T. W. Manson explains, "We find in the late Jewish literature a tendency to speak of the attributes of God as if they had a separate existence. This tendency is specially marked in the Wisdom literature. The passages that are specially relevant to our present problem are those in which the wisdom of God is to some degree personified."[81] British New Testament scholar James D. G. Dunn affirms that most specialists "would agree that the principal background against which the Logos prologue must be set is the Old Testament itself and the thought of inter-testamental Hellenistic Judaism, particularly as expressed in the Wisdom literature."[82]

In the eighth chapter of Proverbs, Wisdom is personified and speaks, claiming both preexistence and involvement in creation. In a major difference with the Logos of John, while the Wisdom of Proverbs exists before the creation of the world, she herself is still created. Wisdom was the result of the first act of divine creation, following which she cooperated with God in creating the world.

Aside from Proverbs, the other important texts that illustrate a Jewish personification of Wisdom exist outside the thirty-nine canonical books of the Old Testament. One of these is the apocryphal book of Ecclesiasticus, where, in 24:1-23, a preexistent Wisdom is identified with Law. Chapters 7–9 of The Wisdom of Solomon constitute another important source. What this literature demonstrates is that if it is necessary to locate some source for John's peculiar use of *logos,* there is no need to consider Philo as the exclusive source. The Wisdom literature shows how, even though totally unfamiliar with Philo, anyone could have started with the Jewish personification of Wisdom (*sophia*).

The Second Alternative

Many scholars prefer a different hypothesis in their search for a non-Philonic source for John's use of *logos.* They note that the phrases "The Word of God" and "The Word of the Lord [Yahweh]" are used throughout the Old Testament in ways that suggest an independent existence and personification (see Pss. 33:6; 107:20; 147:15, 18; Isa. 9:8; 55:10ff.). James D. G. Dunn explains that such texts present the word of Yahweh "as Yahweh himself acting, acting decisively in creation, in judgment, in salvation. When a sovereign speaks his subjects obey; when he commands it is done. So the utterance and command of Yahweh are simply ways of saying that Yahweh brought his will to effect, that Yahweh achieved his purpose; when Yahweh speaks things happen."[83] Dunn doubts that the personifications of Wisdom and the Word in the Old Testament really mean a literal personalization. They are simply different ways of describing God's acts.

It is a mistake, then, to assume that the early

Christian use of *logos* had to be derived from Alexandrian Judaism. There are at least two separate Old Testament traditions that could have given rise to the teaching found in the Prologue to the Fourth Gospel. Practically speaking, it is probably both unnecessary and impossible to choose between the available hypotheses noted in this chapter. While T. W. Manson prefers the second alternative (the personification of the Word of God), he does not rule out the possibility that the notion of a personified Wisdom also rests somewhere in the background. But, he insists,

> With regard to Philo I do not think that John is dependent on him at all. The similarities between them are not due to the borrowing by John from Philo, but to the fact that both have borrowed from the same source—the Old Testament. The points of similarity are just those that both have in common with the Old Testament notion of the "word of God." Philo's *logos* is really Stoicism blended with the Old Testament "word of God." John's *logos* is Jesus Christ understood in the light of the same Old Testament "word of God."[84]

Wholly apart from his sources, the author of the prologue to the Fourth Gospel was, as James Dunn explains, "*the first to take that step which no Hellenistic-Jewish author had taken before him, the first to identify the word of God as a particular person;* and so far as our evidence is concerned *the Fourth Evangelist was the first Christian writer to conceive clearly of the personal preexistence of the Logos-Son and to present it as a fundamental part of his message.*"[85]

Thus it is wrong to hold that the biblical teaching about the divine Logos is a synthesis developed from earlier Jewish and Hellenistic speculation about mediators and then applied to Christ. On the contrary, L. W. Bard argues, the early Christian theologians, like John, begin with Jesus as the fulfillment of God's purposes, the logos which God has spoken and who lived a historical life on earth. The logos had become flesh—that was the line which divided Christian speculation from the speculations of Hellenistic and Rabbinic Judaism and Philo. However, in using the idea of the logos early Christian writers no doubt were appealing obliquely to the contemporary world so that both Jewish and Greek readers would understand their meaning.[86]

After the close of the New Testament canon, some of the early church fathers made a rather extended use of the Logos concept. For example, Justin Martyr (about A.D. 100–163) argued that every apprehension of truth (whether by believer or unbeliever) is made possible because humans are related to the Logos, the ground of truth.[87] Further advances in the development of a philosophical use of *logos* appear in the later work of Clement of Alexandria (about A.D. 150–211) and Augustine (A.D. 354–430).[88]

SUMMARY

We have examined the charge that the author of the Fourth Gospel borrowed the term *logos* from Hellenistic philosophy, more specifically from the work of the Jewish Platonist, Philo; specific objections to that thesis will appear in chapter 6. We have noted two alternative sources in the Old Testament for John's Logos doctrine, sources that could also have influenced Philo in the development of his particular synthesis of Hellenistic philosophy and Judaism. The presence of these alternatives shows clearly how unnecessary it is to seek a Hellenistic source for the Johannine Logos. In the next chapter, we will examine the possibility of another alternative that has not yet received the attention it deserves.[89]

chapter six

The Book
of Hebrews:
A Test Case

In addition to further discussion of the Logos concept, the author uses the New Testament Epistle to the Hebrews as a test case, offering an alternative explanation of the epistle's relationship to Alexandrian Judaism.

In addition to concluding the discussion of the relationship between early Christianity and Hellenistic philosophy, this chapter will attempt to reach several other goals. For one thing, we will examine the argument that there is an important but often unrecognized Logos-Christology in the Epistle to the Hebrews. We will explore that book's *implicit* use of the notion of Logos and its possible affinities to Philo and Alexandrian Judaism. I will present and defend the view that the anonymous writer of Hebrews both knew and utilized language and concepts learned while he himself was an active participant in the 89 thought world of Alexandrian Judaism *prior* to his conversion to Christianity. I will argue, however, that this falls far short of illustrating what I called in chapter 1 *dependence in the strong sense*. My hypothesis illustrates a way in which the writer of a canonical book could have known and used the concepts and terminology of a non-Christian system without thus compromising his status as an inspired and therefore authoritative writer. It pictures one sense of what I have earlier called *dependence in the weak sense*. Finally, this chapter suggests a way in which my approach to the Book of Hebrews may provide a new answer to questions about the source of the Johannine Logos.*

THE ALEXANDRIAN BACKGROUND OF HEBREWS

The writer of Hebrews demonstrates a familiarity with the tenets of Hellenistic Judaism as these are known from documents written in Alexandria. The text of Hebrews clearly indicates his knowledge of the Platonic philosophy that Hellenistic Jews like Philo had sought to harmonize with Judaism. He also knew the Alexandrian teachings about Divine Wisdom (*sophia*) and the Logos. In particular, the writer evidences familiarity with the Alexandrian work The Wisdom of Solomon. Although the extent of his knowledge of Philo's thought and writings is debatable, at the very least the writer of Hebrews and Philo shared a common education in Alexandrian thought. Moreover, the writer of Hebrews assumes a familiarity with Alexandrian theology and philosophy on the part of his readers.[90] The view that the Book of Hebrews is

---

*The reader should recognize the speculative nature of this chapter. I first broached these suggestions in a 1977 paper read to the Biblical Theology Society at Tyndale House, Cambridge, England. That paper (somewhat modified) was published later that year in the *Westminster Theological Journal* (see n. 89). I have no reason, after the passage of seven years, to doubt the value of my approach. In fact, continued reflection during these intervening years has strengthened my convictions.

a legacy to Christianity from the Hellenized Judaism of Alexandria is shared by many, to a greater or lesser degree.[91]

There are two diametrically opposing views concerning the relationship between the Book of Hebrews and the thought of Philo and Alexandrian Judaism. The one extreme, typified by French scholar C. Spicq,[92] holds that the author of Hebrews was definitely influenced in a direct manner by the writings of Philo. The writer may have known Philo personally; he certainly read some of his writings; he may have been a Philonic convert to Christianity. More moderate versions of this thesis have for years found expression in the literature about Hebrews. Spicq's commentary on Hebrews remains one of the most detailed and fully documented works arguing for a strong, direct Philonic influence on Hebrews.

Recently, however, Ronald Williamson has challenged Spicq's contentions. Williamson succeeds in pointing out a large number of weaknesses in the case built by Spicq. Although Williamson strays too far in the opposite direction in his effort to rule out any Philonic influence, he is correct in his claim that interpreters have tended to exaggerate Philo's influence on the Book of Hebrews. Williamson concludes: "The Writer of Hebrews had never been a Philonist, had never read Philo's works, had never come under the influence of Philo directly or indirectly."[93]

Fortunately, we do not have to choose simply between the extremes of Spicq and Williamson. In spite of Williamson's strong antipathy to a Philonic influence on Hebrews, he is forced to admit that the writer of Hebrews "almost certainly lived and moved in circles where, in broad, general terms, ideas such as those we meet in Philo's works were known and discussed; he drew upon the same fund of cultured Greek vocabulary upon which Philo drew."[94] Williamson's important study cannot be ignored.

It is no longer possible to glibly presuppose a Philonic background to every concept and term in Hebrews with affinities to Philo. But whatever the actual relationship between the writer of Hebrews and Philo (or Philo's writings), both share the common heritage of the Hellenistic Judaism of Alexandria.[95] An examination of the Book of Hebrews reveals at least five testimonies to its Alexandrian background.

1. *Hebrews contains an implicit Wisdom-Christology that has affinities to the Alexandrian teaching about Sophia.* The fact that Hebrews does not actually apply the term *sophia* to Jesus is not decisive.[96] Anyone familiar with the Wisdom doctrine will recognize its echoes in the proem of Hebrews (1:1–4).[97] For example, the rare term *apaygasma* ("effulgence") is used in Hebrews 1:3 to describe Jesus in a manner reminiscent of the way Wisdom is described in the Wisdom of Solomon (7:25–26). Hebrews 1:1–4 does recall the personification of divine Wisdom in Proverbs 8:22ff., but it is likewise true that the vocabulary of Hebrews is indebted to the Alexandrian author of the apocryphal Wisdom of Solomon.

Not only does Hebrews describe Jesus in terms that the Alexandrian literature applied to Sophia; it also ascribes to Jesus the same functions as those fulfilled by Divine Wisdom. He mediates God's revelation, is the agent and sustainer of creation, and reconciles men to God (compare Wisdom of Solomon 7:21–8:1).[98] There seems to be sufficient evidence to support the claim that the Epistle to the Hebrews contains or implies a Wisdom-Christology that draws on the Alexandrian teaching about Sophia.

2. *Hebrews contains an implicit Logos-Christology similar to the Alexandrian Logos doctrine.* Just as the Book of Hebrews does not explictly call Jesus "Sophia," so it does not apply to Him the name "Logos." But there can be no doubt that it contains an implicit Logos-Christology.[99] Predicates that, in the pertinent

Alexandrian literature, are applied to both Logos and Sophia, are applied by the writer of Hebrews to Jesus (for example, Heb. 1:3, "the radiance of his glory, the exact representation of his nature").[100] It is thus clear that the writer believes that Jesus is the *true* Logos and Sophia.

Philo wrote of the Logos as Mediator (*mesitēs*)[101] and Image (*eikon*—cf. Heb. 1:3, where the parallel term *charakter* occurs) of God.[102] The world was created through the agency of the Logos.[103] Philo described the Logos as neither unbegotten (and thus like God) nor begotten (thus like man).[104] As such, the Logos is on the borderline between God and man—mediating from God to man as an ambassador, and from man to God as a suppliant.[105] The Logos is called the "First born Son"[106] (cf. Heb. 1:6) and the "Chief born."[107] The Logos is both Light[108] and the very shadow of God.[109]

The appearance of some of these (e.g., mediator, firstborn, radiance) as predicates of Christ in Hebrews makes it highly likely that the writer of Hebrews was familiar with the Alexandrian Logos doctrine. Even Williamson admits that Hebrews contains "a rudimentary form of Logos Christology."[110]

3. *Hebrews assigns mediatorial functions to Jesus that are similar to the functions of Alexandrian mediators.* Since the writer of Hebrews had knowledge of Alexandrian Judaism, we should expect to find an acquaintance with that culture's promotion of an assortment of mediators that fulfilled certain requirements of Old Testament Wisdom theology and of Platonic philosophy (for example, the need for cosmological mediators between God and an evil, material world). The mediators of Hellenistic Judaism fulfilled at least two specific functions, both of which appear in Hebrews.[111]

a. *The Cosmological Function of the Logos.* The Hellenistic mediators were postulated primarily because of the ontological gap between God and the world. Because Philo stressed the divine transcendence, he faced the problem of how a pure, transcendent Spirit can be related to an evil, material world without compromising either His transcendence or His holiness.[112] Since God could not contaminate His own being by contact with the material world, His action upon the world would have to be through an intermediary being. Thus the first function of the Logos is to act both as an agent through which God brings the world into existence and as an intermediary in God's sustaining relationship with the world.

b. *The Epistemological Function of the Logos*. Philo saw two epistemological questions that demanded answers. How can God make Himself known to man, and how can man attain knowledge of God?[113] Philo maintained that man could know God only through the medium of the Logos, which works in man's reason.[114] "What Philo appears to mean [in passages like *On the Special Laws* 3, 207] is . . . that for ordinary men knowledge of God is obtained through rational contemplation of the invisible world of Ideas."[115] According to Philo's Platonism, man can know the world only via the eternal archetypes (forms) in the Logos. Since the earthly, corporeal world is but a shadowy reflection of the eternally existent forms, any knowledge of the material world is dependent on a prior knowledge of the eternal pattern.

c. *The Cosmological and Epistemological Logos of Hebrews*. The Epistle to the Hebrews begins by describing Christ as the Epistemological Logos, who mediated the revelation of God to men. Before Christ's first coming, God spoke in various ways through the prophets. But that partial and incomplete word is now presented in its final, complete form by God's speaking "in One who was Son." This Son reveals God by being the very effulgence, or radiance, of His being (Heb. 1:1-3). The writer then describes Jesus as the Cosmological Logos,* who mediates as both the creator (Heb. 1:2) and sustainer (1:3) of the universe.†

To the cosmological and epistemological functions of mediation already present in Alexandrian thought, the Epistle to the Hebrews adds a third function, that of the soteriological Logos.[116] In Christianity, people can be redeemed and their sins forgiven only through the efforts of one who mediates between God and man. And so, after the writer of Hebrews has described Jesus as cosmological and epistemological mediator, he continues: "When he had made purification for sins, he sat down at the right hand of the Majesty on high" (Heb. 1:3, RSV). As the later argument of Hebrews makes clear, this is *not* simply an addendum. It anticipates the primary emphasis of the writer of Hebrews. While the cosmological and epistemological functions of the Mediator are not mentioned again in Hebrews, Christ's work as savior and redeemer is studied and examined from every possible angle. Jesus is the soteriological

---

*Paul also uses the notion of the Cosmological Logos when he describes the preexistent Christ as the mediator of creation (see 1 Cor. 8:6 and Col. 1:16).

†The order in Hebrews is reversed in the prologue to John's Gospel, where Christ the Logos is described first in His cosmological function (John 1:3) and then in His epistemological function. Jesus is not only the mediator of divine special revelation (John 1:14); He is also the ground of all human knowledge (John 1:9). Consider Cullmann's perceptive comments: "Whether Heb. 1:1ff. is earlier or later than John 1:1ff., one must in either case notice that it connects the Old Testament word of God with *the* revelation which is the Son himself as the reflection of the glory of God. Hebrews does not call the Son 'Logos.' The first chapter of John does so because it is a prologue to a life of Jesus, which in itself is the starting point for all further Christological reflection. God's revelation is presented in this life not only in the words but also in the actions of Jesus. Jesus himself *is* what he *does*. The Hebrew term *debarim* (words) can also mean 'history,' and when one thinks primarily in terms of the life or 'history' of Jesus, it becomes natural to identify Jesus with the Word" (Cullmann, *Christology*, p. 261).

Logos, who as both priest and sacrifice effects the salvation of the human race.

4. *Hebrews asserts the superiority of Jesus over a group of individuals and classes that served mediatorial functions in Alexandrian thought.* The mediators of the Alexandrian community included Logos, Sophia, the angels, Moses, Melchizedek, and the high priest. Philo had even applied the term *logos* to every member of this list. Attention has already been drawn to the implicit Logos-Christology and Wisdom-Christology of Hebrews. More explicit is the prominence of discussions about angels, Moses, Melchizedek, and the Aaronic high priest throughout the Epistle to the Hebrews. Perhaps a major purpose of the book is the demonstration of the superiority of Jesus (the sole mediator between God and men) to the assorted mediators of Alexandrian Judaism.

5. *The Epistle to the Hebrews manifests a Platonic distinction between a shadowy and less perfect earthly temple and the perfect heavenly temple.* Hebrews 8:5 describes the earthly temple as a "shadow of the heavenly sanctuary," language that seems too reminiscent of Plato's allegory of the cave to be coincidental. Philo had earlier drawn a contrast between an earthly priest and a heavenly priest,[117] from which it is but a small and natural inference to contrast an earthly and a heavenly sanctuary.[118] Philo made frequent use of the Platonic distinction[119] between the real, ideal world and the shadowy replica that humans contact through their physical senses.[120] While James Moffatt's comment is lengthy, it represents the way a number of scholars have reacted to Hebrews 8. For the author of Hebrews, Moffatt writes,

> trained in the Alexandrian philosophy of religion, the present world of sense and time stands over against the world of reality, the former being merely the shadow and copy of the latter. There is an archetypal order of things, eternal and divine, to which the mundane order but dimly corresponds,

and only within this higher order, eternal and invisible, is access to God possible for man. On such a view as this, which ultimately . . . goes back to Platonic idealism, and which has been worked out by Philo, the real world is the transcendent order of things, which is the pattern for the phenomenal universe, so that to attain God man must pass from the lower and outward world of the senses to the inner. But how? Philo employed the Logos or Reason as the medium. Our author similarly holds that men must attain this higher world, but for him it is a *skēnē*, a sanctuary, the real Presence of God, and it is entered not through ecstasy or mystic rapture, but through connection with Jesus Christ, who has not only revealed that world but opened the way into it. The Presence of God is now attainable as it could not be under the outward cultus of the *skēnē* in the OT, for the complete sacrifice has been offered "in the realm of the spirit," thus providing for the direct access of the people to their God.[121]

I will argue shortly that too many commentators have exaggerated the supposed philosophic significance of Hebrews 8:5ff. For now, however, the text provides one more example of the Alexandrian intellectual background of the Book of Hebrews.[122]

HEBREWS AND ALEXANDRIAN JUDAISM

The discussion to this point has shown that the writer to the Hebrews shared the thought world of Alexandrian Judaism. The notion that humans require a mediator between God and themselves or between God and His world is not unique to the New Testament. The concept of mediator pervaded the intellectual milieu to which the writer of Hebrews owed his education. It is a safe assumption that the concept was known and accepted in other parts of the Dispersion as well. Even though the notion of mediator is not unique to the New Testament, and several New Testament declarations about the Mediator may draw on earlier views, the application of the concept of mediator to the person and work of Christ in Hebrews *is* unique.

A Different Hypothesis Presented

Earlier, I drew attention to the contrasting views of Spicq and Williamson regarding an Alexandrian influence on Hebrews. Regarding that, I have an alternative hypothesis to present, namely, *that one purpose, if not the major purpose, of the writer of Hebrews was to expose the inadequacy of the Alexandrian beliefs about mediators.* "Jesus is superior," the writer of Hebrews affirms. "In fact, he is superior to your Alexandrian Logos and Sophia; he is superior to your angelic and priestly mediators; he is superior to Moses and Melchizedek. Jesus is the true Logos, the true Sophia, and the Great High Priest." This superiority of Jesus is demonstrated by showing significant ways in which Jesus differs from the Alexandrian *logoi*. In part, this demonstration of the superiority of Jesus may have been made necessary by the life situation of his readers. The Book of Hebrews suggests that its readers may have been tempted to return to one or more of the "older" mediators because of pressure brought to bear on the Christian community.

I offer this as a hypothesis. Even though, like many hypotheses, irrefutable proof of its truth is not available, the theory has much to commend it. First, it explains the distinctive echoes of Hellenism that can be found in Hebrews. The writer employs a vocabulary that was appropriate to the world of discourse in which one spoke of a mediator. Second, it can account for those forms of statement in which Hebrews *conflicts* with Alexandrian thought.[123] Third, the hypothesis provides a perspective for interpreting many of the key passages in Hebrews. In fact, its success or failure in illuminating these texts should be regarded as the ultimate test of its value.

In spite of the author's apparent affinity to Platonism, by the time he came to write his epistle he was determined to *contrast* his present Christian position with those elements of Platonic philosophy that were incompatible with it. His rejection of Alexandrian Platonism is evident in at least three ways.

1. *The two-story universe of Hebrews 8 is less an endorsement than a correction of Platonism.* Anyone who reads the eighth chapter of Hebrews as a simple application of Platonism to elements of Judaism and Christianity is guilty of a gross inattention to detail.[124] While there is in Hebrews 8 an incontestable familiarity with the thought of Alexandrian Platonism, the chapter evidences even more dramatically a *break* with the content of that philosophy. Platonism has been altered in the service of a distinctively different and quite contrary Christian emphasis. As Williamson explains,

> If the contrast in 8.5 were really Platonic we should have found the Writer of Hebrews explaining that the ministry of Jesus in the heavenly sanctuary had been going on eternally, that the priestly ministry of the Jewish priests over the centuries had been all the time an imperfect copy and shadow of an eternal and timeless ministry exercised by Christ in heaven. The idea that such a heavenly ministry could begin as a result of an event on earth, the crucifixion of the Word made flesh, is about as far removed from Platonism as one could wish to get, and a Philonist would never have wished to get that far away from the Master's teaching while he still remained in any significant way a Philonist. . . . in Platonism the idea is always antecedent to the copy, the copy always an earthly object which can exist only in virtue of the prior and fuller reality of its related idea. The language of 8.5 then, is not proof of the Platonism of Hebrews, but simply an example of how even the language of the philosophers, with which the Writer was clearly familiar, could be used by him to express his own non-philosophical ideas.[125]

Williamson is surely correct in his observation that in Hebrews 8 the writer is neither teaching Platonism nor subordinating revealed truth to Platonic philosophy. *Rather, the writer is adapting the language and perhaps some concepts of Platonism to illustrate a distinctive feature of Christian theology.* These comments on Hebrews 8 lead naturally into the next contrast.

2. *The writer of Hebrews and the Alexandrian Platonists hold conflicting theories about time and history.* The Stoics taught that after the world runs its course, it will be destroyed in a universal conflagration. The world then begins anew and proceeds through a precise repetition of its history in earlier cycles. This creation and destruction and re-creation continue eternally.[126] Philo accepted this view of the cyclical nature of time.[127] For someone holding this notion, events in history could never attain the dramatic significance or ultimate value we find assigned to some historical occurrences in the Book of Hebrews.

The writer of Hebrews repeatedly stresses the historical uniqueness of what Jesus did to effect the redemption of the human race. Jesus "has no need, like those [Levitical] high priests, to offer sacrifices daily . . . he did this *once for all* when he offered up himself" (7:27, RSV, my emphasis). It is not necessary, he adds later, that Christ should "offer himself repeatedly" like the sacrifices offered through the Jewish high priest. "But as it is, he has appeared *once for all* at the end of the age to put away sin by the sacrifice of himself . . . so Christ [has] been offered *once* to bear the sins of many" (9:25–28, RSV, my emphasis). Similar comments about the finality of Christ's redemptive work are made in Hebrews 10:10–14.

The once-for-all, fully completed, never-to-be-repeated, and final character of Jesus' sacrifice contrasts sharply with the continuing sacrifices of the Levitical priests. Unlike the Old Testament priest, whose work of sacrifice was never done, Jesus' redemptive work is finished. Jesus has done it once-for-all. A Hellenist could not help but notice the writer's explicit disavowal of the Stoic and Philonic view of time and history. Williamson states this forcefully: "For Hebrews, time matters, does not repeat itself (events happen within it 'once for all') . . . events in time can be decisive, crucial and climactic. . . . Events in time could never hold for Philo that eternal significance and final value they held for the Writer of Hebrews."[128] The author of Hebrews perceives time, not as cyclical, but as *linear*. This perspective makes it possible to see history as progressing towards a goal, the final victory of God. The linear view of history allows the writer to see particular moments in history, such as the crucifixion, as unique and nonrepeatable events. Thus, this emphasis of Hebrews clashes irreconcilably with the Alexandrian mind-set about time.

3. *Hebrews and Alexandrian Platonism represent conflicting views about the earthly material world.* One of the central and most familiar tenets of Platonism was its disparagement of this earthly world in comparison with the ideal world of rational forms. Philo shared Plato's disregard for the corporeal, sensible world. The writer of Hebrews did not do so. For him, the stage of God's drama of redemption is not heaven or some ideal world but earth itself. It is not eternity but time in which God acts to redeem the human race. God's final revelation, as defined by the Letter to the Hebrews, is given in a sphere unacceptable to a Platonist like Philo.

What becomes clear in a study of Hebrews is not that the writer was unfamiliar with Platonism but that he self-consciously and intentionally set himself to contrast his understanding of the Christian message with the philosophy he himself may have once accepted and that his audience may still have found attractive.

It remains only to consider more specific differences between the Alexandrian mediators and the Mediator portrayed in Hebrews. I shall note, in order, the intentional contrasts drawn in Hebrews between Jesus and Philo's Logos, the angels, Moses, and the High Priest.

1. *The Logos-Mediator of Hebrews is not Philo's metaphysical abstraction but a specific, individual, historical person.* The Logos of Philo was *not* a person. To be sure, Philo wrote about the Logos in personal terms, but his personifications were metaphors for a metaphysical abstraction. According to A. H. Armstrong, the precise degree of the independent existence of Philo's Logos "must remain doubtful because Philo is so vague about it, and it certainly cannot be said to be a person, still less a Divine Person."[129] There is absolutely no support for the position that Philo believed the Logos to be personal, let alone a person living in history. Philo's Logos is especially lacking in the personal, messianic, and soteriological traits so prominent in the Christian account of Jesus, the soteriological Logos. Philo's Logos is not a person or messiah or savior but a cosmic principle, postulated to solve assorted metaphysical and epistemological problems.[130] Our conclusion on this point must be that of Copleston, that "in the Philonic doctrine of the Logos there is no reference to an historic man."[131]

2. *Philo's philosophical system is totally incompatible with the notion of the Incarnation.* Philo's view of man was, of course, Platonic: man is a dualism of a material body and an immaterial soul.[132] The body is a prison house for the soul, which longs to break free from the body and its senses and wing its way back to God.[133] Although we should not expect to find in Philo's writings the Bible's teaching about the

Incarnation, the more important question is the logical incompatibility of such a doctrine with Philo's stated positions. Since this doctrine is so crucial to the argument of Hebrews (see 2:5–16; 10:4ff.), a discovery of the impossibility of such a doctrine in Philo's thought must be regarded seriously.

It certainly seems unlikely that Philo could have made peace with the notion of incarnation, given his disparagement of the body as a tomb of the soul.[134] The doctrine would also be out of place in Philo's system because of his extreme emphasis on the impossibility of God's contact with matter. Copleston comments that it "does not require much thought to recognize that the Philonic philosophy could never admit the Christian doctrine of the Incarnation—at least if Philonism were to remain self-consistent—since it lays such stress on the Divine Transcendence that direct contact with matter is excluded."[135] As if these observations were not enough, there are passages in Philo that denounce any attempt to bring God and man together. Philo derides the Epicurean position that the gods exist in human form.[136] He shuns anthropomorphic language about God.[137] On several occasions, he repeats the words, "God is not as a man."[138] Clearly, Philo would have found the Incarnation both incomprehensible and abhorrent.

But the Jesus described in Hebrews not only becomes man but participates in a full range of that which is human, including temptation to sin. Cullmann is correct when he notes there is no trace of Docetism in Hebrews. "Jesus was really a man, not just God disguised as a man."[139] The evidence seems clear that the writer of Hebrews had a previous relationship to Alexandrian Platonism and is now determined to attack major aspects of that philosophical position in an effort to show the superiority of Christ and the Christian scheme of mediation and redemption.

3. *The description in Hebrews of Jesus' compassion for His brethren is incompatible*

with Philo's view of the emotions. Philo appears to have been influenced by the Stoic disparagement of emotion. While the writer of Hebrews repeatedly stresses Jesus' compassionate concern for His brethren,[140] it is clear that Philo views the attainment of *apatheia* (freedom from passion, emotion, and affection) as a much more important achievement than *metriopatheia*.[141] For Philo, compassion can only be second best to *apatheia*. The author of Hebrews saw Jesus' complete possession of compassion as one significant sign of His superiority over the Jewish priests, while Philo maintained that the high priest was not supposed to mourn. In Philo's words, the high priest "will have his feelings of pity under control and continue throughout free from sorrow."[142] Or to cite another text, "the high priest is precluded from all outward mourning."[143] But contrast this with the account of Jesus in Hebrews. Jesus is "not a high priest who is unable to sympathize with our weaknesses" (4:15, RSV). Rather, Jesus "can deal gently with the ignorant and wayward, since he himself is beset with weakness" (5:2, RSV). During His earthly ministry, "Jesus offered up prayers and supplications, with loud cries and tears, to him who was able to save him from death" (5:7, RSV). Hebrews pictures Jesus as compassionate to His lost brethren and able to experience the full range of human emotions.

4. *Philo's Logos could never be described, as Hebrews pictures Jesus, as either suffering, being tempted to sin, or dying.* The claims of Hebrews 2:17; 4:15; and 5:7 are even more extraordinary when seen against the backdrop of the Alexandrian Logos. Williamson notes:

> One of the dominant themes of the Epistle to the Hebrews is the full and authentic reality of the humanity of Jesus. It was this, according to the Writer, which fitted Him to be "a merciful and faithful high priest" (2:17). It was because Christ has "suffered and been tempted that He is able to help those who are tempted" (2:18; cf. 4:14–16).

The Writer of Hebrews was convinced that it was Jesus' genuine involvement in human life, suffering and temptation which has equipped Him, as nothing else could have done, to help ordinary, sinful, suffering men and women.[144]

The idea of a mediator who has "in every respect . . . been tempted as we are" (4:15, RSV), who "has suffered and been tempted" (2:18, RSV) and who "himself is beset with weakness" (5:2, RSV) would have been repugnant to an Alexandrian like Philo. The last straw, for Philo, would have been, as it was for the Greek mind,[145] the death—no, not just the death—the *crucifixion* of the Christian Mediator. The idea of the Logos becoming incarnate would have been hard enough for Philo to take. To compound the foolishness by the Logos's submitting to death by crucifixion would have been unthinkable. But the writer of Hebrews does not apologize for his emphasis on Jesus' death. He stresses it and glories in it. The death of Jesus was not incidental to His work as Mediator. Jesus' self-sacrifice through His ignominious death was the very ground of His work as Mediator (9:15).

Unlike Philo's impersonal Logos, Jesus is a unique, historical, individual person, the incarnation of God, who suffered, was tempted, and died for the sins of mankind. What is important here is the truly significant contrasts between the Mediator of Hebrews and the mediators of Philo, of the other Alexandrians, and perhaps of the proto-Gnosticism Paul appears to warn against in Colossians.[146] There are unmistakable echoes of an Alexandrian influence in Hebrews. But the author places all of his emphasis on the differences that make Christ superior to anything the Alexandrians had to offer.[147]

The Superiority of Jesus to the Angels

The suddenness of the transition from the proem to the subject of angels at Hebrews 1:4 suggests that something of immediate importance was on the writer's mind. Of the assorted theories offered to explain this shift,[148] the one that makes the most sense is that the writer's audience held false views of the angels as mediators, views that posed a threat to the supremacy of Jesus. Galatians 3:19 is evidence of a Jewish belief in an angelic mediation with respect to the giving of the Law, a point alluded to in Hebrews 2:2. Paul's reference to this belief forms a part of his argument to the Galatians that the Law that was "ordained through angels" is inferior to the unmediated promise God made to Abraham. In Williamson's words:

> For the Writer of Hebrews angels may have been an anxiety because of a tendency on the part of his readers to worship or give undue reverence to them, or because they were regarded as the mediators of a revelation of God which he was doing his best to convince his readers had now been replaced by a new and final revelation mediated by Christ alone. For him therefore the problem of angels was one to be dealt with by showing what was, according to a Christian interpretation, the true relationship of angels to Christ and their comparatively lowly office of spiritual ministers to those who have become heirs of salvation.[149]

If we continue to suppose the writer's intent to contrast the biblical Mediator with the Alexandrian mediators, the place of Hebrews 1:4–2:18 in his argument becomes clearer when the following points are considered. Philo applied the term *logos* (pl., *logoi*) to angels at least seventeen times.[150] He described angels as ambassadors between God and men,[151] a function that implies a mediatorial role. In other passages, he actually used the term *mesitēs* (mediator) of angels.[152]

What stands out in any analysis of the Hebrews' account of angels is the major differences between the angelic *logoi* of Alexandria and the true Logos of the New Testament. First, Philo's angels were not personal beings; they were only powers of God, that is, impersonal elements of the Stream of "Powers" radiating out from God's own being. Second, the writer of Hebrews will have nothing to do with the multiple mediators of the Alexandrians.[153] He implies, rather, that there is only *one* mediator. Because Christ mediates a better covenant than the old, His priestly ministry is superior to that of the priests under the old covenant (Heb. 8:6). Since the new covenant Jesus mediates has as its sacrifice a death that has the power to redeem people from the penalties for sin that are set forth under the old covenant, those who believe are able to receive the promised inheritance of eternal life and cleansing from sin (9:15). The Jesus who mediates the new covenant (12:24) does not call the believer to a frightful Mount Sinai (12:18). The believer is called rather to Mount Zion and the city of the living God (12:22). Third, unlike Philo,[154] the author of Hebrews never applies Old Testament statements about the angels to the Logos. Fourth, the writer uses seven quotations from the Old Testament to prove the superiority of Christ the Mediator[155] to the angels.[156]

More problematic is the purpose of the writer in Hebrews 2:5–18. Most likely, these verses respond to a possible objection to the superiority of Christ over the angels, an objection grounded on the Christian's belief in the Incarnation. If, as the psalmist suggests (Psalm 8), humans are lower than the angels, and Christ became a man, how is it still possible to maintain His superiority over the angels? Complicating this problem is the additional fact that Christ *died*. The writer of Hebrews answers such objections by pointing out three facts: (1) if it is true that Christ became lower, then it must also be true that He was originally higher; (2) Jesus became lower than the angels for a little while, that is, His lowering was temporary (2:9); and (3) His humiliation (the Incarnation) was essential to God's plan of salvation and it was followed by His permanent exaltation (2:7–8).[157] Jesus is now "crowned with glory and honor" (2:9), that is, He has been

elevated to a rank and dignity that again is higher
than that of the angels (cf. 1:4).

The writer in this passage (2:14–16) also
suggests that since it was human beings, not
angels, that Christ came to save, this salvation
required a real incarnation—a savior like Jesus,
not an impersonal, heavenly Logos. It required a
mediator who could experience temptations,
suffer, and die. Jesus' fulfillment of this divinely
appointed role in the plan of salvation does not,
in any way, make him inferior to the angels.
Rather, it qualifies him to be a compassionate
Mediator. This is the clear message of the
second chapter of Hebrews.*

**The Superiority of
Jesus to Moses**

Because of its brevity, clarity, and simplicity,
Hebrews 3:1–6 can be handled more quickly.
Philo viewed Moses as a mediator.[158] In fact, he
occasionally identified Moses with the Logos.
"The estimate of Moses found in Philo's work is
so lofty that one is almost bound to ask the
question: Was Moses, in Philo's view, human or
divine?"[159] The writer's effort, then, to prove the
superiority of Christ to Moses is compatible with
my hypothesis. Moses was simply one of the
Alexandrian *logoi,* and Christ is better than he.

**The Superiority of
Jesus to the
Aaronic High Priest**

The primary concern of Hebrews is not the
cosmological and epistemological dimensions of
a Logos Christology, but the soteriological
Logos, the Mediator who secures the forgiveness and redemption of a fallen human race
through His priestly office.

Philo frequently referred to the Logos in
priestly terms.[160] He did this, apparently, because the Logos was the mediator by which men
approach God. When the High Priest performed

*Jesus' superiority to the angels conflicts not only with
their role as mediators in Alexandrian Judaism but also with
their important place in some Gnostic systems. See part 3 of
this book.

his priestly work, he stood between man and God and, indeed, became something greater than man but less than God.[161] The High Priest, Philo wrote, is a mediator who stands on the "borderline" between man and God.[162] As Logos, the High Priest is even described in language that suggests his sinlessness.[163]

But even when Philo's Logos is described in priestly terms, it is still a nonpersonal principle abiding in the world of Ideas. It is not a man such as we find described in Hebrews 2:17–18. The Christian's Great High Priest is the incarnate Logos, whose sinlessness was maintained while He shared the lot of humankind (Heb. 4:15). The author of Hebrews unites the idea of the High Priest's sacrifice for the sins of the people with the notion of the Suffering Servant of Yahweh to provide a concept of self-sacrifice (9:12). The concept of the Suffering Servant had carried the idea of *passive* suffering. In Hebrews, this suffering appears as an *active* self-sacrifice that becomes the highest expression of the high priestly ministry of atonement and reconciliation. The same act of self-sacrifice that provides an effectual ground for God's forgiveness of human sin also fulfilled the priesthood of the old covenant at the same time that it abolished it. The readers of Hebrews must never again think of the old covenant as God's final word. God's Word in these last days, His Word "in One who is Son," includes a replacement of the old covenant with a new covenant that is accompanied by a final and perfect priesthood. Now that Jesus is the Great High Priest in the highest sense, all other high priests have become superfluous.

The priestly mediatorial work of Jesus has three dimensions—past, present, and future. With respect to the past, Jesus is the source, or cause (*aitios*), of our salvation (5:9). The Christian can look back and see the fully completed sacrificial work of Christ that constitutes the ground of his redemption (9:12, 28). So far as the believer's present is concerned, he has an advocate in heaven "who always lives to make intercession" for him (7:25; cf. 9:24). With respect to the future, there is an unmistakable eschatological dimension to Christ's high priestly work. The same High Priest who accomplished so much for the believer in His past work and whose continuing advocacy is so important to the believer's present life still has something to do in the believer's future. "Christ . . . will appear a second time . . . to save those who are eagerly waiting for him" (9:28, RSV).[164]

One of the more important elements of Hebrews' depiction of Christ's high priestly work is found in Hebrews 7:22. In this text, a different term (*engyos*) is used, a term that conveys an idea not found in *mesitēs*.[165] As F. F. Bruce explains:

> In common Greek [*engyos*] is found frequently in legal and other documents in the sense of a surety or guarantor. The *engyos* undertakes a weightier responsibility than the *mesitēs* or mediator . . . he is answerable for the fulfillment of the obligation which he guarantees. . . . The old covenant had a mediator (cf. Gal. 3:19) but no surety; there was no one to guarantee the fulfillment of the covenant which He mediates, on the manward side as well as on the Godward side. As the Son of God, he confirms God's eternal covenant with His people; as His people's representative, He satisfies its terms with perfect acceptance in God's sight.[166]

Jesus the guarantor (*engyos*) is not simply a go-between; He is personally responsible for that which He guarantees. The old covenant lacked anyone who could guarantee it. But Jesus guarantees the new covenant on both sides— God's and man's. Jesus is not simply a mediator (*mesitēs*) who happens to bring two opposed parties together. In Jesus, God and man are conjoined. As God's Son, Jesus ensures God's side of the compact. He fulfills the human side of the covenant as the perfect representative of the entire race. As *mesitēs*, Jesus is superior to the mediators of the Alexandrians. But Jesus is superior in an even greater sense, inasmuch as He performs a function unlike that of any Alexandrian mediator. Only one who is both God and man can perfectly guarantee the new covenant.

CONCLUSIONS

By design, this chapter is the most complex and detailed of the book. Earlier chapters started slowly so that readers approaching this subject for the first time could get their feet wet. I think it is clear that if the influence of Hellenistic philosophy can be detected anywhere in the New Testament, it can be found in the Book of Hebrews. I have argued that attempts to find traces of such philosophy in the writings of Paul fail to persuade. Likewise, the Logos doctrine of John's Gospel proves unsatisfactory as evidence of a philosophical influence, since there are Old Testament sources for it as well as manifest differences between it and Hellenistic philosophy. But the Epistle to the Hebrews is another story.

It is clear that the writer of Hebrews knew personally the language and teachings of Alexandrian Judaism. In all likelihood, he knew the writings of Philo. But what stands out in our study of Hebrews is the fact that the author uses the language and ideas he knew before his conversion to confute the Alexandrian philosophy and theology and to prove the superiority of Christ and the Christian message. Is there any way, then, in which it makes sense to say that the writer of Hebrews was dependent on, or borrowed from, Philo or Alexandrian Judaism? I judge that the use of words like *influence, dependence,* and *borrow* in this context are inappropriate. To use a modern example, imagine someone who prior to his conversion is involved in some contemporary anti-Christian movement. Suppose further that he is one of a number of people in that movement who are converted to Christianity. But then imagine that some of these new converts, for one reason or another, are strongly tempted to return to their former anti-Christian position. If, in preaching to these potential backsliders, our author uses the terminology and ideas of his former position in an effort to refute it and demonstrate the superiority of Christian truth, does it make sense to speak of him as being influenced by, or dependent on, that earlier set of beliefs? Surely not.

What all this shows is that attempts to prove the dependence (in the strong sense) of the first-century church on alien ideas or terminology require far more than the discovery of parallels. One must also show that it was the author's intention to incorporate the alien ideas into Christianity. As I have shown, the intention of the writer of Hebrews was just the opposite. This apologetic (or missionary, or evangelistic) motive could explain any real parallels in thought or language that might pop up elsewhere in the New Testament. Effective preaching (and Hebrews is an extended sermon) will use language and ideas that are most likely to affect the audience being addressed.

My hypothesis about the apologetic purpose of Hebrews' use of Alexandrian terminology and ideas is relevant to speculation about the source of the Johannine Logos. The Book of Hebrews demonstrates that there was a circle of believers who knew and used terms like *logos* early in the history of the church.* Whether or not the Fourth Gospel was written after Hebrews, perhaps its use of such terminology only points to its author's personal contact with such Christians.[167]

---

*I agree with those commentators who conclude that the fact that Hebrews repeatedly refers to temple sacrifices points to its being written before the destruction of the temple in A.D. 70.

Part Two:

The Mystery Religions

chapter seven

The Mystery Religions: An Overview

Numerous claims have been made by modern scholars that the Hellenistic mystery religions influenced early Christianity. Besides introducing those claims, this chapter overviews the history, development, and characteristics of the mystery religions.

Other than Judaism and Christianity, the most influential religions in the Hellenistic age were the so-called mystery religions. The mystery religions are relevant to this book because of repeated claims in this century that early Christianity was influenced (in the strong sense) by one or more of them. These Hellenistic religions are called mystery religions because of their use of secret ceremonies that were thought to bring their initiates such benefits as "salvation."

It would be wrong to think that the mystery religions were the only manifestations of the 115 religious spirit in the Orient or the eastern reaches of the Roman Empire. One could also find public cults that were not exclusive. But the mystery religions were popular in their day for much the same reason that they retain an interest for scholars today: they claimed to satisfy the hunger of their age for some kind of salvation, for the successful attainment of a higher level of life.

Each region of the Mediterranean world seems to have produced its own mystery religion.* Out of Greece came the cults of Demeter and Dionysus, as well as their later developments, the Eleusinian and Orphic mystery religions. Asia Minor (more specifically, the region known as Phrygia) gave birth to the cult of Cybele and Attis. The cult of Isis and Osiris (later Serapis) originated in Egypt, while Syria and Palestine saw the rise of the cult of Adonis. Finally, Persia (Iran) was a leading early locale for the cult of Mithras.

The mystery religions came in two major forms. The earlier Greek mystery religions (such as the Eleusinian mysteries) were civil or state religions in the sense that they attained the status of a public or civil cult. While these civil mystery religions had their private and personal dimensions, they also served a national or public function. In Greece, they were associated with a national festival observed throughout that land. The later non-Greek mystery religions were personal, private, and individualistic.

THE MYSTERY RELIGIONS AND CHRISTIANITY

Proponents of an early Christian dependence on the mystery religions have stated their case in different ways. Among the many claims published in this century are the following:

1. Early Christianity was just another Hellenistic mystery religion.

---

*Each mystery religion named in this paragraph will be discussed more fully in chapter 8.

2. Important Christian beliefs and practices were either borrowed from, or were heavily dependent on, similar beliefs and practices in the mysteries.

3. Both baptism and the Lord's Supper evidence the influence of similar rituals in the mystery cults.

4. Among the many Christian beliefs drawn from the mysteries is the Pauline doctrine of salvation, which parallels the essential themes of the mysteries: a savior-god dies violently for those he will eventually deliver, after which the god is restored to life.

Claims like these were frequently encountered in scholarly publications from about 1890 to 1930 or 1940. A major movement in the development and promotion of such theories was the History of Religions School (*Religionsgeschichtliche Schule*). The two most influential members of this school were German New Testament scholar Wilhelm Bousset* and German classicist and historian Richard Reitzenstein.† At first Reitzenstein argued that the Christian belief in rebirth was derived from an ancient Iranian mystery religion. Later he modified his position and taught that the original source of this doctrine was a Gnostic cult known as Mandaeanism.[168] Reitzenstein denied that either the teachings of Jesus and the early church or Paul's own Judaism was the primary source of Paul's gospel. He thought the most likely sources were elements of the mystery cults and especially Gnosticism.‡ In fact, he went so far as to call Paul the greatest of the Gnostics.[169]

Bousset focused his quest for the source of Paul's religion on the Hellenistic mystery religions. In his 1913 book *Kyrios Christos*,[170] he argued that these mysteries subconsciously

---

*Bousset (1865–1931) taught New Testament at the universities of Göttingen and Giessen.

†Reitzenstein (1861–1931) served as professor at the universities of Strasbourg and Göttingen.

‡Gnosticism is treated in part 3 of this book.

influenced Hellenistic Christians in places like Antioch, helping to transform the original, simple gospel of Jesus into a redemptive religion with strong affinities to the mystery religions. Bousset thought that one important evidence of this pagan Hellenistic influence in early Christianity was the application of the pagan term *Lord* to Jesus.

An even more radical view was set forth by Alfred Loisy,* who maintained that Christianity and the mysteries shared an essential belief in, and ceremonial enactment of, the death and resurrection of a dying and rising savior-god.[171] Although Samuel Angus, another member of the school, adopted the same basic position, he advanced it in more cautious terms.[172] Among those who stressed a major dependence of early Christianity on the mysteries and whose works were published in English are: Edwin Hatch, Percy Gardner, John Glasse, Arthur Weigall, Shirley Jackson Case, W. H. Hyde, and William Vassall.[173]

The list of early twentieth-century opponents of the claim of a primitive Christian dependence on the mystery religions is equally impressive. It included, for example, such distinguished German scholars as Carl Clemen[174] and Adolf von Harnack. Harnack argued:

> We must reject the comparative mythology which finds a causal connection between everything and everything else, which tears down solid barriers, bridges chasms as though it were child's play, and spins combinations from superficial similarities. . . . By such methods one can turn Christ into a sun god in the twinkling of an eye, or one can bring up the legends attending the birth of every conceivable god, or one can catch all sorts of mythological doves to keep company with the baptismal dove; and find any number of celebrated asses to follow the ass on which Jesus rode into Jerusalem; and thus, with the magic wand of

---

*Loisy (1857–1940) was a radical Roman Catholic who, in 1908, was finally excommunicated for his views.

"comparative religion," triumphantly eliminate every spontaneous trait in any religion.[175]

Other scholars (whose works are available in English) who believed the mystery religions exercised little if any substantive influence on early Christianity include Samuel Cheetham, H. A. A. Kennedy, J. Gresham Machen, and A. D. Nock.[176]

For a number of years now, the consensus among biblical scholars has been that the earlier opponents of a primitive Christian dependence on the mystery religions got the better of their debate. Younger scholars now returning from doctoral studies in Germany report that, over there at least, the question of a mystery influence on the New Testament is a dead issue. Once again, however, we find that news like this has been slow to reach American scholars in fields other than biblical studies. For example, Edwin Burtt, a distinguished Cornell University philosopher for many years, was still too close to ideas picked up in his younger days when he wrote that the result of Paul's mature reflection about his own religious experience "may be briefly described as a remolding of the moralized cult of Yahweh, developed by the Hebrew prophets, into a mystery religion of personal salvation, in which the crucified Jesus of Nazareth appears not merely as the promised Messiah but also as a savior-god."[177]

Burtt published his views in the 1950s, but claims like this still show up in works published during the last decade or so. In a 1981 book, Colgate University professor Joscelyn Godwin essentially reduces Christianity to the status of just another mystery religion.[178] In a 1982 book entitled *The Sacred Executioner,* Hyam Maccoby sets forth a thesis that would have been much less surprising fifty years ago:

> Thus, though the outward limbs of Paul's system are those of Gnosticism, the heart of it is derived from the mystery religions, which preserved the

ancient concept of the sacrificial death of a god. Whenever Paul writes about the sacrificial efficacy of the Crucifixion, he uses the language of the mystery religions.[179]

The distinguished Columbia University philosopher John Herman Randall, Jr., continuing his quest for pagan roots of early Christianity, wrote:

> Christianity, in the hands of Saul of Tarsus, the real formulator of Christian theology, and of certain other early Christians, notably the author of the Fourth Gospel, became one such incarnation and mystery cult among many other competitors. It became the Jewish rival of the cults of Isis, of the Great Mother [Cybele], of Mithras, and of many Gnostic sects.[180]

And not surprisingly, philosopher W. T. Jones also has an opinion on this subject:

> For Paul understood his vision of Jesus, the anointed of the Lord, not in the narrowly Jewish sense of Jesus' disciples, but in the light of the wider Hellenistic culture in which he had been born and which he had put aside when he went to Jerusalem to study under the rabbis. That is to say, Paul naturally interpreted his mystical experience in the light of his knowledge of the mystery cults already popular and widespread in the East. Thus, though there seems to have been nothing mystical in the teachings of Jesus nor in the earliest interpretation of them, Paul understood the Jesus movement as a mystery religion.[181]

A few pages later, Jones adds the following:

> If he [Paul] had been a Greek, not a Jew, the religion he fathered would probably have been just another Eastern mystery cult—an ethical and metaphysical dualism to which was attached the notion of a savior god dying for his worshipers. Because he was a Jew, and a Jew of the Diaspora, he superimposed a mystery cult on a Judaic base. It is precisely because his understanding of Jesus' message was compounded of so many elements— traditional Judaism, the Messiah cult, the mystery

of a resurrected god—that his teaching of the message had so universal an appeal.[182]

What shall one say to such an assortment of claims? After reviewing similar charges, one historian of philosophy (Gordon Clark) could only conclude: "Such surmises are not so much bad scholarship as prejudiced irresponsibility."[183] As strong as Clark's statement is, it does not even address the extent to which assertions like those quoted are out of step with the tide of contemporary scholarship.

Those who advocated an early Christian dependence on the mystery religions were a diverse group. Some, like Reitzenstein and Bousset, drew up extensive lists of parallel ideas and language. They said that Christianity began as a mystery religion and grew even more syncretistic after the first century A.D. A more moderate group acknowledged early Christian accommodation to some Hellenistic elements but saw Judaism as the dominant influence on first-century Christianity. Others detected some accommodation by primitive Christianity to Hellenistic culture but regarded it as rather insignificant.

Much confusion results at this point from inattention to questions about the degree of accommodation. Suppose a biblical writer, in order to communicate his distinctive message more effectively, adopts certain pagan language used by his audience. Is that accommodation? Imagine that a New Testament author refers to pagan ideas in order to contrast more sharply his own distinctive Christian beliefs.* Is that accommodation? I judge not. Once again, we find that it is not the mere presence of genuine parallels in thought and language that proves dependence and accommodation. We must analyze the biblical writing to see if the author's Christian beliefs have been shaped by, or derived from, the non-Christian parallel. Hugo

*As I pointed out in chapter 6, this was likely true of the Book of Hebrews.

Rahner declares that even if early Christians like Paul did borrow "words, images, and gestures from the mysteries, they did so not as seekers but as possessors of a religious substance; what they borrowed was not the substance but a dress wherein to display it. . . ."[184] Commitment to a high view of Scripture is not at all inconsistent with saying that biblical writers could have adapted language and ideas from their culture for the specific purpose of explaining and communicating the Christian message. Contemporary missionaries do this all the time.

BASIC TRAITS OF THE MYSTERY RELIGIONS

It will be helpful at this point if I gather together a complex mass of material and identify those features that the mystery religions shared in common. Whenever this is done, however, it is important to avoid a mistake found in many writings on the subject. Many authors have written about the mystery religions in such a way as to suggest that there was one common, or general, mystery religion. Later I will point out how this serious error is the basis of a number of the claims about an early Christian dependence on the cults. While a tendency towards eclecticism among several of the mysteries developed rather late (after A.D. 300), they were distinct religions during the century when Christianity began. Moreover, each mystery cult itself assumed different forms in different locales and underwent significant changes, especially after A.D. 100.

1. Central to the mysteries was their use of the annual vegetation cycle, in which life is renewed each spring and dies each fall. Followers of the mystery cults found deep symbolic significance in the natural process of growth, death, decay, and rebirth. According to Rahner, "We know definitely that, at a very early date, hopes of an afterlife became associated with the mystical rites of these vegetation cults, and the gods of growth are in large part also gods of the dead.

And so the primordial mystery, after its purification by the Greek spirit, became a symbol of the whole mystery of life, a consecration of the chain of the generations forever engendering new life. . . ."[185]

2. Not surprisingly, each mystery religion made important use of secret ceremonies, often in connection with an initiation rite. The mystery rites tied the initiates together at the same time they separated them from outsiders. In addition to the secret ceremony that marked a person's entrance into the cult, every mystery religion also "imparted a 'secret,' a knowledge of the life of the deity and the means of union with him. There was a sacred tradition of ritual and cult usages expounded by hierophants [interpreters] and handed down by a succession of priests or teachers."[186] Whatever place particular mysteries allowed knowledge to have in their cult, it was a secret, or esoteric, knowledge, attainable only by the initiated and never revealed to those outside the circle of the religion. While several cults did stress the role of knowledge (*gnōsis*) in achieving redemption, the term referred not so much to the cognizance of a set of truths as to a "higher knowledge" associated with their secret ceremonies.

3. A basic element of the mystery religions was a myth in which the deity either returned to life after death or else triumphed over his enemies. Implicit in the myth was the theme of redemption from everything earthly and temporal. The secret meaning of the cult and its accompanying myth was expressed in "a Sacramental drama . . . which portrayed before the wondering eyes of the privileged observers the story of the struggles, sufferings, and victory of a patron deity, the travail of nature in which life ultimately triumphs over death, and joy is born of pain."[187] The dependence of both the myth

and the drama upon the annual cycle of nature is obvious.* As Angus explains, the drama "appealed primarily to the emotions and aimed at producing psychic and mystic effects by which the neophyte might experience the exaltation of a new life."[188]

4. The mysteries had little if any use for doctrine or correct belief. They were primarily concerned with the emotional state of their followers. According to Angus, "the Mysteries, with the exceptions of the Hermetic theology and Orphism, were never conspicuously doctrinal or dogmatic: they were weak intellectually and theologically."[189] Speaking generally, Angus notes that "the Mysteries made their appeal not to the intellect, but through eye, ear, and imagination to the emotions."[190] Even Aristotle observed that "the *mystai* are not intended to learn anything, but to suffer something and thus be made worthy."[191] The mysteries used many different means to affect the emotions and imaginations of their followers in order to quicken their union with the god: processions, fasting, a play, acts of purification, blazing lights, and esoteric liturgies.

5. The immediate goal of the initiates was a mystical experience that led them to feel that they had achieved union with their god. But beyond this quest for a mystical union were two more ultimate goals: some kind of redemption, or salvation, and immortality. The initiation ceremony was supposed to end the alienation of the *mystes* (initiate) from his god, making possible communion with the deity and eventual triumph over death. Angus states that the mysteries

> professed to remove estrangement between man and God, to procure forgiveness of sins, to furnish mediation. Means of purification and formulae of access to God, and acclamations of confidence and

---

*It is important to keep in mind that the myth and the rites of the cults developed from original fertility rites.

victory were part of the apparatus of every Mystery. . . . These redemption-religions thus promised salvation and provided the worshiper with a patron deity in life and death. This salvation consisted in release from the tyranny of Fate, alleviation from the burdens and limitations of existence, comfort in the sorrows of man's lot, a real identification with his god guaranteeing *palingenesia* (rebirth), and hope beyond.[192]

Many who write about the mysteries describe how the initiates of the various cults shared in the "resurrection" and subsequent "immortality" of their deity, terminology that I shall shortly criticize. Supposedly, as the initiate achieved union with his god, he himself attained a state of deification. In this identification with the god, mysticism and a magical view of certain "sacraments" (another questionable term often used in this context) play an important role. German New Testament scholar Rudolf Bultmann (1884–1976), perhaps the most influential recent proponent of ideas rescued from the work of Bousset and Reitzenstein, defines "the general sense of the mysteries . . . as the imparting of 'salvation.'" For this reason, he observes, the gods of the mystery cults are regarded as "saviors." The salvation that they promise "includes all the blessings it is possible to desire; deliverance from all the perils of life, such as storm and shipwreck, protection from sickness and misfortune. But above all it includes the salvation of the soul and immortality."[193]

PRELIMINARY WARNINGS

Before this chapter closes with a brief historical overview of the development of the mystery religions, some preliminary warnings are in order. Many of the publications that purport to find signs of an early Christian dependence on the mystery religions repeat a number of fundamental errors. In many cases they ignore important differences between different cults or between different stages of the same religion so as to suggest too great an agreement among the mysteries. Sometimes they go so far as to imply that the Hellenistic world contained but one basic mystery religion. This can be seen, for example, in a 1973 book by Joseph B. Tyson, who blurs important distinctions within the development of the various mysteries, ignores crucial information about changes during the evolution of the cults, and leaves the impression that first-century Christianity was confronted by and was influenced by one basic mystery religion.[194]

Another common fault encountered in many discussions of the mystery religions is the use of careless language. One frequently encounters scholars who first use Christian terminology to describe pagan beliefs and practices and then marvel at the awesome parallels they think they have discovered. One can go a long way towards "proving" early Christian syncretism by describing some mystery belief or practice in Christian terminology. A good recent example of this can be found in Godwin's book *Mystery Religions in the Ancient World*, which describes the *criobolium** as a "blood baptism" in which the initiate is "washed in the blood of the lamb."[195] An uninformed reader might be stunned by this remarkable similarity to Christianity (see Rev. 7:14), whereas a more knowledgeable reader will regard Godwin's description as the reflection of a strong, negative bias against Christianity.

One should also be on the watch for the exaggerations and oversimplifications that abound in this kind of literature. One will encounter exaggerated claims about alleged likenesses between baptism and the Lord's Supper

---

*I explain the *criobolium* and the more common rite known as the *taurobolium* later. Since the taurobolium went through several major stages of development, it would be misleading for me to offer a general description or definition now.

and similar "sacraments" in certain mystery cults. Attempts to find analogies between the resurrection of Christ and the alleged "resurrections" of the mystery deities involve massive amounts of oversimplification and inattention to detail. Furthermore, claims about the centrality of a notion of rebirth in certain mysteries are greatly overstated.[196]

The Three Stages of Development

Hugo Rahner has provided a helpful service by dividing the historical development of Christianity and the mystery religions into three periods: (1) the first two centuries after Christ (A.D. 1–200); (2) the third century (A.D. 200–300); and (3) the fourth and fifth centuries (A.D. 300–500).[197]

1. *Christianity and the Mystery Religions in the first two centuries A.D.* According to Rahner, it is extremely important to realize how relatively new the introduction of a mystery element into the religious experience of the Hellenistic world still was during the first century. While it is possible to speak of an atmosphere of mystery during the years when Christianity was getting its start, the practice of the mystery cults was still largely localized. However, a number of important changes took place soon after A.D. 100. One of these "was a solar pantheism, centering round the ascent of the salvation-hungry souls by lunar ways to a blissful hereafter, which is no longer conceived as a subterranean Hades, but as an astral-celestial heaven." [198] All of the still localized mystery cults began to exhibit this theme. After A.D. 100, the mystery religions gradually began to attain a widespread popular influence throughout the Roman Empire. But they also underwent transformation through a process of synthesis. As devotees of the mysteries became increasingly eclectic, new and odd combinations of the older mysteries began to develop. As the cults continued to tone down the more objectionable features of their older

practices, the number of people who found them attractive naturally increased.

The starting point for any adequate comparison between early Christianity and the mystery religions is recognition of the fact that *early Christianity was an antimystery religion.** To quote German scholar Carl Clemen:

> Christianity was distinguished from the mystery religions by its historical character and the entirely different significance it imputed to the coming and death of the Christian redeemer . . . and thus we may say with Heinrici: an inquiry into the general character of early Christianity shows it to be more in the nature of an antimystery religion than of a mystery religion.[199]

2. Christianity and the Mystery Religions in the third century A.D. It really is not until we come to the third century that we find sufficient source material to permit a relatively complete reconstruction of the content of the Hellenistic mysteries. It takes great care not to confuse the "cosmopolitan mysteries" of the third century A.D. with the "original localized indigenous cults" of earlier times.[200] Far too many writers on this subject use the available sources to form the plausible reconstructions of the third-century mystery experience and then uncritically reason back to what they think must have been the earlier nature of the cults. We have plenty of information about the mystery religions of the third century. But important differences exist between these religions and earlier expressions of the mystery experience (for which adequate information is extremely slim). We must be careful not to take the information we have about the third century and uncritically read it back into earlier centuries.

Two very important things happened to Christianity during the third century. First of all, the church began to give definite form to its worship

---

*Later chapters contain an elaboration of this point.

and organization and began systematically to elaborate important elements of its doctrine. In almost every case, this latter development was a response to a threat from one heresy or another. Moreover, it was in the third century, and not before, that the first real meeting took place between Christianity and the mystery religions. It was after A.D. 300 that the terminology of the mystery cults first began to appear in the language of the church.[201]

3. *Christianity and the Mysteries in the fourth and fifth centuries A.D.* During these two centuries, the mysteries became dying movements, although they did experience brief and localized revivals. Yet, as Rahner notes, "the spirit of this dying adversary imposed on victorious Christianity what might almost be called a mannered mystery terminology, a secret discipline, and certain liturgical acts. . . . It was in this process that the last faded remnants of the mysteries passed into Christianity, there to take on an entirely new meaning and radiance."[202] Rahner's attitude toward this intrusion of a mystery element into fourth- and fifth-century Christianity is not altogether clear. Perhaps because he is a Roman Catholic and thus required in some sense to approve medieval developments in the church's belief and practice, Rahner states his point more positively than would a Protestant who views the Reformation as a necessary reaction to a large number of essentially pagan elements that had become a part of the church's faith and practice. But putting this disagreement in attitude aside, Rahner is correct in pointing out that attempts to compare Christianity and the mysteries must keep in mind the transformation that took place in fourth- and fifth-century Christianity. The study of the intrusion of ideas and language from the mysteries into fourth- and fifth-century Christianity, along with a discussion of the steps that were necessary to correct these deviations from early Christianity, belongs more properly to another kind of book.

Informed Christians acknowledge the church's continuing need for reformation, for a return to the truth and purity of the early faith as it is reflected in the New Testament. For such people, the crucial question is not what possible influence the dying mysteries may have had on Christianity after A.D. 400 but what effect the emerging mystery cults may have had on the New Testament in the first century. Rahner's helpful history of the parallel development of these two movements weakens considerably the allegations of a first-century dependence on the mysteries. However, much more needs to be said before this tentative conclusion can be asserted with the confidence we seek.

chapter eight

The Specific Mystery Religions

Each of the major mystery religions is examined in depth.

The purpose of this chapter is to provide the essential information about each of the major mystery religions. The chapter begins with the early mysteries of ancient Greece, moves to the Isis cult that began in Egypt, discusses the cult of the Great Mother (Cybele) that originated in Asia Minor, and concludes with an analysis of Mithraism, which entered the Roman Empire from roots in Iran and Syria.

THE EARLY MYSTERY RELIGIONS OF GREECE

Religion assumed two fundamentally different forms in the Greek world: the Olympian religion and the Greek mystery religions. As described in the writings attributed to Homer and Hesiod, the

131

Olympian religion centered around a collection of superhuman beings said to dwell on Mount Olympus, Greece's highest mountain. The dedicated followers of the Olympian religion held a general belief in the existence of good and evil spirits. They centered their efforts on getting the spirits on their side, especially when important events were imminent. Generally speaking, the Olympian religion had little effect on the life of the typical Greek farmer or tradesman.

Both Homer and Hesiod describe a polytheism in which the gods are limited by their own weaknesses (both physical and moral), by the actions of other gods, and, above all, by fate (*moira*). Greek gods like Zeus, Hera, Apollo, Poseidon, and Pluto were certainly not models for humans to emulate. They were prey to all the vices that afflict the human race. Given their greater power, the gods' proneness to vice often produced gigantic calamities. In Homer, the human heroes were actually more noble than the gods.

The Greek gods were worshiped because of their superior power, not because of their greater goodness. It was useful to have these powerful beings on one's side and dangerous to have them as enemies. The gods in Homer's works are childish beings who just happen to have superhuman powers. In Homer's writings, when men were punished, it was not for doing wrong, but for being insubordinate to the gods. In Hesiod's writings, Zeus begins to assume the character of a moral deity. Hesiod's Zeus was a god of justice who existed to correct wrongs. Hence, in Hesiod's account, the gods are depicted as subject to a natural law of morality in addition to the physical laws that govern the natural world.

Alongside the Olympian religion in ancient Greece was a movement of mystery religions. They were mystery religions in the sense that their beliefs and practices were esoteric, or secret, known only to an exclusive group of initiates. Because of the success they had in maintaining their secrets, reconstructing a picture of their beliefs and ceremonies must be done from surviving artifacts. Their ceremonies, limited to initiates and usually held at night, were performed in mountain forests away from the inquiring eyes of the unconsecrated.

Some interesting attitudes toward the Greek mysteries show up in the extant fragments of early Greek philosophers. Heraclitus of Ephesus (flourished about 500 B.C.) had nothing but contempt for the mystery religions. This is not to say that he defended the Olympian religion; but he found it incredible that intelligent people could get caught up in the frenzy of the more excessive mystery rites.*

The Greek mystery religions possessed a universal character; they transcended tribal, geographical, and even racial boundaries. Within them, there was less emphasis on material prosperity and the city-state and more stress on the spiritual well-being of the individual.

The older Greek mysteries revolved around Demeter (goddess of the soil and of farming) and Dionysus (god of the vine and of wine). In the myth of Demeter, her daughter Persephone was carried away by the god of the underworld. Stricken with grief, Demeter wandered widely, searching for her lost daughter. During her absence, vegetation stopped growing. Finally, Zeus arranged a temporary reunion for a part of each year during which Demeter once again allowed vegetation to grow. Because of its strict secrecy, we still know very little about the teachings of the cult of Demeter.

The annual vegetation cycle, so prominent in the religion of Demeter, reappears in later

---

*Xenophanes, another pre-Socratic philosopher, criticized and ridiculed the anthropomorphism of the Olympian religion. Socrates and Plato represent still another ancient Greek attitude toward religion—a kind of piety that recognizes that humans exist alongside a deity but that leaves the picture of this god or gods extremely unclear.

mysteries. Spring's annual triumph over the death of winter came to symbolize the human hope for victory over death. The human hope for immortality that is expressed each spring in the rebirth of nature could be fulfilled only by participating in the nature of the god. The search for this immortality was directed, not toward the gods on Olympus, but towards gods or goddesses who, like Demeter, were thought to have conquered death.

Because the Great Mysteries associated with Demeter were held each September near the town of Eleusis, fourteen miles west of Athens, they are known as the Eleusinian Mysteries. In all likelihood, this was the oldest mystery cult practiced in Greece. Temple ruins as old as the fifteenth century B.C. have been discovered. We know of several stages, or levels, of initiation in the Eleusinian Mysteries. First were certain rites of purification; these were followed by the so-called Lesser Mysteries, which took place each February near Athens. During the third stage, in September, white-robed initiates formed a spectacular procession that followed a sacred route from Athens to the "Great Mysteries" at Eleusis. Finally, after a full year of probation, the initiate gained admission to the highest level, which included the right to view the secret contents of a sacred ark.

The cult of Dionysus (Greek), or Bacchus (Roman), apparently began in Thrace before moving to Greece.* Dionysus was said to have been born from a union between Zeus and a human mother. He came to be associated both with the natural cycle of vegetation and with certain animals thought to embody him. The purpose of the Dionysian rites was to bring the initiate into union with "the god of life," who was thought to be master over death. The cultic

---

*Ancient Thrace occupied the southeastern part of the Balkan peninsula, the part that today comprises Bulgaria, the far western stretches of Turkey, and a part of northern Greece.

rites were held at night on an isolated mountain top. After a torch-lit processional, the participants worked themselves into a drunken frenzy that led Dionysus' followers, mostly women, into an orgiastic revelry in which they attacked and dismembered an animal, ate its raw flesh, and drank its blood.* By eating their god, who was supposedly embodied in the animal they had torn apart, they thought they reached a state of divine possession that made them divine as well.

> The divine union, the contact with the divinity, marked the beginning of a new life for the initiate. He became a superior human being, God's own, who, thereafter, lived a dynamic, a Dionysian life. And since Dionysus was not only the Lord of Life but also of Death, the devotee believed that his union with God would continue even after death, that even immortality was within his grasp, since his patron God had attained it, that the joy and exaltation he experienced during his initiation was but a foretaste of the bliss to be experienced both in this life and after death.[203]

As the cult of Dionysus moved from Thrace to Greece, it became more civilized. What is known as the Orphic religion was a reformation and purification of the earlier, more savage cult. Orpheus was a legendary Thracian singer who charmed the Queen of Hades with his playing of the lyre. He was dismembered by the Maenads, the female worshipers of Dionysus. By the middle of the sixth century B.C., the Orphic mystery religion had already spread widely throughout Greece. The Orphics eliminated the orgiastic element of the earlier Dionysiac rites and introduced a sacred literature composed of hymns and prayers that interpreted the rites. While the Orphic movement is distinguished by its organization into brotherhoods, it remained an individualistic religion that described a per-

---

*Normally, the followers of Dionysus preferred a bull for this rite; but they are also known to have used goats and fawns.

sonal plan of salvation utilizing purifications, sacraments, and mystic ceremonies.

The Orphics taught a radical body-soul dualism coupled with a belief in reincarnation. They regarded human nature as the embodiment of a constant struggle between good and evil, which were thought to reside in the soul and body respectively. The body is the prison house of the soul.* Every human being has the duty of seeking the release of his soul from the corrupting influence of the body. While the Orphics did not invent the notion of the transmigration of the soul, they used it in conjunction with the belief that the soul can achieve greater degrees of purity through successive reincarnations. It is impossible now to say what the content of the Orphic mysteries was, but we do know that the earlier stages of initiation involved fasting, hymns, prayers, purifications, and sacrifices.†

The Cult of Isis and Osiris

The three most important mystery religions of the Hellenistic age were the cults of Isis, Cybele, and Mithra. The cult of Isis originated in Egypt and went through two major stages.[204] In its older Egyptian version, which was *not* a mystery religion, Isis was regarded as the goddess of heaven, earth, the sea, and the unseen world below. In the Egyptian stage of the cult, Isis had a husband named Osiris. The cult of Isis became a mystery religion only after Ptolemy the First introduced major changes into the older worship of Isis.‡ In the post-Ptolemaic version of the religion, a new god, named Serapis,§ replaces Osiris.[205] Ptolemy's motive for changing the Isis

---

*A number of these Orphic beliefs reappear later in Plato's philosophy. They came to Plato by way of the Pythagorean movement in Italy, which first learned them from the Orphics.

†The Orphics retained the practice of dismembering a live bull and eating its flesh raw.

‡Ptolemy the First became king of Egypt around 300 B.C.

§An implicit identification of Serapis with the older Osiris may have been part of the newer religion.

cult seems to have been a desire to synthesize Egyptian and Greek concerns in his new kingdom, thus hastening the Hellenization of Egypt. From Egypt (Alexandria), the cult of Isis gradually made its way to Rome. Its success in the Roman Empire seems to have been a result of its impressive ritual and the hope of immortality it offered its followers. While the city of Rome was at first repelled by the cult, the religion finally entered Rome during the reign of Caligula (A.D. 37–41). During the next two centuries its influence spread gradually, and it became a major rival of Christianity.

I mentioned earlier that each mystery religion centered around a myth concerning its god. The basic myth of the Isis cult concerned Osiris, her husband during the earlier Egyptian stage of the religion. According to the most common version of the myth, Osiris was murdered by his brother Seth, who then sank the coffin containing Osiris's body in the Nile. Isis discovered the body and returned it to Egypt. But Seth once again gained access to the body of Osiris, this time dismembering it, cutting it into fourteen pieces, which he scattered widely. Following a long search, Isis recovered each part of the body. It is at this point that the language used to describe what follows is crucial. Sometimes those telling the story are satisfied to say that Osiris came back to life.* But some writers go much too far and refer to Osiris's "resurrection." A statement by Joseph Klausner, a New Testament scholar, illustrates how easily some writers add still another parallel to the myth: "The dead body of Osiris floated in the Nile and he returned to life, this being accomplished by a baptism in the waters of the Nile."[206]

This kind of language suggests three misleading analogies between Osiris and Christ: a savior god dies and then experiences a resurrection

---

*As I shall point out later, even this statement claims too much.

accompanied by water baptism. But the alleged similarities as well as the language used to describe them turn out to be fabrications of the modern scholar and are not part of the original myth. Comparisons between the resurrection of Jesus and the resuscitation of Osiris are greatly exaggerated.[207] Not every version of the myth has Osiris returning to life; in some he simply becomes king of the underworld.[208] Equally far-fetched are attempts to find an analogue of Christian baptism in the Osiris myth.[209] The fate of Osiris's coffin in the Nile is about as relevant to baptism as the sinking of Atlantis. There are reports of a ritualistic washing as part of the cult's secret initiation. But these reports concern second-century A.D. practices, and as German scholar Günter Wagner explains: "This washing has as little as possible the appearance of a sacrament; evidently it was not intended to produce 'regeneration' or anything of the sort. The purpose of it seems to have been cleanliness, which was naturally regarded as a preparation for the holy rite that was to follow."[210]

During its later, mystery stage, the male deity of the Isis cult is no longer the dying Osiris but Serapis; and Serapis is often thought of as a sun god. It is clear that the Serapis of the post-Ptolemaic, mystery version of the cult was not a dying god. Obviously then, neither could he be a rising god. It requires a fertile imagination to discover any significant parallels between either version of the Isis cult and the Christian understanding of Jesus Christ.

THE CULT OF CYBELE AND ATTIS

Cybele, also known as the Great Mother, was worshiped throughout much of the Hellenistic world.[211] The cult of Cybele underwent a number of significant changes over a period of several hundred years. Cybele undoubtedly began as a goddess of nature; the early worship of her in Phrygia was not unlike that of Dionysus. But it went beyond the sexual orgies that were part of the primitive Dionysiac cult, as the frenzied male worshipers of Cybele were led to castrate themselves. Following their act of self-mutilation, these followers of Cybele became "Galli," or eunuch-priests of the cult. From her beginnings as a Nature-goddess, Cybele eventually came to be viewed as the Mother of all gods and the mistress of all life.

Most of our information about the cult describes its practices during its later, Roman period. Details about the early Phrygian cult are slim. But even with regard to our information about the cult in Rome, the sources are relatively late. For this reason, reconstructions of the beliefs and practices of the religion are very tenuous. We do know that during its Roman stage, an important part of the cult was a festival of Attis that took place each spring. But the sources do not make it clear if this festival was an extension of an earlier Phrygian practice.

In 204 B.C., the cult of Cybele became the first mystery religion to be introduced into Rome. But its worship was too barbaric even for Roman tastes, so it was conducted in secret for several hundred years. Although the Romans came to support its religious ceremonies, the cult itself was led by a eunuch priesthood of non-Romans. Roman citizens were forbidden to participate until the reign of Claudius (A.D. 41–54), who honored Cybele and Attis by introducing a spring festival (held from March 22 to 27).

According to the central myth of the cult, Cybele loved a handsome Phrygian shepherd named Attis. Because Attis was unfaithful, Cybele drove him insane. Overcome by his madness, Attis castrated himself and died shortly after that. This produced great mourning on Cybele's part and introduced death into the world. But then Cybele restored Attis to life, and his restoration brought the world of nature back to life. Here as before, the presuppositions of the interpreter often determine the language used to describe what followed Attis' death.

Many writers refer carelessly to the "resurrection of Attis." But surely this is an exaggeration. As Machen explains, "The myth contains no account of a resurrection; all that Cybele is able to obtain is that the body of Attis should be preserved, that his hair should continue to grow, and that his little finger should move."[212] In some versions of the myth, Attis's return to life took the form of his being changed into an evergreen tree. Since the basic idea underlying the myth was the annual vegetation cycle, any resemblance to the bodily resurrection of Christ seems largely coincidental.[213]

Many worshipers of Cybele believed that an annual rehearsal of the Attis myth was a way of guaranteeing a good crop. Eventually the rehearsal of the myth became a way by which worshipers could share in Attis' immortality. Each spring the followers of Cybele would mourn for the dead Attis in acts of fasting and flagellation. The more fanatical followers would castrate themselves, an act that preceded their becoming priests of the Great Mother.*

During the later Roman celebrations of the spring festival, the notion of resurrection in connection with Attis assumed more prominence. Samuel Angus describes the proceedings:

> At the spring festival of the Great Mother the myth of Attis was rehearsed in a passion-play. The sacred pine-tree under which the unfaithful youth had mutilated himself was cut down. The tree then, prepared like a corpse, was carried into the sanctuary, accompanied by a statue of the god and other symbols. Then followed the lamentation of Attis, with an appropriate period of abstinence. On the *Day of Blood* the tree was buried, while the *mystae* in frenzied dances gashed themselves with knives to prove their participation in the sorrows of the

---

*Wagner suggests that "The self-emasculation of the Gallic is not a genuine, deliberate *imitatio* of Attis; its object is rather assimilation to the goddess." Günter Wagner, *Pauline Baptism and the Pagan Mysteries* (Edinburgh: Oliver and Boyd, 1967), p. 266.

god that they might have fellowship in his joy. Next night the *Resurrection of Attis* was celebrated by the opening of the grave. In the darkness of the night a light was brought to the open grave, while the presiding priest anointed the lips of the initiates with holy oil, comforting them with the words: "Be of good cheer, ye *mystae* of the god who has been saved; to you likewise there shall come salvation from your trouble." The initiates gave vent to their emotions in a wild carnival: they made their confession that by eating out of the *tympanum* and drinking out of the *cymbalum* they had been rendered communicants of Attis.[214]

According to Günter Wagner, author of perhaps the definitive work on the independence of Christian baptism from the mysteries, the Attis myth is exclusively an initiation-myth; it has nothing to do with death and resurrection. All versions of the myth agree that after Attis died, he remained dead. As Wagner explains, "In its various forms, from the oldest traditions right down to the versions received in the fourth century A.D., the Attis myth knows nothing of a resurrection of Attis. The Attis of the myth is not a dying and rising god."[215] Wagner goes on to discuss a disputed passage in the writings of Firmicus Maternus[216] in which the resurrection of the god may be read into the myth. Angus's allusions to resurrection in his lengthy description of the spring festival appear to rely on this source. However, the language Firmicus used is ambiguous, making disputable any reading of resurrection into it. The source is also very late (fourth century A.D.) and appears inconsistent with known elements of the cult. Hence, the reliability of the text is highly questionable.[217]

The most well-known rite of the cult of the Great Mother was the *taurobolium*. Initiates reclined in a pit under a platform of boards on which a bull was slaughtered. As the blood of the dying bull dripped through the cracks between the boards and onto the initiates, they would often throw back their heads to allow the blood to wet their face, nostrils, and lips. Often, initiates would drink the hot blood. This rite is frequently described in pseudo-Christian terminology. Later commentators, for example, refer to it as a "baptism of blood" and describe the initiate rising from the pit as one who has died and risen with his savior-god. The frequency with which this kind of language appears in the literature should not obscure its questionable character.

Gordon J. Laing, one author who uses such careless language, describes the taurobolium as "literally a baptism of blood. It cleansed the sins away. The person who submitted to it was 'born again.' "[218] Every element of Laing's account can be challenged. It is an odd kind of scholarship that first describes a pagan rite in Christian terminology and then marvels at the alleged parallels. Ironically, after Laing has finished describing the taurobolium in such question-begging language, he admits that the parallelism is only coincidental. "It is a manifestation in two contemporary religions of an idea that was then filtering through the Mediterranean world. There is certainly no evidence that the Christians derived it from the cult of the Great Mother. The earliest known taurobolic inscription is dated A.D. 133, but Paul had preached the doctrine that men must be born again long before."[219] While we welcome Laing's admission that the taurobolium could not have influenced first-century Christianity, his assertion that Paul preached the new birth is another piece of misinformation. The term *born again* does not appear in Paul's writings.

In chapter 9 we will examine in greater detail the claims made about the taurobolium.* Over-enthusiastic commentators on ancient religion also write carelessly about the act of eating the

---

*Earlier I mentioned the *criobolium*. This was a similar practice in which a ram was substituted for the bull. It seems to have been a late modification of the taurobolic rite, especially for poorer people who could not afford a bull.

god, thus suggesting an analogy with Christian Communion. Colgate University professor Joscelyn Godwin maintains that Christians sublimated the "crudely physical rite" of the taurobolium by not actually slaughtering an animal but "by drinking their saviour's blood in the form of sacramental wine."[220] Most scholars dismiss such statements as gross distortions.

Other writers depict the taurobolium as a kind of baptism, thereby planting the seed that a specific relationship existed between the taurobolium and Christian baptism. Later we will examine how tenuous such claims are. In that discussion, significance will be attached both to the date for the introduction of the taurobolium and the major stages of its subsequent development. For now, it is important to note that the taurobolium was *not* part of the Mother cult in the beginning. It entered the cult of Cybele and Attis sometime *after* the middle of the second century A.D.

THE CULT OF MITHRA

Mithraism was easily the most significant of all the mystery religions.[221] While Mithraism eventually became Christianity's most serious rival, it had no importance in the Roman world during the first century; it could not possibly have influenced early Christianity. Later, Mithraism came close to becoming the dominant religion of the Roman Empire, only to lose out to Christianity. A major element in its defeat was the emperor Constantine's conversion to Christianity. A later emperor, Julian the Apostate (emperor from A.D. 360 to 363), made one final attempt to restore Mithraism to a position of dominance, but he failed. The cult disappeared slowly both in the West and in the East, though it reappeared as one element of the religion known as Manichaeanism. Mithraism's final disappearance in the East was helped by the eventual rise of Islam, which opposed images.

The worship of Mithra began in what is today

Iran. The subsequent history of the religion is a story of how an ancient tradition became a part of different religions in different countries, being modified in the process by each of the cultures that adopted it. Mithra appears first in Iranian religion as the twin brother of the Zoroastrian god Ahura Mazda. In later Zoroastrian literature he assumes more prominence as a judge of the dead; but it was the Syrian version of the cult of Mithra that finally reached Rome. Attempts to read facets of the later Syrian development of the cult back into the Iranian version must be questioned.

Roman soldiers learned of the worship of Mithra during military journeys to what are today Iraq and Iran, and converts to the religion within the Roman army helped spread Mithraism throughout the empire. Traces of the religion have been found in Britain, North Africa, central Europe, and Spain.

Attempts to reconstruct the beliefs and practices of Mithraism face enormous challenges because of the scanty information that has survived. We do know that Mithraism, like its mystery competitors, had a basic myth. Mithra was supposedly born when he emerged from a rock; he was carrying a knife and torch and wearing a Phrygian cap. He battled first with the sun and then with a primeval bull, thought to be the first act of creation. Mithra slew the bull, which then became the ground of life for the human race.

Given its roots in Zoroastrianism, it is not surprising that a metaphysical dualism lay at the center of the Mithraic system. In other words, the world must be explained in terms of two ultimate principles, one good (depicted as light) and the other evil (darkness). The universe is the battleground where these ultimate powers struggle. Human beings must choose which side they will fight for; they are trapped in the conflict between light and darkness. Mithra came to be regarded as the most powerful mediator who could help humans in their attacks from demon forces. Mithraism's frequent use of the imagery of war and conflict enhanced its appeal among Roman soldiers. Astrology also served as an important backdrop for Mithraic beliefs. The seven known planets and the dozen signs of the Zodiac make frequent appearances in the symbolism of the cult. Each of the seven planets was thought to control a different day of the week.

Mithraism taught that the human soul has fallen or descended from its original home in heaven through seven layers of reality, each identified with one of the seven known planets. At each stage of its descent, the soul lost more of its original heavenly characteristics and acquired more defects associated with the sphere of the body. Man's present existence on earth is a time of testing. If the soul passes its tests, its eventual reunion with the good god is made more likely. If the soul fails, it will be sentenced to unending suffering with the forces of evil.

Mithra was believed to have two vital functions in the testing of the human soul. First, he was the judge who would weigh the good and evil effects of each human trial. But he was also viewed as a savior who would help his followers in their fight against evil, eventually rewarding the faithful by giving them the final victory over evil. The seven levels of man's fall reappear as seven stages that each initiate had to pass through as symbols of his gradual elevation to the purity and communion of his original life.*
Before the initiate could proceed to a new stage, he had to pass a test that demonstrated his worthiness for the new level. Worshipers of Mithra believed that after death the souls of Mithra's true disciples are led by Mithra himself through the spheres of the seven planets to their final blessed destination. This belief allows

---

*Women were never admitted as initiates in the cult of Mithra.

Mithra to be called, rather loosely, a "redeemer-god."

The Romans knew Mithra as *Sol Invictus*. Since dualisms like Mithraism normally represented good and evil in terms of light and darkness, the eventual relating of Mithra with the sun was perhaps to be expected. The worship of Mithra was often associated with stages of the sun (dawn, midday, and sunset). The major Mithraic festival occurred on December 25, the date of the winter solstice.*

Mithraism was the one mystery religion that seems to have promoted an ethical life. It "imposed upon its adherents a code of virtue similar to what is now understood by the word *honor*. In addition to this, there was engendered an *esprit de corps* and true brotherhood which was a real binding force in such an extensive and heterogeneous empire like the Roman."[222] Mithraism also promoted purity as an ideal. "Mithra as the enemy of every kind of impurity stood forth as an ideal and perfect man. The ceremonies and the various degrees imparted to the initiates all tended to emphasize grade by grade the ideal of purity."[223] The high moral tone of Mithraism, compared to the lack of purity of the other mystery deities, made it look good by comparison.

Mithraism came to have a sacred meal of bread and water along with a ritual that some regard as analogous to baptism. Justin Martyr, an early father of the church, referred to the Mithraic meal as a Satanic imitation of the Lord's Supper.[224] The taurobolium came to play a role in later Mithraic worship. The symbol of the bull had always been part of the cult, and this may explain the ease with which Mithraism borrowed the taurobolium from the cult of Cybele. However, the Mithraic taurobolium had no relation to the cult's rite of initiation. By

---

*The relatively late Christian adoption of December 25 as the date of Christ's birth is irrelevant to the concerns of this book inasmuch as it is a nonessential matter.

definition, initiation rites are not repeated, whereas the Mithraic taurobolium was.[225]

Allegations of an early Christian dependence on Mithraism have been rejected on many grounds. Mithraism had no concept of the death and resurrection of its god and no place for any concept of rebirth—at least during its early stages. Whereas other mystery cults had a cyclical notion of life-death-rebirth based on the vegetation cycle, the Mithraic view of history was linear, not cyclical. During the early stages of the cult, the notion of rebirth would have been foreign to its basic outlook. If rebirth appears at all in the cult, it was a late addition. Moreover, Mithraism was basically a military cult. Therefore, one must be skeptical about suggestions that it appealed to nonmilitary people like the early Christians.

Perhaps the most important argument against an early Christian dependence on Mithraism is the fact that the timing is all wrong. The flowering of Mithraism occurred after the close of the New Testament canon, too late for it to have influenced the development of first-century Christianity.[226] Recently, however, several attempts have been made to support an earlier major presence of Mithraism in the Roman Empire. In one of these moves, Swedish scholar G. Widengren claimed that an excavation at Dura (Europos) is a Mithraeum that points to the possible presence of a Mithraic cult before the end of the first century A.D.* If this dating were to stand up, it would at least make more plausible the possibility of a first-century Christian contact with Mithraism. But Widengren's suggested dating has been rejected. He himself admitted that "the evidence is very uncertain."[227] According to other scholars, including M. J. Vermaseren, excavation reports suggest that the Dura Mithraeum that Widengren dated

*Widengren suggested A.D. 80–85 as the dates.

so early should be dated much later, in A.D. 168.[228] In his book on the cult of Mithra, Vermaseren states that "no Mithraic monument can be dated earlier than the end of the first century A.D., and even the more extensive investigation at Pompeii, buried beneath the ashes of Vesuvius in A.D. 79, have not so far produced a single image of the god."[229]

An initially more plausible argument for an early Mithraic presence in the Roman world appeals to a text in one of Plutarch's writings.* Plutarch mentions Pompey's military excursion against certain pirates in Cilicia who, according to Plutarch, practiced mystery rites, including Mithraism. This text has been used to support the claim that the mysteries of Mithra were practiced in Italy before 67 B.C. But any conclusion along this line can be, at best, only an inference from Plutarch's text, which itself makes no such claim. All Plutarch states explicitly is that some of the pirates practiced Mithraic mysteries and that some of them in all likelihood were taken to Rome as trophies of Pompey's victory. But Plutarch himself does not state that Mithraism was established in Italy in or before 67 B.C. Historian Edwin Yamauchi has examined the entire matter on several occasions and considers groundless the case for any significant Mithraic influence on Roman society.[230] His conclusion is that "apart from the visit of the Armenian king, who was a worshiper of Mithra, to Nero, there is no evidence of the penetration of Mithra to the west until the end of the first century A.D."[231] Chronological problems, then, make the possibility of a Mithraic influence on early Christianity unlikely. These difficulties have not been eased by any of the issues we have considered.[232]

---

*Plutarch, a Middle Platonist, lived from A.D. 34 to 125.

The Mystery Religions and the Christian Sacraments

Alleged dependence of the Christian sacraments on the ceremonies of the mystery religions is examined. The meanings behind the mystery rites are compared to the meanings behind Christian baptism and the Lord's Supper.

In this and the following chapter, we will examine more closely claims of a mystery influence on early Christian belief and practice. Because several foundational issues fit better in discussions of alleged pagan influences on the Christian sacraments, we will deal with this matter first. Chapter 10 will consider whether the mysteries influenced essential Christian beliefs.

Most claims of an early Christian dependence

on the "sacraments" of the mystery religions focus on the view of baptism and the Lord's Supper in the writings of Paul. A Hellenistic influence on Paul's view of the sacraments has been advanced on two grounds: (1) the mere fact that both Christianity and the mysteries had apparently similar rites in which there was eating and a washing of the body; and (2) the fact that Paul had any sacraments at all, regardless of the outward form that they took.

THE MEANING OF THE PAGAN PRACTICES

The mere fact that Christianity had a sacred meal and a baptism is supposed to prove that it borrowed these ceremonies from similar meals and washings in the pagan cults. By itself, of course, such outward similarity would really prove nothing. After all, religious rituals can assume only a limited number of forms, and they will naturally relate to important or common aspects of human life. Alleged similarities might reflect only common features of a time or culture, rather than genetic dependence. Consequently, we need to dig below the surface of apparent similarities and ask the more basic question, *What did the pagan practices mean?* Regarding the pagan washings, Machen observes:

> The various ablutions which preceded the celebration of the mysteries may have been often nothing more than symbols of cleansing; and such symbolism is so natural that it might appear independently at many places. It appears, for example, highly developed among the Jews; and in the baptism of John the Baptist it assumes a form far more closely akin to Christian baptism than in the washings which were connected with the pagan mysteries. The evidence for a sacramental significance of the ablutions in the mysteries, despite confident assertions on the part of some modern writers, is really very slight.[233]

Many proponents of early Christian syncretism simply assume that acts of washing (and eating) in the mystery religions were sacraments. But as Metzger counters,

> Actually it is only in Mithraism, of all the cults, that one finds evidence that washing with water was part of the ritual by which a new member was admitted to one or other of the grades in the Mithraic system. Similarly with respect to sacramental meals reserved for those who had been initiated into the community of devotees, there is singularly little evidence. Nothing is heard of sacramental meals in Orphism. The drinking of the *kykeon* in the rites at Eleusis, which has sometimes been thought to be the prototype of Paul's teaching and practice regarding the Lord's Supper, is as different as possible from the Christian Communion.[234]

Ceremonial washings that antedate the New Testament have a different meaning from New Testament baptism, while pagan washings after A.D. 100 come too late to influence the New Testament and, indeed, might themselves have been influenced by Christianity.

What did the sacred meals in various mystery cults mean? While sacred meals played a role in the Eleusinian mysteries, their purpose is unclear and may have served only as some kind of preparation for the mystery without actually being part of it. The sacramental function of the Mithraic ceremony in which initiates ate bread and drank water seems well established. But the major problem with the Mithraic rite is its late date, which precludes its having any influence on Paul. Attempts to find a Dionysiac source for Paul's teaching about the Lord's Supper (1 Cor. 10:14–22; 11:17–34) or the words of Jesus in John 6:53–56 face at least one major obstacle: the chronology is all wrong. As we have seen, many times the belief or practice that is supposed to have influenced first-century Christians is too late; it developed after A.D. 100. In this case, the Dionysiac practice is too early! The savage practice of eating one's god appears to have long since disappeared by the time we get to Jesus and Paul.

If Paul is dependent upon the pagan notion of eating the god, he must have deserted the religious practice which prevailed in his own day in order to have recourse to a savage custom which had long since been abandoned. The suggestion does not seem to be very natural. It is generally admitted that even where Christianity is dependent upon Hellenistic religion, it represents a spiritualizing modification of the pagan practice. But at this point it would have to be supposed that the Christian modification proceeded in exactly the opposite direction; far from marking a greater spiritualization of pagan practice, it meant a return to a savage stage of religion which even paganism had abandoned.[235]

The advocate of early Christian syncretism cannot have it both ways. While almost all of his case for syncretism alleges that Christianity elevated and spiritualized the pagan ideas and rites it borrowed from its own milieu, attempts to locate the source of the Lord's Supper in the savage practice of eating the god would have the early Christians borrowing a primitive act that had been abandoned even by its contemporary pagan competitors. As I point out later in this chapter, both the meaning and symbolism of the Christian act are adapted from the Old Testament Passover.

A MAGICAL VIEW OF THE SACRAMENTS?

Putting aside any visible similarity between ritual forms, some allege that the mere presence of sacraments in Paul's writings points to a connection between Paul himself and the mystery religions. The major problem with this argument is its assumption that the sacraments, in Paul's view, operated in a purely external, mechanical, or even magical way. That is, the efficacy of the sacrament depended solely on the performance of the rite, independent of the faith,

attitude, or intentions of the worshiper. As
Bruce Metzger explains:

153

The Mystery
Religions
and the
Christian Sacraments

> Both of the Christian sacraments, in their earliest
> phase, were considered to be primarily *dona data*,
> namely blessings conveyed to those who by nature
> were unfit to participate in the new order inau-
> gurated by the person and work of Jesus Christ.
> Pagan sacraments, on the contrary, conveyed their
> benefits *ex opere operato*.[236]

The phrase *ex opere operato* describes the pagan
belief that their sacraments had the power to
give the individual the benefits of immortality in
a mechanical way without his undergoing any
moral or spiritual transformation. This certainly
was not Paul's view, either of salvation or of the
operation of the Christian sacraments.[237] So once
again we find that attempts to discover significant parallels between mystery rites and
early Christian practice founder on inattention to
detail. The religion of Paul was not a sacramen-
tarian religion.

THE TAUROBOLIUM

The taurobolium was described earlier in
connection with the cult of the Great Mother.
Initiates would stand or recline in a pit as a bull
was slaughtered on a platform above them. The
initiate would then be bathed in the warm blood
of the dying animal. The taurobolium has been
alleged to be a source for Christian language
about being washed in the blood of the lamb
(Rev. 7:14)* or sprinkled with the blood of Jesus
(1 Peter 1:2).[238] William Fairweather, himself a
proponent of syncretism in other areas, judged
the connection as "no more feasible than that
which derives the idea of Christ's descent into
Hades from the visits paid . . . by Greek heroes
to the infernal regions."[239] As Fairweather not-

---

*The use of a ram in the criobolium rather than a bull was
probably due to economic considerations; bulls cost more
than rams.

ed, the cult of Cybele made no use of the taurobolium until the second century A.D. [240]

The taurobolium has often been cited as the source for Paul's teaching in Romans 6:1–4, where he relates Christian baptism to the Christian's identification with Christ's death and resurrection. As the baptized Christian is lowered below the water, he is symbolically buried. His rising from the water symbolizes his resurrection to newness of life.* Günter Wagner has countered such claims by arguing that no notion of death and resurrection was a part of the taurobolium. "It is important that the taurobolium-initiation is not to be regarded as a dying and rising again, an after-fulfillment of the destiny of Attis. This thesis, with its various presuppositions, is in my opinion quite untenable. At any rate, the comparison of Rom. vi with taurobolium-initiation is to be dismissed as an anachronism." [241] The reason the comparison is anachronistic, of course, is that the best available evidence requires us to date the origin of the taurobolium about one hundred years after Paul wrote his words. According to Robert Duthoy, not one existing text supports the claim that the taurobolium memorialized the death and resurrection of Attis. [242] Therefore, the pagan rite could not possibly have been the source of Paul's teaching.

The proper dating of the taurobolium is critically important in this entire matter. Scholarly opinion favors the view that the taurobolium first appeared in the West in the second century A.D. The most frequently cited date is A.D. 160. According to Wagner,

> the taurobolium in the Attis cult is first attested in the time of Antoninus Pius for A.D. 160. As far as we can see at present it only became a personal consecration at the beginning of the third century A.D. The idea of a rebirth through the instrumentality

---

*This interpretation of Romans 6 views immersion as the mode of baptism.

of the taurobolium only emerges in isolated instances towards the end of the fourth century A.D.; it is not originally associated with this blood bath.[243]

The best available evidence also suggests that the taurobolium underwent a number of significant changes in the centuries after A.D. 160. Although his views are not always accepted in every detail, Robert Duthoy has argued that the taurobolium went through three major stages, evolving gradually from being a sacrifice into being a rite of consecration that involved a descent into the pit.[244]

In the first stage of this process (about A.D. 160–250), the taurobolium was primarily a bull-sacrifice in honor of Cybele. Duthoy describes the second stage (about A.D. 228–319) as a period of transition to the third stage. During this intermediate period, the blood of the bull became increasingly important. The blood was caught in a vessel and given to the dedicator. Duthoy suggests that since the blood came to be associated with the power of purification, the possibility of a Christian influence cannot be ruled out.[245]

It was after A.D. 300 that the rite evolved into the blood bath used as a rite of purification. In this third stage of the development of the taurobolium, "the killing of the bull was no longer a sacrifice, but merely the only means to obtain the purifying blood."[246] Duthoy is convinced that a Christian influence is at work during this third stage. "It is obvious," he writes, "that this alteration in the taurobolium must have been due to Christianity, when we consider that by A.D. 300 it had become the great competitor of the heathen religions and was known to everyone. The complete submersion that purified the aspirant Christian of all his sins may quite possibly have inspired in the worshipers of Cybele the desire to be sprinkled all over with the purifying blood."[247] Duthoy stresses "that the transitions from one form of the rite to the next were gradual and did not take place overnight. Indeed the whole of the second phase was itself a transition."[248]

Although I hesitate to push dogmatically every element of Duthoy's theory,[249] all of the extant evidence points to a chronology that makes it impossible for the taurobolium to have influenced first-century Christianity. Moreover, the evidence supports the hypothesis that the later changes in the blood bath reflect a Christian influence. It is clear, then, that the New Testament emphasis on the shedding of blood should not be traced to any pagan source. The New Testament teaching should be viewed in the context of its Old Testament background—the Passover and the temple sacrifices.

CHRISTIAN BAPTISM

While the independence of Christian baptism from the taurobolium is assured, other problems remain. Various proponents of an early Christian syncretism maintain that Paul's account of baptism in Romans 6 (as well as the entire Christian view of the sacrament) is analogous to initiation-rites in the mystery religions. For example, Alfred Loisy regarded Christian baptism, in which the Christian believer died a symbolic death and underwent a symbolic resurrection, as an initiation rite influenced by similar pagan ceremonies.[250] More recently, Rudolf Bultmann advanced a similar claim.[251]

Claims like this are helped considerably by a consolidation of all the specific mysteries into one general mystery cult. Since they differed greatly in form and meaning, it is important to ask, Which specific initiation rite does the advocate of syncretism have in mind? Wagner argues, "The mystery religion *par excellence* has never existed, and quite certainly did not in the first century A.D. One has only to bear in mind the vast difference there was between the magical sprinkling rites in the Osiris cult and the initiation undergone by Lucius, after diligent preparation in prayer and with absolute and ardent trust in the grace of the goddess.''[252] Moreover, these washings differed significantly from the initiation rite of the Eleusinian mystery, which symbolized the initiate's descent to the Nether World. None of these can be matched with Paul's teaching in Romans 6.

The oversimplifications that abound in the syncretists' cases are clearly seen in the way they slight the significant differences between baptism and the pagan initiation rites. While Paul clearly associated baptism with the death, burial, and resurrection of Christ (Rom. 6:3–4; Col. 2:11–14), it is clear, according to Herman Ridderbos, that

> (a) nowhere in the mystery religions is such a symbolism of death present in the "baptism" ritual, and that (b) in Romans 6 and Colossians 2 Paul does not portray baptism itself as a symbolic or sacramental representation of the going down into death (the so-called "death by drowning," about which Lietzmann speaks) and rising up again to life. Thus in the area of the sacraments every deeper link with the ritual acts in the mystery religions has become illusory.[253]

Mircea Eliade, author of a definitive study of pagan initiation rites, argues that

> it would be useless to seek a parallel to Christian baptism in the lustration rites of the mysteries or other ceremonies of pagan antiquity. Not only the Essenes but other Jewish movements were familiar with it. But baptism could become a sacrament for the earliest Christians precisely because it had been instituted by Christ. In other words, the sacramental value of baptism derived from the fact that the Christians saw Jesus as the Messiah, the Son of God.[254]

The fact that some initiation theme may appear in first-century Christianity does not prove that it was borrowed from one of the mystery cults. Rather, Eliade counters,

Such a theme could have been taken directly from one of the esoteric Jewish sects, especially the Essenes, concerning whom the Dead Sea manuscripts have now added sensationally to our knowledge. Indeed, it is not even necessary to suppose that an initiatory theme was "borrowed" by Christianity from some other religion. As we have said, initiation is coexistent with any new reevaluation of spiritual life.[255]

Unlike the initiation rites of the mystery cults, Christian baptism looks back to what a real, historical person, Jesus Christ, did in history. The event of baptism is explained by the prior Christ-event.[256] In contrast with pagan initiation ceremonies, Christian baptism is not a mechanical, or magical, ceremony. An attitude of faith on the part of the Christian recipient is regarded as a necessary condition for receiving baptism.

It is clear that the sources of Christian baptism are not to be found either in the taurobolium or in the washings of the pagan mystery cults. Its sources lie rather in the washings of purification found in the Old Testament and in the Jewish practice of baptizing proselytes, the latter being the most likely source for the baptistic practices of John the Baptist.

THE LORD'S SUPPER

Claims that the Lord's Supper was derived from pagan sacred meals can be disposed of quickly. For one thing, we still know very little about the sacred meals of the ancient pagan cults. No information has survived that enables us to say with any certainty which specific concepts and practices turned the eating and drinking into a sacrament. As Albert Schweitzer pointed out decades ago, it is therefore impossible to set up a meaningful comparison between the pagan sacred meals and the Lord's Supper.[257] Schweitzer goes even further and suggests that this scarcity of information may imply an important truth: "If we possess so few typical statements about the Mystery-feasts, is it not partly because they had no very remarkable features and did not take a very exalted position in the hierarchy of the cultus acts?"[258]

Of all the mystery cults, only Mithraism had anything that resembled the Lord's Supper. A piece of bread and a cup of water were placed before initiates while the priest of Mithra spoke some ceremonial words. But the chronology of Mithraism precludes its sacred meal from influencing first-century Christianity.

Once again, claims that the Lord's Supper was derived from pagan sacred meals are grounded on exaggerations and oversimplifications. Careful study reveals that the supposed parallels and analogies break down completely.[259] Any quest for the historical antecedents of the Lord's Supper is more likely to succeed if it stays closer to the Jewish foundations of the Christian faith than if it wanders off into the practices of the pagan cults. As noted in the case of Christian baptism, the Lord's Supper looked back to a real, historical person and something he did in history during the Last Supper. And as every student of the New Testament knows, the occasion for Jesus' introduction of the Christian Lord's Supper was the Jewish passover feast. Metzger is correct when he notes that "the Jewishness of the setting, character, and piety expressed in the [Christian] rite is overwhelmingly pervasive in all the accounts of the origin of the supper."[260] We must conclude, then, that attempts to find pagan sources for such essential Christian practices as baptism and the Lord's Supper are failures.[261]

chapter ten

The Mystery Religions and Essential Christian Beliefs

Several essential Christian beliefs—Christ's deity, His resurrection, Christian rebirth, and Pauline conceptions of salvation—are examined in light of claims of alleged dependence on the beliefs of the mystery religions.

When proponents of early Christian syncretism turn their attention to essential Christian beliefs, they usually focus on one or more of four related topics: (1) the early Christian ascription of deity to Christ; (2) the belief that Jesus was a dying and rising savior-god like the deities of the mystery cults; (3) the doctrine of rebirth; and (4) the Pauline teaching about salvation.

THE DEITY OF JESUS CHRIST

Attempts to show that the early Christian belief in the deity of Christ was influenced by Hellenistic thought usually center on the   161 church's ascription of the title "Lord" to Jesus.* The title "Lord" was one way in which the early church expressed its conviction that Christ was God. In Philippians 2:6–11, Paul speaks of the coming day when "at the name of Jesus every knee should bow . . . and every tongue confess that Jesus Christ is Lord . . ." He refers to Jesus as "my Lord" (Phil. 3:8). Revelation 19:16 names the coming Christ as "King of kings and Lord of lords." Paul even made the confession "Jesus is Lord" a necessary condition of salvation (Rom. 10:9).

The Alleged Pagan Source of the Title "Lord"

The major inspiration behind the search for a pagan source of the early church's use of "Lord" was Wilhelm Bousset's book *Kyrios Christos,* already mentioned in chapter 7. Like other members of the History of Religions School, Bousset popularized the view that early Christianity borrowed heavily from the mystery religions. According to Bousset, the transformation of Christianity that took place during its early years was so dramatic and so extensive that it could not have been the work of just one man, even a man as dynamic as Paul. Therefore, Bousset argued, both Paul and the early Christian communities must have borrowed from their pagan environment. How did the simple gospel of Jesus become transformed into a redemptive religion with strong affinities to the mystery cults? In Bousset's thinking, this new version of Christianity arose primarily in Hellenistic churches like the ones at Antioch and Damascus, and this Hellenistic Christian view of Jesus

*For reasons of space, I must pass over similar attempts to show that the early church's belief that Jesus was "the Son of God" was dependent on the rather widespread use of the phrase in the Hellenistic world. The apparent linguistic parallel becomes insignificant in light of the fact that early Christians understood the phrase in a distinct way. Worth consulting in this regard is the discussion in James D. G. Dunn, *Christology in the Making* (Philadelphia: Westminster, 1980), pp. 17ff.

differed markedly from that of Palestinian Christians.

Bousset claimed that the early Palestinian church never called Jesus "Lord" (*Kyrios*). The Palestinian church viewed Jesus rather as the Son of Man, a title rooted in Jewish apocalyptic literature. Bousset believed that the title "Lord" was first applied to Jesus in Antioch as a result of pagan influence on the Hellenistic Christians there. Since their pagan neighbors used *kyrios* as a name for their gods, the Antioch Christians could hardly use a lesser title as their designation for Jesus. Prior to their conversion, such Gentiles were accustomed to referring to their pagan gods as "Lord." It was only natural, then, that they would build on this earlier practice and worship Jesus as Lord.

But according to Bousset, more than just a name was involved in the transference of the pagan title "Lord." Since the word contained a number of theological connotations, including an implicit recognition of the divinity of the bearer, Bousset suggested that this transference explains how the early church first came to think of Christ as God. John W. Drane explains the implications of Bousset's thesis:

> Consequently, when the New Testament writers refer to Jesus as *ho Kyrios* [the Lord] they are demonstrating their theological isolation from the historical Jesus, and their close association with the pagan theology of the Hellenistic world. Far from being the guardians of the truth revealed once and for all by Jesus the Christ, the apostles were religious plagiarists of the worst sort, attempting to conceal the rags of a discredited Jewish apocalyptist beneath the rich robes of Hellenistic deity.[262]

Bousset's influence led Rudolf Bultmann to speak of Paul's Hellenistic Christianity as an essentially new position in the early church, distinct from the Christianity of the Palestinian church. It was also instrumental in leading

Bultmann to place Pauline Christianity within the sphere of the mystery religions.[263]

Bousset's thesis has been attacked on at least five grounds.[264]

1. *Critics have pointed out the lack of evidence needed to support Bousset's key claims.* For one thing, evidence for the allegedly widespread use of *kyrios* as a title for the pagan gods of the Hellenistic age is spotty at best.[265] For another, there is no evidence to support belief in the existence of a pagan Kyrios cult in either Antioch or Damascus. And finally, there is no evidence to support the claim that the Christianity Paul found in Damascus and Antioch was radically different from that of the church in Jerusalem. If the churches of Damascus and Antioch had begun to incorporate pagan elements into their theology, the New Testament would be full of signs of conflict between them and the Christians in Jerusalem. All of our evidence indicates that Hellenistic Christians had no such differences with the Jerusalem church. As New Testament scholar Oscar Cullmann points out,

> The assertion of Bousset and Bultmann that there is a complete break between the original Palestinian Church and Hellenistic Christianity is simply a construction which is neither justified by the elements handed down to us from the very early Church, nor able to explain the origin of Hellenistic faith in the *Kyrios Jesus*. It is clear that whenever Paul mentions the confession of Christ as Lord, he draws upon an old tradition and presupposes acquaintance with it as the foundation of all proclamation of Christ.[266]

Cullmann maintains that one simply "cannot say that Jesus was first *worshiped* as *The* Lord in a Hellenistic environment" instead of in the original Palestinian environment.[267]

2. *Bousset's opponents also criticize him for faulty reasoning from his premises.* For example, even if Bousset had succeeded in proving the existence of a Hellenistic Kyrios cult, it still would not follow that the Hellenistic churches borrowed from it. This is especially true given the more plausible alternative sources for the Christian use of *kyrios* to be noted later in this chapter.

3. *Bousset's detractors also object to his faulty methodology.* Bousset created any number of methodological problems for himself. For one thing, his claim that Pauline Christianity was derived from Hellenistic churches that differed markedly from the Jerusalem church made it necessary for him to reconstruct the Hellenistic Christianity of Antioch. In order to do this he first had to distinguish what Paul learned from what Paul himself produced. But then Bousset also had to distinguish between what Paul learned from the church at Antioch and what he received from the church at Jerusalem. Many of Bousset's critics regarded the difficulty of establishing the latter distinction as the Achilles' heel of his theory.[268] We know from passages like 1 Corinthians 15:1–7 that a distinction can be made between what Paul received from others and what he himself produced by direct revelation from God. The text itself tells us some of the things he learned from others. But how can someone like Bousset determine whether the source of what Paul received was the church at Antioch or the church at Jerusalem?

Bousset tried to use the Book of Romans as the ground of his reconstruction of the Hellenistic Christianity of Antioch, assuming a basic similarity must underlie all Gentile Christianity (whether of Rome or Antioch). But this assumption begs an important question. As Machen asks, "What reason is there to assume that the pre-Pauline Christianity of Rome was the same as the pre-Pauline Christianity of Antioch and Damascus? Information about the pre-Pauline

Christianity of Antioch and Damascus is, to say the least, scanty and uncertain. And it is that Christianity only . . . and not the Christianity of Rome, which can be of use in explaining the origin of Paul's religion."[269]

4. *Bousset's theory conflicts with the evidence we do have.* Several points are relevant here.

a. First of all, we have already noticed the complete silence of the New Testament regarding any possible disagreement or conflict between Paul and the leaders of the Jerusalem church regarding their understanding of Jesus. Herman Ridderbos draws attention to an important point to be learned from this silence:

> When one remembers that the apostles were eye-witnesses and that Paul was called to be an apostle only a short time after Jesus' death, it is historically unthinkable that Paul could have proclaimed a different gospel concerning Christ without getting into difficulty with "Jerusalem." This historical circumstance is . . . one of the most powerful counter arguments against the opinion that Paul introduced an entirely new proclamation of Jesus as the Christ, and was even the second originator of Christianity. . . . [Nor was there ever] any indication of a difference between the apostles or the early church concerning the content of [Paul's] gospel.[270]

Bousset's claim of an essential disagreement between the Hellenistic and Palestinian interpretations of Jesus is contradicted by the New Testament's clear implication that on this point the churches were in agreement.

b. Our evidence also indicates that those who first took the Christian gospel to Antioch were Jews of the Dispersion who received their own understanding of Jesus from Jesus' closest followers, the apostles. Machen finds it incredible that "such men would so soon forget the impression that they had received, and would transform Christianity from a simple acceptance of Jesus as Messiah with eager longing for His return into a cult that emulated the pagan cults of the surrounding world."[271]

c. The evidence also reveals the short period of time between the first proclamation of the gospel in Antioch—by Jews who had learned it at the feet of the apostles in Jerusalem—and the amazingly swift paganization of the Hellenistic churches (according to Bousset). After all, Paul's conversion took place within three years of Jesus' death.

> If, therefore, the paganizing Hellenistic Christianity of Damascus and Antioch was to be the spiritual soil in which Paul's religion was nurtured, it must have been formed in the very early days. The pagan influences could hardly have begun to enter after the conversion of Paul. For then Paul would have been conscious of their entrance, and all the advantages of [Bousset's] hypothesis would disappear—the hypothesis would then be excluded by the self-testimony of Paul. For the formation of a paganizing Christianity at Antioch and Damascus, in the very early days and by the instrumentality of men who had come under the instruction of the intimate friends of Jesus, and despite the constant intercourse between Jerusalem and the cities in question, is very difficult to conceive. At any rate, the separation between what Paul received from Antioch and Damascus and what he received from Jerusalem is quite impossible.[272]

d. Bousset's claim that *kyrios* was a pagan title that was first applied to Jesus in Hellenistic churches like Antioch is contradicted by the fact that the early church frequently used *kyrios* (Matt. 7:21; 8:25; 21:3ff.; Mark 12:35-37; Luke 5:8). First Corinthians 16:22, where Paul uses the Aramaic word *maranatha*, has become a pivotal verse in the debate over Bousset's theory. What makes the text significant is the fact that Paul here uses the Aramaic word for Lord to refer to Jesus. Since it is extremely doubtful that the Antioch Christians spoke Aramaic, the word *maranatha* most likely originated in the Jerusalem church. This fact has led scholars like A. D. Nock to conclude that "*Kyrios Christos* probably comes therefore from the language of the original community at Jerusalem."[273] This means that it was not Hellenistic churches like the one at Antioch that brought into the Christian church the concept of faith in Jesus as Lord. The worship of Jesus as Lord began with the Jewish Christians in Jerusalem.

5. *Bousset's theory is in complete conflict with the exclusive nature of early Christianity*. The religion of the New Testament is totally alien to any spirit of compromise or cooperation with anything that might undermine the supremacy of Christ. Machen observes that Bousset's theories are rendered improbable

> by the sturdy monotheism of the Christian communities. That monotheism was not at all impaired by the honor which was paid to Jesus; the Christian communities were just as intolerant of other gods as had been the ancient Hebrew prophets. This intolerance and exclusiveness of the early Church constitutes a stupendous difference between the Christian "Jesus-cult" and the cults of the other "Lords."[274]

The uncompromising monotheism and the exclusiveness that the early church preached and practiced make the possibility of any pagan inroads like those suggested by Bousset unlikely, if not impossible.

Alternatives to Bousset's Theory

Two alternative accounts of what led the early church to call Jesus *Kyrios* are more plausible than the view of Bousset. One of them suggests that the early Christians simply took a common Greek word and adapted it to meet the demands of the particular message they wished to proclaim. As Machen observes,

> Certainly the mere fact that the Christians used a title which was also used in the pagan cults does not establish any dependence upon paganism. For the title "Lord" was almost as well established as a

designation of divinity as was the term "God." Whatever had been the origin of the religious use of the word, that use had become a part of the Greek language. A missionary who desired to proclaim the one true God was obliged, if he spoke in Greek, to use the term *God*, which of course had been used in pagan religion. So if he desired to designate Jesus as God, by some word which at the same time would distinguish Him from God the Father, he was obliged to use the word "Lord," though that word also had been used in paganism. Neither in the one case nor in the other did the use of a Greek word involve the slightest influence of the conceptions which had been attached to the word in a polytheistic religion.[275]

But even more important is the fact that, in the Septuagint, *Kyrios* is the Greek translation of Yahweh.[276] The Christian message was first proclaimed to people who used the Septuagint as their Bible. This important truth suggests that when the earliest Christians called Jesus *Kyrios*, they were not just transferring a pagan title of deity to Him. Rather, they were proclaiming that Jesus is the Yahweh of the Old Testament.

Summary

The early church clearly believed that Jesus Christ is God. One of the several ways in which it expressed this conviction was its calling Jesus "Lord." An examination of the evidence reveals that neither the title nor its meaning was borrowed from pagan sources. The term was first used by the Jerusalem church and was in all likelihood adapted from the Septuagint's use of *Kyrios* as a translation of Yahweh.

JESUS' DEATH AND RESURRECTION

The early church believed that Jesus Christ, God incarnate, died to save the human race from its sins and then rose triumphantly from the dead. Many proponents of an early Christian syncretism have maintained that this picture is borrowed from the dying and rising savior gods of the mystery cults.

Early in the twentieth century, Alfred Loisy taught that Paul regarded Jesus as "a savior-god, after the manner of an Osiris, an Attis, a Mithra. Like them, he [Jesus] belonged by his origin to the celestial world; like them, he had made his appearance on the earth; like them, he had accomplished a work of universal redemption, efficacious and typical; like Adonis, Osiris, and Attis he had died a violent death, and like them he had returned to life . . ."[277] Loisy claimed that because Paul had been influenced by the savior-god myths of the time, he was led to create a myth of his own, namely, that the world is redeemed by Christ. In this supposed Pauline myth, Christ, the Christian's savior-god, dies and rises. Baptism is a rite of initiation by which the Christian dies a symbolic death and undergoes a symbolic resurrection.

In the 1920s, American scholar George Holley Gilbert put forth the same general thesis.* As Gilbert wrote, "The nucleus of the popular cults, as the cults of Attis, Osiris and Adonis, is this: a divine being comes to earth, assumes human form, dies a violent death, rises, and, through union with him . . . men are redeemed. And what does Paul teach? A being who existed in the form of God appeared on earth in the likeness of sinful flesh, was crucified, and rose from the dead. Men, through their relation to this experience of a celestial being, are redeemed."[278]

In the 1950s, American philosopher Edwin Burtt argued that Paul's theology "may be briefly described as a remolding of the moralized cult of Yahweh, developed by the Hebrew prophets, into a mystery religion of personal

---

*In fact, a close reading of Loisy's 1911 article and Gilbert's 1928 book suggests that Gilbert was paraphrasing Loisy.

salvation, in which the crucified Jesus of Nazareth appears not merely as the promised Messiah but also as a savior-god."[279] And even more recently, philosopher W. T. Jones has claimed that "Paul first made the historical Jesus into a savior god and then built up a mythical setting for this god out of the Jewish legends and stories that he and Jesus, as Jews, knew in common."[280] These few examples that cover most of the twentieth century make it clear that the enemies of biblical Christianity think highly of this argument.*

The Death of Jesus and That of the Mystery Gods

The best way to evaluate the alleged dependence of early Christian beliefs about Christ's death and resurrection on the pagan myths of a dying and rising savior-god is to examine carefully the supposed parallels. The death of Jesus differs from the deaths of the pagan gods in at least six ways. (1) None of the so-called savior-gods died for someone else. The notion of the Son of God dying in place of his creatures is unique to Christianity.[281] (2) Only Jesus died for sin. It is never claimed that any of the pagan deities died for sin. As Wagner observes, to none of the pagan gods "has the intention of helping men been attributed. The sort of death that they died is quite different (hunting accident, self-emasculation, etc.)."[282] (3) Jesus died once and for all (Heb. 7:27; 9:25–28; 10:10–14). In contrast, the mystery gods were vegetation deities whose repeated death and resuscitation depict the annual cycle of nature. (4) Jesus' death was an actual event in history. The death

---

*Rudolf Bultmann's variation of the thesis that Jesus was a descending and ascending savior-god stresses the dependence of this belief less on the pagan mystery religions than on a similar theme within Gnosticism. For that reason, his particular statement of the theory will be discussed in part 3 of this book. See Rudolf Bultmann, *Theology of the New Testament*, 2 vols. (New York: Scribner, 1955), 2:6, 12–13, 66.

of the god described in the pagan cults is a mythical drama with no historical ties; its continued rehearsal celebrates the recurring death and rebirth of nature. The incontestable fact that the early church believed that its proclamation of Jesus' death and resurrection was grounded upon what actually happened in history makes absurd any attempt to derive this belief from the mythical, nonhistorical stories of the pagan cults.[283] (5) Unlike the mystery gods, Jesus died voluntarily. Nothing like the voluntary death of Jesus can be found in the mystery cults. Machen states, "Osiris, Adonis, and Attis were overtaken by their fate; Jesus gave his life freely away. The difference is stupendous; it involves the very heart of the religion of Paul."[284] (6) And finally, Jesus' death was not a defeat but a triumph. Christianity stands entirely apart from the pagan mysteries in that its report of Jesus' death is a message of triumph. Even as Jesus was experiencing the pain and humiliation of the cross, He was the victor. The New Testament's mood of exultation contrasts sharply with that of the mystery religions, whose followers wept and mourned for the terrible fate that overtook their gods.[285]

The Risen Christ and the "Rising Savior-Gods"

The significant differences between the death of Jesus and the mythical deaths of the pagan deities must be coupled with the equally serious errors made by those who write of the "resurrections" of the mystery gods.

Which mystery gods actually experienced a resurrection from the dead? Certainly no early texts refer to any resurrection of Attis.[286] Attempts to link the worship of Adonis to a resurrection are equally weak.[287] Nor is the case for a resurrection of Osiris any stronger. After Isis gathered together the pieces of Osiris's dismembered body, he became "Lord of the Underworld." As Metzger comments, "Whether this can be rightly called a resurrection is questionable, especially since, according to Plutarch, it was the pious desire of devotees to be buried in the same ground where, according to local tradition, the body of Osiris was still lying."[288] One can speak then of a "resurrection" in the stories of Osiris, Attis, and Adonis only in the most extended of senses.[289] And of course no claim can be made that Mithras was a dying and rising god. French scholar André Boulanger concludes: "The conception that the god dies and is resurrected in order to lead his faithful to eternal life is represented in no Hellenistic mystery religion."[290]

Summary

The tide of scholarly opinion has turned dramatically against attempts to make early Christianity dependent on the so-called dying and rising gods of Hellenistic paganism.[291] German scholar Günter Wagner aptly summarizes the situation in these words: "That Paul modeled his Christ 'myth' on the myths about other 'dying and rising' gods is now no more seriously held than is the derivation of the observance of Sunday and of the resurrection on the third day from the mystery cults."[292] Therefore, in the case of this theory, our examination of the evidence shows that it too must be rejected.

THE NEW BIRTH

Any claim that the Christian doctrine of rebirth was borrowed from pagan Hellenistic sources would, if true, constitute a serious blow to the traditional understanding of Christianity.[293] The two relevant Greek words in this debate appear in just four New Testament verses. First Peter 1:23 uses *anagennaō* ("to be born again"): "For you have been born again, not of perishable seed, but of imperishable, through the living and enduring word of God." And Titus 3:5 uses *palingenesia* (regeneration): "He saved us through the washing of rebirth and renewal by the Holy Spirit." *Palingenesia* is found in a different sense in Matthew 19:28; but the idea of rebirth, if not the exact language, is prominent throughout the New Testament (e.g., John 3:3–8; 2 Cor. 5:17; Eph. 4:24; Rev. 2:17).

Sample Claims

A number of scholars have argued that the early Christian belief in rebirth was borrowed from similar teaching in religions of the Hellenistic world. Samuel Angus, a proponent of Christian syncretism in the 1920s, claimed: "Every Mystery-Religion, being a religion of redemption, offered means of suppressing the old man and of imparting or vitalizing the spiritual principle. Every serious *mystes* [initiate] approached the solemn sacrament of Initiation believing that he thereby became 'twice-born,' a 'new creature,' and passed in a real sense from death unto life by being brought into a mysterious intimacy with the deity."[294] British scholar W. L. Knox agreed: "It is a matter of common form in primitive initiation rites that the initiate underwent a new birth."[295] As recently as 1956, Rudolf Bultmann described the pagan initiates as "born again," "changed," "deified," and "enlightened."[296]

Rebirth in the Mystery Religions?

In this section, each of the major mystery religions will be examined to see if it really taught a doctrine of rebirth analogous to the Christian view. Attempts to find a notion of rebirth in the Eleusinian mysteries hinge largely on appeals to this cult's practice of washings, references to which are found in the church father Tertullian (A.D. 160–222). A careful analysis of the Eleusinian practices reveals that the washings carried no idea of rebirth or regeneration and served only as preparatory cleansings prior to the initiate's entrance to the temple. Nowhere in the ritual was there any notion of rebirth.[297]

With regard to the cult of Cybele and Attis,

there is only one major literary connection between the religion and the notion of rebirth. It is a philosophical interpretation of the myth of Cybele and Attis by a fourth-century A.D. thinker named Sallustius. But it is unclear why any testimony this late should be regarded as a reliable clue to the beliefs and practices of the cult in the first century or before. Since the source is so late, the possibility exists that *it* was influenced by Christianity. In fact, it is possible that Sallustius wrote his work as part of the pagan reaction against Christianity during the reign of Julian the Apostate (A.D. 361–363). The pagan desire to counteract the growing influence of Christianity is often said to have resulted in its imitation of Christian language and practice. It is extremely risky, therefore, to use Sallustius as a witness to what the cult of Cybele believed and practiced during its pre-Christian stage.

With regard to the cult of Isis and Osiris, only two sources (both from the second century A.D.) use the imagery of rebirth: Apuleius's *Metamorphoses* and Plutarch's *On Isis and Osiris*.[298] In both cases, the claim that the source actually refers to rebirth depends on a debatable interpretation. Attempts to make Apuleius teach that the *mystes* is reborn are contradicted by Lucius's disclaimer that the rebirth took place only "in a sense." In all likelihood, Apuleius simply borrowed a metaphor from common speech to illuminate his own personal experience with the cult.

Plutarch did actually use the word *palingenesia* several times, but it is unclear whether he borrowed it from the mysteries or from philosophical sources. While it was a convenient term for him to use to describe Osiris's "return to life" in the Nether World, it is anything but clear that Plutarch applied *palingenesia* to the followers of Osiris; and it would be this latter usage that would be crucial for our problem. Plutarch's account hardly justifies the interpretation that the person who undergoes initiation in the mysteries of Isis is "reborn." Moreover, the use of a particular term by someone describing something within a cult does not prove that the word itself was actually part of the cult's terminology. Since Plutarch was reinterpreting the myth, it remains an open question as to what extent his report contains personal emendations, including, possibly, his borrowing *palingenesia* from the philosophical literature he knew so well.

While there are several sources that suggest that Mithraism included a notion of rebirth, they are all post-Christian. The earliest, a wall painting in what is now the church of Santa Prisca, dates from the end of the second century A.D.[299] But, of course, this earliest source still postdates by one hundred years the early Christian adoption of the imagery and terminology of rebirth. Another source that connects Mithraism and the notion of rebirth is an inscription usually dated A.D. 391, obviously too late to help the proponent of syncretism.

The most frequently discussed evidence alleged to prove the presence of rebirth in a mystery religion is an inscription on a Roman altar that appears to connect the taurobolium with a belief in rebirth. The Latin inscription *taurobolio cribolioque in aeternum renatus* can be translated "reborn for eternity in the taurobolium and criobolium." Proponents of an early Christian syncretism refer to the phrase *in aeternum renatus* as clear evidence that the Christian belief in rebirth was derived from beliefs associated with the taurobolium. But the problems connected with this hypothesis are enormous. For one thing, the Roman altar containing the inscription dates from A.D. 376.[300] Machen's discussion of the inscription is instructive:

> The phrase, "reborn for eternity," occurs in connection with the bloodbath of the taurobolium. How significant, it might be said, is this connection

of regeneration with the shedding of blood! How useful as establishing the pagan origin of the Christian idea! From the confident way in which the phrase "reborn for eternity" is quoted in discussions of the origin of Christianity, one would think that its pre-Christian origin were established beyond peradventure. It may come as a shock, therefore, to readers of recent discussions to be told that as a matter of fact the phrase does not appear until the fourth century, when Christianity was taking its place as the established religion of the Roman world. If there is any dependence, it is certainly dependence of the taurobolium upon Christianity, and not of Christianity upon the taurobolium.[301]

According to F. C. Grant, the formula comes from a time when pagan religions were attempting a resurgence against Christianity. They were trying hard to "copy and take over the more appealing elements in Christianity. . . ."[302] The inscription was dedicated by a Roman named Sextilius Agesilaus Aedesius, known to be an enemy of Christianity, whose effort may well have been an attempt to counter its growing influence.[303]

We must beware of the common practice of starting with what we know about a cult during a late stage of its development and reading some belief or practice back into some earlier stage. All of the Hellenistic religions underwent major developments. Both the Isis cult as practiced in Greece and the Mithraism of Rome were significantly different from earlier forms of these religions in Egypt and Iran. Thus, what we may learn about the beliefs of a cult in the fourth century A.D. will not necessarily be true of the cult several hundred years earlier.

Although rebirth would have been a fitting metaphor for the mystery cults and perhaps they could have used it, we should not assume that they did use it. Whether it was fitting or not, the mystery cults prior to A.D. 100 did not use the metaphor of rebirth. Günter Wagner goes even further than this and maintains that the notion of an initiate's rebirth bringing him into union with his god was not really part of the mystery theology. Consequently, he concludes, we cannot even say that a doctrine of rebirth was compatible with their systems.[304]

Conclusion

We began this section by noting several sweeping generalizations to the effect that early Christianity borrowed its notion of rebirth from the pagan mysteries. But now that we have examined the evidence, we find that there was no pre-Christian doctrine of rebirth for the Christians to borrow. As we have seen, there are actually very few references to the notion of rebirth in the evidence that has survived, and even these are either very late or very ambiguous. They provide no help in settling the question of the source of the New Testament use of the concept. The claim that pre-Christian mysteries regarded their initiation rites as a kind of rebirth is unsupported by any evidence contemporary with such alleged practices. Instead, a view found in much later texts is read back into earlier rites, which are then interpreted quite speculatively as dramatic portrayals of the initiate's "new birth." The belief that pre-Christian mysteries used *rebirth* as a technical term is unsupported by even one single text.

Most contemporary scholars maintain that the mystery use of the concept of rebirth (testified to in the late evidence noted earlier) differs so significantly from its New Testament usage that any possibility of a close link is ruled out. The most that such scholars are willing to concede is the *possibility* that some Christians borrowed the metaphor or imagery from the common speech of the time and recast it to fit their distinctive theological beliefs. So even if the metaphor was Hellenistic, its content within Christianity was unique.[305]

Reitzenstein and others in the History of Religions School maintained that the Pauline doctrine of redemption was derived from the pagan mystery religions. MacGregor and Purdy provide one statement of this thesis:

> It is, however, when we pass from Christology to Soteriology that the full flood of Hellenistic influence is apparent. The salvation brought by Christ, instead of being related, as it originally was, to the Jewish apocalyptic scheme of a coming Kingdom of God introduced by a great day of judgment, is now conceived rather as a redemption of mankind from bondage to the evil forces of a lower material world; salvation is not merely a deliverance promised for the future, but the present gift of a new kind of life guaranteed through mystical union with a Savior-Redeemer.[306]

Such advocates of Christian syncretism find the whole Pauline teaching about redemption to be dependent on Hellenistic sources.

Granted, there is a similarity between Paul's writings and Hellenistic thought on the human need for redemption. But does the mere presence of this similarity prove Paul's dependence? As Machen observes:

> Both Paulinism and the Hellenistic mystery religions were religions of redemption. But there have been many religions of redemption, in many ages and among many peoples, which have been entirely independent of one another. It will probably not be maintained, for example, that early Buddhism stood in any fundamental causal relation to the piety of the Hellenistic age. Yet early Buddhism was a religion of redemption.[307]

The independent appearance of a doctrine of redemption at different times and in different cultures is well established. Thus, the mere fact that Paul teaches that human depravity must be delivered by a divinely conferred redemption and that this view is superficially similar to other views of his time fails to prove anything.

180

The Gospel
and
The Greeks

The Christian and
Pagan Doctrines of
Redemption

The Christian and pagan doctrines of redemption differ in at least three major respects:

1. Redemption in the mystery religions was concerned primarily with deliverance from burdens—such as fate, necessity, and death—that form the basic constraints of human life.[308] On the other hand, Christian doctrine maintains that humans need to be saved from *sin*. The basic problem for human beings is not fate or circumstances, in short, things external to man. The human problem lies within. Man is sinful and thus unable to meet the requirements of a holy God and powerless to overcome his sin by his own effort. Even Reitzenstein was forced to admit that Christianity taught something totally different from the mysteries: "The new element in Christianity is redemption as remission of sins. The terrible seriousness of the doctrine of guilt and atonement is lacking in Hellenism."[309]

2. Paul's doctrine of salvation differed from pagan notions by being forensic. As explained by Machen:

> Salvation, according to Paul, is not only salvation from the power of sin; it is also salvation from the guilt of sin. Not only regeneration is needed, if a man is to be saved, but also justification. At this point, there is apparently in the mystery religions no parallel worthy of the name. . . . Without the slightest question Paul did maintain a forensic view of salvation. The believer, according to Paul, is in himself guilty in the sight of God. But he is given a sentence of acquittal, he is "justified," because Christ has born on the cross the curse of the Law which rightly rested upon those whom Christ died to save.[310]

This judicial dimension to salvation is central to Paul's view, as its prominence in the Book of Romans attests.

3. While pagan salvation most certainly did not produce a moral change, Pauline salvation resulted in a transformation of human character and the imposition of moral obligations (Rom. 8:12; 2 Cor. 5:14–15, 17).[311] The absence of any

strong moral influence within the mystery cults is not really that surprising, given their origin in ancient fertility rites replete with sexual overtones. While there was, to some extent, an ethical content in the older Greek mysteries such as Orphism, the mystery cults that came from the Orient were almost completely lacking in ethical content at first. This led Hugo Rahner to state:

> Measured by the standards of ethical content, Christianity and the mysteries are worlds apart. Mystery religion at best is man's earthbound tragic attempt to purge and raise himself morally (and sometimes only ritually) by his own resources— while in Christianity it is not man who raises himself up but *God* who descends, conferring upon man the divine grace that makes possible his moral regeneration in the love of Christ.[312]

We have examined only three of the significant ways in which Paul's doctrine of redemption differs from the pagan view. Since some of the other differences will be discussed in chapter 11, I close here by noting that I have found no reason to believe that any of the four major Christian beliefs discussed in this chapter was borrowed from the mystery religions. As Rahner says, "Christianity, as revealed by God in Christ, has in neither its genesis nor its growth anything fundamental in common with the ancient mysteries."[313] Once again we find that first-century Christianity has no clear and direct dependence on the mystery cults.[314]

Conclusion

chapter eleven

Paul and the Mystery Religions

The author examines possible connections between the apostle Paul and the mystery religions: terminology, personal contact, and theological meaning. He marshals eight arguments against such a connection.

This final chapter on the mystery religions will cover three additional issues relating to claims of an early Christian dependence on the mysteries. It will then conclude with a summary of the weaknesses of such claims.

THE QUESTION OF PAUL'S TERMINOLOGY

Considerable attention has been paid to the presence or absence of key mystery terms in Paul's vocabulary. If we were to discover that Paul actually used technical terms from the mystery religions, it is unlikely that anything of significance would follow. Even MacGregor and

183

Purdy, strong proponents of an early Christian syncretism, find little substance in this line of thinking. They point out that however striking the resemblances between Christianity and the mysteries may appear,

> they are in vocabulary and outward form rather than in essential thought and content. The Mysteries and Christianity, being products of the same age, were almost certain to use the same forms of expression. But there is no greater fallacy than to assume that because Christianity took over, or developed independently, a number of terms and rites familiar also to the Mysteries, the thought and experience symbolized in them are equally comparable to, and do not entirely transcend, the pagan analogy.[315]

Martin Hengel, a German critic of syncretism, argues that the language of the mystery cults had attained widespread usage independent of the actual practice of the religions. The appearance of this language in The Wisdom of Solomon and in the writings of Philo indicates its likely use in synagogues outside of Palestine. Even so, Hengel concludes, evidence of mystery language "in the New Testament still does not mean direct dependence on the mystery cults proper."[316]

Paul's Vocabulary in General

A number of scholars are willing to admit the presence of pagan terms in Paul's writings while still insisting that he imbued those words with a new meaning. As Albert Schweitzer put it, "Paulinism and Hellenism have in common their religious terminology, but, in respect of ideas, nothing. The Apostle did not Hellenize Christianity. His conceptions are equally distinct from those of Greek philosophy and from those of the Mystery-Religions."[317] Historian E. Glenn Hinson allows for similar words but a different meaning: "Whatever words were imported from the Hellenistic milieu, they were reshaped by biblical nuances."[318]

While any biblical writer, including Paul, could have used pagan language and given it a new meaning, many scholars are unwilling to concede that Paul used any technical pagan terms. Expressing his reservations about alleged linguistic similarities between Paul and the mystery religions, A. D. Nock wrote, "It is not clear that St. Paul's linguistic practice points to first-hand knowledge of the mysteries, still less to the reading of theological literature about them."[319] Günter Wagner also objects to statements assuming there is mystery language in Paul's writings:

> When those terms that frequently occur in the mystery cults are compared with Paul's vocabulary, one comes to the conclusion that Paul knows only those words that have been common property for a long time, and that he uses them in a sense that does not correspond with the specific meanings accorded them in the mysteries. . . . It is thus no exaggeration to declare that the vocabulary of the mysteries is foreign to the apostle.[320]

Putting aside for the moment the term *mysterion*, one must be impressed by all the technical mystery terms that are missing from Paul's writings.[321] For example, Paul never uses such key pagan terms as *mystes* ("initiate") or *telestheis* ("made perfect"). "The few words which are common to the New Testament and the texts of the Mysteries either are so infrequent in the New Testament as to be inconclusive in establishing religious affinities . . . or have an entirely different meaning in the two corpora of sources."[322] A word like *teleios* ("perfect" or "mature") was such a common Greek word that its appearance in the New Testament signifies nothing.[323]

186

The Gospel
and
The Greeks

Paul's Use of
Mysterion

But a number of people have thought that the frequent use of *mysterion* in Paul's writings deserves another look.* Paul mentions "the revelation of the mystery hidden for long ages past" (Rom. 16:25) as well as the mystery of God's will (Eph. 1:9) and the mystery he learned through revelation (Eph. 3:3). He wrote of "God's secret wisdom" (1 Cor. 2:7) and "the mystery of the gospel" (Eph. 6:19). But neither these nor any other New Testament uses of *mysterion* imply dependence on the vocabulary of the mystery cults. Even before Paul, Jesus had referred to the mysteries of the kingdom (Matt. 13:11; Mark 4:11; Luke 8:10)—the king's secret counsels that are communicated in parables to those close to him and hidden from everyone else. Nothing of real significance follows from Paul's frequent use of *mysterion*. While the word was sometimes used outside the New Testament in a technical way to refer to the mysteries, it was also used in nontechnical ways in common Greek. Paul's meaning clearly relates to the word's more popular usage. Machen elaborates:

> The Christian "mystery" according to Paul is not something that is to be kept secret on principle, like the mysteries of Eleusis, but it is something which, though it was formerly hidden in the counsels of God, is now to be made known to all. Some, it is true, may never be able to receive it. But that which is necessary in order that it may be received is not "gnosis" or an initiation. It is rather acceptance of a message and the holy life that follows.[324]

Put in its simplest terms, the word *mystery* in the New Testament usually refers to the gospel, God's good news that through Christ the redemption of human beings is now possible (Rom. 16:25; Eph. 6:19; Col. 2:2).[325] The word is

---

*Of the twenty-seven times the word is used in the New Testament (not including one questionable variant reading in 1 Corinthians 2:1), it occurs twenty times in the writings of Paul.

also used occasionally in a more restricted sense to refer to a specific doctrine (1 Cor. 15:51; 1 Tim. 3:16). As Mircea Eliade explains,

> It is true that he [Paul] uses *mysterion,* but in the sense given it in the Septuagint, that is, "secret." In the New Testament, *mysterion* does not refer to a cult act, as it does in the ancient religions. For St. Paul, the mystery is God's secret, that is, his decision to save man through his son, Jesus Christ. The reference, then, is basically to the mystery of redemption. But redemption is an idea that is incomprehensible except in the context of the Biblical tradition; it is only in that tradition that man, originally the son of God, had lost this privileged station by his sin.[326]

It is clear, then, that nothing about the vocabulary of the New Testament in general, or the writings of Paul in particular, forces us to conclude that any signs of a mystery influence appear in the language of the New Testament.[327]

THE TARSUS CONNECTION

One theory often used to explain how paganism came to influence the Apostle Paul can be called the Tarsus connection. Members of the History of Religions School worked hard to show that Paul was an easy target for influences from the pagan surroundings in which he was raised and educated. Save for a few years spent in Jerusalem, Paul lived most of his life in a pagan environment. How likely is it, advocates of Christian syncretism ask, that anyone under such constant bombardment from, or exposure to, pagan ideas and practices could have remained free of their influence?

Tarsus, Paul's boyhood home, was known as the "Athens of Asia Minor." It was a major center of trade and culture. Paul, the syncretists argue, could not help but encounter public ceremonies of some of the pagan religions that

An Analysis of the Tarsus Connection

thrived in Tarsus. Years later, according to the theory, memories of Paul's youth would merge with impressions from his later years and give birth to his distinctive view of Jesus as a dying and rising savior-god.[328]

The inconclusiveness of this kind of reasoning should be obvious. Even though Tarsus was a city where one could easily encounter pagan philosophy and religion, it was also a place where a strict Jew of the Dispersion could have consciously avoided such an influence. As Albert Schweitzer pointed out decades ago, Paul's independence of pagan influence seems reasonable. Even though Paul may have lived in the middle of Hellenistic paganism, Schweitzer observed, "it is possible that Paul absorbed no more of it than a Catholic parish priest of the twentieth century does of the critical theology, and knew no more about it than an Evangelical pastor knows of theosophy."[329] Any final judgment on this question must be based on what Paul actually stated in his writings, and they clearly display his resolve to remain free of paganism.

Even though Paul could have seen paganism at work in Tarsus, there is an important difference between noting that he grew up in a pagan city and concluding that this strict young Jew was influenced by the paganism around him. If Paul had been a liberal Jew, a Sadducee for example, the supposition that he had acquired pagan ideas in his youth would make more sense. But as Paul himself made clear, he was anything but a liberal Jew (Phil. 3:4–6).* "It is very difficult," wrote Machen, "to conceive of such a man—with his excessive zeal for the Mosaic Law, with his intense hatred of paganism, with his intense consciousness of the all-

---

*Other verses that testify to Paul's pride in his Jewishness include: Acts 22:3; 23:6; 26:4–5; Rom. 1:16; 2:9–10; 11:1; 2 Cor. 11:22; Gal. 2:15. F. C. Grant states that Paul's Judaism was that of the Western Dispersion. See Grant, *Roman Hellenism*, p. 146.

sufficiency of Jewish privileges—as being susceptible to the pagan influences that surrounded his orthodox home.''[330] The very most that a syncretist can maintain is that if any pagan influences were operative in Paul's life, they affected him subconsciously. Even if we suppose that pagan ideas lay dormant in Paul's subconscious for years, we must still find some event that suddenly triggered the more favorable attitude that would have been required before he incorporated these ideas into his "new" religion. "When," Machen asks, "did he overcome his life-long antagonism to everything connected with the worship of false gods? Such a change of attitude is certainly not attested by the Epistles.''[331] Machen counters the most popular answer to his question:

> When Paul was converted, it is said, he was converted not to the Christianity of Jerusalem, but to the Christianity of Damascus and Antioch. But the Christianity of Damascus and Antioch, it is supposed, had already received pagan elements; hence the influx of pagan ideas. Of course Paul did not know that they were pagan ideas; he supposed that they were merely Christian; but pagan they were, nevertheless. The Hellenistic Jews who founded the churches at Damascus and Antioch, unlike the original apostles at Jerusalem, were liberal Jews, susceptible to pagan influence and desirous of attributing to Jesus all that the pagans attributed to their own cult-gods. Thus Jesus became a cult-god like the cult-gods of the pagan religions, and Christianity became similar, in important respects, to the pagan cults.[332]

We have already evaluated this line of reasoning in chapter 10. The weaknesses that we noted there apply with equal force to the position now in view.[333]

Many contemporary scholars counter the alleged Tarsus connection with what might be called the Jerusalem connection. Like W. C.

An Alternative to the Tarsus Connection

Van Unnik, they discount Tarsus as a major influence on Paul and argue instead that the dominant influences in his life came from Jerusalem.[334] Even though Paul was born in Tarsus, he grew up and was educated in Jerusalem. "The real possibility of Paul's upbringing and education in Jerusalem weakens the basis of the view that his Tarsus background was an important factor for his becoming a missionary to the Gentiles later."[335]

It would appear, therefore, that the thesis I have called the Tarsus connection must be rejected because it conflicts with the only evidence available to us—Paul's own written testimony. The strict, conservative Pharisee who was so proud of his Jewishness would never have consciously included pagan elements in his religion. The hypothesis of an unconscious influence founders on its inability to identify any event that might have altered Paul's hostile attitude toward paganism. And the entire theory is made even more unlikely by the strong possibility that the major religious and educational influences in Paul's life came, not from Tarsus, but from Jerusalem.

The Origin of Paul's Religion

The question of the source or sources of Paul's religion lies in the background of much of this book. Of course, this sort of question becomes a problem primarily for someone who rejects the traditional Christian interpretation of Christianity and the relation of Paul's gospel to Jesus, to the Jerusalem church, and to the Old Testament. Early in the twentieth century, it was fashionable in some theological circles to set up a dichotomy between the religion of Jesus and the theology of Paul. Paul, it was sometimes said, effectively gave the world an entirely new religion, different in essentials from the simple gospel of Jesus. If Paul's religion really did differ from that of Jesus, then Paul could not have derived his religion from Jesus. But where, then, did Paul get his religion?

Our argument thus far certainly implies that the religion of Paul is an extension of the religion of Jesus and is implicit in the Old Testament. Everything that Paul teaches about the person and work of Jesus has its source in what Jesus Himself actually was, taught, and did. There is nothing new about this claim. It was the view that Paul himself held about his own teaching. It is the position of traditional Protestants and Roman Catholics. It is a view that has been examined and defended in many books written in this century, including a book by J. Gresham Machen, *The Origin of Paul's Religion,* written sixty years ago, and a recent book by Korean scholar Seyoon Kim, *The Origin of Paul's Gospel.*

The central task in understanding the origin of Paul's religion is grasping Paul's close, personal, and loving relationship with Jesus Christ. Paul's personal and saving relationship with Christ began, of course, in his encounter with the risen Christ on the Damascus road. Seyoon Kim traces Paul's theology back to that crucial event: "Thus it is clear that Paul's gospel and apostleship are grounded solely in the Christophany on the Damascus road. . . . *Paul received his gospel from the Damascus revelation of Jesus Christ.* We submit that *only when this insistence of Paul is taken seriously can we really understand Paul and his theology.*"[336] But this fact, Kim hastens to add, should not lead us to think that prior to his conversion, Paul's mind was just a blank tablet.

Paul certainly had known the messianic beliefs, the conceptions of the law and Wisdom, and other ideas and concepts in Judaism and the primitive Christian kerygma, and perhaps also became acquainted with some Hellenistic ideas and concepts later in his mission field. But these *religionsgeschichtlichen* materials neither made Paul a Christian nor produced his theology. They were suspended, needing a catalyst for solution into Paul's theology. Only when there was the catalyst of the living experience of seeing the crucified Jesus as the exalted Messiah, the Lord, and the Son and image of God on the Damascus road, were these materials precipitated into Paul's Christian theology. To put it another way, the real experience of the Damascus revelation led Paul to use all these *religionsgeschichtlichen* materials as interpretive categories and concepts for his Christian theology. That is to say, those materials provided Paul only with certain categories and concepts with which he could interpret the Damascus experience and produce his theology. But without the real experience of the Damascus revelation Paul could not have had his gospel at all, not to mention his unshakable and lively conviction in it.[337]

Nor does any of this mean that Paul's theology came to him in one sudden flash. "Further reflections on the revelation in the light of the OT Scriptures, his experience in the mission field and his controversies with his opponents led him to deepen and sharpen his understanding of the gospel revealed on the Damascus road."[338] The weakness of attempts to trace Paul's beliefs back to the pagan philosophical and religious systems of his day helps us appreciate anew the unique truth revealed in Paul's writings.

CONCLUSION TO PART TWO

The best way to conclude our study of the mystery religions is to review the most serious weaknesses of attempts to make early Christianity dependent (in the strong sense) on the pagan cults.

1. The arguments of the syncretist illustrate the logical fallacy of false cause. This fallacy is committed whenever someone reasons that just because two things exist side by side, one of them must have caused the other. As we all should know, mere coincidence does not prove causal connection. Nor does similarity prove dependence. American theologian E. Earle Ellis

was right when he criticized the History of Religions School for its tendency "to convert parallels into influences and influences into sources."[339]

2. Many alleged similarities between Christianity and the mystery religions are either greatly exaggerated or invented. As we have seen, scholars often describe pagan rituals in language borrowed from Christianity. The careless use of language could lead one to speak of a Last Supper in Mithraism or the baptism of the Isis cult. It is inexcusable to take the word *savior* with all of its New Testament connotations and apply it to Osiris or Attis as though they were savior-gods in any similar sense. Many of the supposed parallels that repeatedly appear in the writings of syncretists turn out to be fictions or imaginary constructs that exist only in the minds of biased seekers who end up finding exactly what they were seeking.

British scholar Edwyn Bevan was correct when he wrote: "Of course if one writes an imaginary description of the Orphic mysteries, as Loisy, for instance, does, filling in the large gaps in the picture left by our data from the Christian eucharist, one produces something very impressive. On this plan, you first put in the Christian elements, and then are staggered to find them there."[340] Critical attention must be drawn to those writers who fill in the gaps between the evidence and their conclusions with details and terminology borrowed from Christianity.

3. With regard to claims about an early Christian syncretism, the chronology is all wrong. Almost all of our sources of information about the pagan religions alleged to have influenced early Christianity are very late. As Machen noted sixty years ago:

In order to reconstruct that Hellenized oriental mysticism from which the religion of Paul is to be derived, the investigator is obliged to appeal to sources which are long subsequent to Paul's day. For example, in reproducing the spiritual atmosphere in which Paul is supposed to have lived, no testimony is more often evoked than the words of Firmicus Maternus, "Be of good courage, ye initiates, since the god is saved; for to us there shall be salvation out of troubles." Here, it is thought, is to be found that connection between the resurrection of the god and the salvation of believers which appears in the Pauline idea of dying and rising with Christ. But the trouble is that Firmicus Maternus lived in the fourth century after Christ, three hundred years later than Paul. With what right can an utterance of his be used in the reconstruction of pre-Christian paganism? What would be thought, by the same scholars who quote Firmicus Maternus so confidently as a witness to first-century paganism, of a historian who should quote a fourth-century Christian writer as a witness to first-century Christianity?[341]

As we have seen, the full development of the mystery religions did not occur until the second century A.D. Moreover, any significant encounter between them and Christianity probably did not take place until the third century A.D. Our extant sources for the mystery cults all belong to periods of time after Paul's death. *The Golden Ass,* a frequently cited source, was written by Apuleius after A.D. 175. It was also impossible for Paul to have been influenced by the Hermetic writings (at least as we know them) or by the magical papyri. While it is possible to claim that Paul could have been influenced by earlier forms of the mystery cults, this hypothesis lacks any supporting evidence. If we consider just the mystery religions as we now know them in their fully developed form, Paul could never have been influenced by them, since they did not then exist in that form.

Machen complains that a "lordly disregard of dates runs all through the modern treatment of the history of religion in the New Testament period."[342] This careless inattention to dates is especially prominent in the very popular writings most likely to affect large numbers of people.

> When the lay reader is overwhelmed by an imposing array of citations from Apuleius and from Lucian, to say nothing of Firmicus Maternus and fourth-century inscriptions, and when these late citations are confidently treated by men of undoubted learning as witnesses to pre-Christian religion, and when the procedure is rendered more plausible by occasional references to pre-Christian writers which, if looked up would be found to prove nothing at all, and when there is a careful avoidance of anything like temporal arrangement of the material, but citations derived from all countries and all ages are brought together for the reconstruction of the environment of Paul—under such treatment the lay reader often receives the impression that something very important is being proved. The impression would be corrected by the mere introduction of a few dates, especially in view of the fact that oriental religion undoubtedly entered upon a remarkable expansion shortly after the close of the New Testament period, so that conditions prevailing after that expansion are by no means necessarily to be regarded as having existed before the expansion took place.[343]

First, we must distinguish between early and later forms of the mystery religions. Second, we must avoid the assumption that just because a cult had a certain belief or practice in the third or fourth century, it therefore had the same belief or practice in the first century. Third, we must avoid any indiscriminate conjoining of facts from different centuries. The relatively late information we have about the pagan religions should not uncritically be read back into earlier stages in their development.[344]

4. Paul would never have borrowed from the pagan religions. All of our information about Paul makes it highly unlikely that he was influenced by pagan sources. He placed great emphasis on his early training in a strict form of Judaism (Phil. 3:5). He warned the Colossians against the very sort of things that advocates of

Christian syncretism attribute to him—namely, letting their minds be captured by alien speculations (Col. 2:8). As Metzger points out:

> The early Palestinian Church was composed of Christians from a Jewish background, whose generally strict monotheism and traditional intolerance of syncretism must have militated against wholesale borrowing from pagan cults. Psychologically it is quite inconceivable that the Judaizers, who attacked Paul with unmeasured ferocity for what they considered his liberalism concerning the relation of Gentile converts to the Mosaic law, should nevertheless have acquiesced in what some have described as Paul's thoroughgoing contamination of the central doctrines and sacraments of the Christian religion. Furthermore, with regard to Paul himself, scholars are coming once again to acknowledge that the Apostle's prevailing set of mind was rabbinically oriented, and that his newly found Christian faith ran in molds previously formed at the feet of Gamaliel.[345]

Even if we suppose that Paul had borrowed from pagan religions, his enemies among the Judaizers would have quickly attacked him for such a serious compromise. Such attacks would have made it necessary for Paul then to explain or defend his use of such ideas. But his writings contain no hint either of such attacks or of Paul's need for a defense.

5. Christianity is a monotheistic religion with a definitive body of doctrine. While the evolution of the oriental mystery cults after A.D. 100 would eventually result in their advancing one solar deity above all the other gods, the earlier mysteries (including those during the first Christian century) reveal a conflicting pantheon of deities and superhuman mythical beings. Moreover, Rahner explains, "the heterogeneous, confused cult legends are utterly irrelevant to the doctrine; and we find a purely emotional longing for a salvation that is conceived in naturalistic terms. It is and remains a riddle how in the period of unrestricted 'comparative reli-

gion' scholars should even have ventured a comparison, not to speak of trying to derive the basic doctrines of Christ from the mystery religions."[346]

6. Early Christianity was an exclusivistic faith. Even though this point has been mentioned before, it is worth repeating; inattention to it is one of the most serious weaknesses of the syncretists' position. Machen explains:

> The oriental religions were tolerant of other faiths; the religion of Paul, like the ancient religion of Israel, demanded an absolutely exclusive devotion. A man could become initiated into the mysteries of Isis or Mithras without at all giving up his former beliefs; but if he were to be received into the Church, according to the preaching of Paul, he must forsake all other Saviours for the Lord Jesus Christ. The difference places the achievement of Paul upon an entirely different plane from the successes of the oriental mystery religions. It was one thing to offer a new faith and a new cult as simply one additional way of obtaining contact with the Divine, and it was another thing, and a far more difficult thing (and in the ancient world outside of Israel an unheard-of thing), to require a man to renounce all existing religious belief and practices in order to place his whole reliance upon a single Saviour. Amid the prevailing syncretism of the Greco-Roman world, the religion of Paul, with the religion of Israel, stands absolutely alone.[347]

This exclusivism should be a starting point for all reflection about any possible relations between Christianity and its pagan competitors. The obvious inference, supported by the clear evidence in the New Testament, is that any hint of syncretism would have caused immediate controversy.

7. Unlike the mysteries, the religion of Paul was grounded on events that actually happened in history. The mysticism of the mystery cults was essentially nonhistorical. Their myths were dramas, or pictures, of what the initiate went through, not real historical events (as Paul

regarded Christ's death and resurrection). "Unlike the deities of the Mysteries," Metzger writes, "who were nebulous figures of an imaginary past, the Divine Being whom the Christian worshiped as Lord was known as a real Person on earth only a short time before the earliest documents of the New Testament were written."[348] Reformed scholar Herman Ridderbos emphasizes the same truth:

> Whereas Paul speaks of the death and resurrection of Christ and places it in the middle of history, as an event which took place before many witnesses, in the recent past, the myths of the cults in contrast, cannot be dated; they appear in all sorts of variations, and do not give any clear conceptions. In short they display the timeless vagueness characteristic of real myths. Thus the myths of the cults . . . are nothing but depictions of annual events of nature in which nothing is to be found of the moral voluntary, redemptive substitutionary meaning, which for Paul is the content of Christ's death and resurrection.[349]

This Christian affirmation that the death and resurrection of Christ happened to a historical person at a particular time has absolutely no parallel in any of the pagan mystery religions.

8. Although many alleged parallels between Christianity and the later mysteries (about which information is available) are imaginary or exaggerated, the genuine parallels that still remain may reflect a Christian influence on the pagan system. Metzger argues, "It must not be uncritically assumed that the Mysteries always influenced Christianity, for it is not only possible but probable that in certain cases, the influence moved in the opposite direction."[350] It should not be surprising that leaders of the cults that were being successfully challenged by Christianity should do something to counter the challenge.

> One of the surest ways would be to imitate the teaching of the Church by offering benefits compa-

rable with those held out by Christianity. Thus, for example, one must doubtless interpret the change in the efficacy attributed to the rite of the taurobolium. In competing with Christianity, which promised eternal life to its adherents, the cult of Cybele officially or unofficially raised the efficacy of the blood bath from twenty years to eternity.[351]

Pagan attempts to counter the growing influence of Christianity by imitating it are also apparent in measures instituted by Julian the Apostate, who was Roman emperor from A.D. 361 to 363.

These eight arguments against Christian syncretism help us understand why biblical scholars today seldom claim any early Christian dependence on the mysteries. They constitute an impressive collection of reasons why scholars in such other fields as history and philosophy should rethink their methods and conclusions and finally put such views to rest.

Part Three:

Christianity and Gnosticism

chapter twelve

The Importance
of the
Gnostic Question

The question of strong Christian dependence on Gnosticism is raised, crucial issues in the debate are overviewed, and a brief history of the debate is offered. The crucial nature of the Gnostic question becomes clear.

The claim that early Christianity was influenced by Gnosticism goes back at least as far as Richard Reitzenstein in the first half of the twentieth century. While the early church fathers depicted Gnosticism as a Christian heresy, Reitzenstein believed that it was actually a pre-Christian movement that in several important ways influenced early Christianity, including the Pauline and Johannine views of Jesus. Closer to our own time, Rudolf Bultmann extended Reitzenstein's position, making it an important part of his interpretation of John's Gospel. As we will see later, Bultmann's theories were attacked and   203 rejected by many scholars. Even while the theory of an early Christian dependence on Gnosticism remained largely in disfavor among biblical scholars, it (like other claims of syncretism noted earlier) continued to be propagated both in popular writings and in textbooks written by specialists in areas other than theology. And so, for example, historian Thomas W. Africa circulated the position in his ancient history text by writing: "Even the canon of the New Testament includes gnostic material. Gnostic themes pervade the Gospel of John, the prologue of which is almost a gnostic hymn."[352]

RENEWED INTEREST IN GNOSTICISM

There are several reasons why Gnosticism commands renewed attention today. Not the least of these is the discovery, translation, and publication of significant Gnostic texts found at Nag Hammadi in Egypt right after World War II. (These finds were in addition to the publication of the better known Dead Sea Scrolls—found at about the same time—and of lesser known texts of the Iranian religion known as Mandaeanism.) Another reason for the new interest in Gnosticism was the publication of English translations of several German books that argued for the existence of a pre-Christian Gnosticism alleged to be a source of important New Testament teachings. These translated works included Wilhelm Bousset's *Kyrios Christos* and Rudolf Bultmann's commentary on the Gospel of John. Thus, at least two motives are operative in the new attention being given to Gnosticism. The more detached motive is the increased scholarly interest in learning more about the past whenever new sources become available. The other, and much less detached, motive is some scholars' hope that new information can help prove Gnosticism's influence on early Christianity.

The general organization of this book into three parts traces the general historical order in which syncretists have alleged a Hellenistic influence on early Christianity. At first, the proponents of syncretism tended to concentrate their charges on primitive Christianity's dependence on Hellenistic philosophy (part 1). As the movement lost steam, many scholars followed the lead of the History of Religions School and sought the roots of early Christian belief and practice in the mystery religions. The fruitlessness of this quest was discussed in part 2. Once it became clear that the mystery religions were not the source that syncretists hoped they would be, attention turned finally to Gnosticism (about which relatively little was known).

A Brief History of the Gnostic Question

The recent history of the Gnostic question can be divided into six stages:

Stage One: Through the eighteenth century, the major sources of information about Gnosticism were the writings of such church fathers as Justin Martyr, Irenaeus, Hippolytus, Origen, and Tertullian.[353] The Fathers depicted Gnosticism as a Christian heresy that began with the Simon Magus mentioned (but not there identified as a Gnostic) in Acts 8:9ff. Major Gnostics after Simon, named in the patristic accounts, included Menander, Saturninus, Cerinthus, Marcion, Basilides, and Valentinus (the most famous). Since the church fathers' purpose in discussing Gnosticism was to attack the movement as a perversion of Christianity, scholars raised questions about the objectivity of the writers and the reliability of the information they presented. For reasons like this, some scholars have tended to look elsewhere for their picture of Gnosticism. Recently, however, confidence in the basic reliability of the patristic picture of early Gnosticism (to about A.D. 150) has been reestablished.[354] Some elements of the patristic account have been confirmed by material found in the Nag Hammadi writings.[355]

Stage Two: Speculation by members of the History of Religions School in the early decades of the twentieth century marks the next significant stage in the history of the Gnostic question. First, rejecting the patristic view that Gnosticism was a Christian heresy, they argued that Gnosticism was a pre-Christian movement. Second, they took the second-century Gnosticism depicted in the patristic writings as merely a late development of ideas that had circulated for years, perhaps centuries. According to Wilhelm Bousset, "Gnosticism is first of all a pre-Christian movement which has its roots in itself. It is therefore to be understood in the first place in its own terms and not as an offshoot or a by-product of the Christian religion."[356] Bousset found this pre-Christian Gnosticism in Philo and in the Hermetic writings.* The major proponent of the view that this pre-Christian Gnosticism heavily influenced first-century Christianity was Richard Reitzenstein.

Stage Three: The influential work of Rudolf Bultmann did more than anything else to establish the significance of the thesis that early Christianity was dependent on a pre-Christian Gnosticism. According to Bultmann, Gnosticism, "a religious movement of pre-Christian origin, invading the West from the Orient, was a competitor of Christianity."[357] Building on the earlier work of such scholars as Reitzenstein and Bousset, Bultmann developed what he called *the myth of the Gnostic Redeemer.*† In his view, the actual point of contact between early Christianity (at least the Fourth Gospel) and this myth was a pre-Christian Gnostic sect in Palestine that centuries later would be represented by the Iranian sect known as Mandaeanism. Bultmann argued that the Mandaean sect originated in Palestine with a group of first-century followers of John the Baptist.

Bultmann believed that the writer of the Gospel of John had been a member of this

---

*But of course, the Hermetic writings as we know them must be dated *after* the origin of Christianity.

†I discuss this myth in the next chapter.

Gnostic sect who was converted to Christianity. Consequently, according to Bultmann, the Fourth Gospel is riddled with Gnostic themes and language. One strange but central feature of Bultmann's theory is his conviction that the New Testament must be viewed as one stage in the development of Gnosticism! This crucial but highly questionable assumption made it possible for Bultmann to find not only New Testament passages that illustrate the introduction of Gnostic ideas into the New Testament but also other texts that depict the transformation of these ideas into the distinctive Christian doctrines we know today. Thus, in Bultmann's view, the New Testament represents two relationships to Gnostic ideas. It both used them and reacted against them. For Bultmann, there was no chronological development in these two steps. Both could and occasionally did exist simultaneously. But generally speaking, he held, the *older* a New Testament writing is, the more likely it is to express opposition to Gnosticism. In addition to John's Gospel, Bultmann declared, other major Gnostic influences are evident in the writings of Paul.*

Stage Four: Bultmann's thesis of Gnostic dependence drew strong opposition from biblical scholars and theologians. Their major objection to Bultmann's speculation was the total lack of any evidence for a pre-Christian Gnosticism. The weak historical basis of Bultmann's theory troubled many scholars who tended, more or less, to stick with the patristic picture of Gnosticism as a Christian heresy. Opponents of Bultmann's thesis included E. Percy, C. H. Dodd, W. F. Albright, and R. P. Casey.[358] In Casey's words, "No one, I fancy, would nowadays take seriously the notion that the Fourth Gospel

---

*For example, Bultmann claims that Paul's Christology is a synthesis of the dying and rising savior-god of the mystery religions, the heavenly Son of Man depicted in Jewish apocalyptic literature, and the Gnostic myth of a heavenly Redeemer who descends to earth.

arose as a Christian adaptation of a Mandaean account of John the Baptist."[359] Supporting this widespread skepticism about Bultmann's position was his failure to present any evidence that the Gnostic Redeemer myth, which was supposed to have influenced New Testament writers, even existed in the first century. C. H. Dodd drew attention to the gigantic chronological gap between Bultmann's late sources, the extant Mandaean writings, and the pre-Christian Gnosticism they were supposed to reflect.

> The compilation of the Mandaean Canon, therefore, cannot be dated much, if at all, before A.D. 700. That is not to say that certain of the writings contained in it may not be earlier, though considerable portions of the Ginza and of the Book of John were certainly written after the appearance of Islam, since they contain references to Muhammad and to the spread of his religion. . . . For any history of the Mandaeans and their beliefs before 700 we are dependent solely on inference and speculation.[360]

In part 2 of this book, I noted the tendency of scholars to criticize proponents of an early Christian dependence on the mysteries for the ease with which they jumped a gap of several hundred years between their sources and the claims they made about the mystery cults in the first century A.D. Compared to Bultmann, those scholars were amateurs. It is little wonder that Bultmann's theories met with such strong resistance.*

Stage Five: But hope springs eternal, even among theologians. A number of Bultmann's followers refused to surrender to attacks on their master's Gnostic thesis, though some of them must have had a few doubts about the theory's shaky historical foundation. Bultmann's speculations were given new life by the accidental 1945 discovery of twelve Coptic codices in the

---

*Bultmann's opponents had plenty of other objections, some of which will be noted later.

region of Nag Hammadi in Egypt. The fifty-three

writings found on the codices were Coptic
translations from earlier Greek versions of such
Gnostic works as *The Gospel of Truth, The
Gospel According to Thomas,* and *The Apocalypse of Adam.* These Gnostic writings were
probably copied around A.D. 350 and then buried
sometime after A.D. 400.* But, of course, the
original writings on which the copies are based
may be dated long before this, since one of
them, *The Apocryphon of John,* is mentioned by
Irenaeus about A.D. 180.[361] The discovery at Nag
Hammadi rivals in importance the discovery of
the Dead Sea Scrolls in 1946. Some scholars
regard them as necessary evidence for a pre-
Christian Gnosticism that was so obviously
missing from Bultmann's speculations.

Scholars disagree sharply over whether the
Nag Hammadi writings actually throw any light
on the question of a pre-Christian Gnosticism.
American scholar James Robinson thinks they
do provide support for a Gnostic movement that
antedates Christianity. He has written: "The
absence of the gnostic redeemer myth at Qumran did seem to diverge from what Bultmann had
anticipated concerning Jordanian baptismal
sects; but this admission would seem to have
been filled in by such Nag Hammadi materials as
the *Apocalypse of Adam.*"[362]

Among the scholars disagreeing with Robinson is Gnostic specialist G. Quispel, who notes
that Robinson "argues that a number of writings
found at Nag Hammadi, which for the greatest
part have not yet been published [at the time
Quispel and Robinson wrote] and which might
be non-Christian, are pre-Christian. But that is
not the question at all. The question is whether
in pre-Christian times there existed a very
specific, coherent myth of the redeemed redeemer. And it appears that that question must be

---

*This kind of dating is based on the writings' allusions to
datable events.

answered in the negative."[363] We will leave open for now the question of possible non-Christian and even pre-Christian Gnostic writings within the Nag Hammadi discovery. The issue will arise later in connection with a more detailed analysis of the possible existence of a pre-Christian Gnosticism.[364]

Stage Six: What is the present state of the debate? Well, on the one hand we have the contemporary disciples of Bultmann who think the case for a pre-Christian Gnosticism has been strengthened as a result of these recent discoveries. But on the other hand, there are scholars (e.g., Edwin Yamauchi) who have examined the full range of claims and found that satisfactory evidence for the existence of a pre-Christian Gnosticism is still absent.

ANOTHER CRUCIAL ISSUE IN THE DEBATE

The issue that rests at the heart of the current debate over the relationship between early Christianity and Gnosticism is Gnosticism's age. Was it, as the church fathers claimed, a post-Christian heresy? Was it an independent movement that began about the same time as Christianity? Or was it a full-blown pre-Christian movement that influenced the early church? Special attention must be given to the ease with which many scholars reason that once the existence of a pre-Christian Gnosticism is established, the dependence of the New Testament on that Gnosticism will be established beyond any doubt. But surely this reasoning is faulty. Even if there were a pre-Christian Gnosticism, why does it follow that Christianity must have been influenced by it? It is clear that the alleged Christian dependence on Gnosticism does not follow solely from the existence of Gnosticism before, or contemporaneous with, Christianity. Without more than this, we would simply have another example of the fallacy of false cause: coincidence does not entail causal connection.

It is at this point that all the putative Gnostic

themes in the Pauline and Johannine writings are supposed to become relevant. But anyone who has read this book through to this point has learned not to accept something as a genuine parallel just because some scholar says it is. We will have to take a careful look at these supposed parallels, just as we did with earlier claims about New Testament similarities to pagan philosophy and religion, and see if they stand up under careful analysis. What explanations other than Gnostic dependence can be offered for those parallels that turn out to be genuine and significant? Our task in resolving the issue of a possible Christian dependence on Gnosticism is a complex one. The first step, to which I turn in the next chapter, is defining Gnosticism and identifying its major beliefs.

chapter thirteen

The Nature of Gnosticism

The doctrinal, historical, and ceremonial aspects of Gnosticism are presented. Its possible sources as a movement are reviewed, and the alleged dependence of Christianity on Gnosticism is surveyed.

The word *Gnosticism* comes from the Greek word *gnōsis,* which means "knowledge." However, the Gnostics gave a special twist to the word, so that for them *gnōsis* meant a special type of revealed knowledge without which human beings could not attain salvation.

VARIETY WITHIN GNOSTICISM

Gnosticism was not a monolithic religion. The term is used to refer to a wide variety of religious views and movements that became influential during the first several centuries A.D. The sources of Gnosticism are difficult to track. 213

According to Scottish New Testament specialist R. McL. Wilson:

> No single tradition yet known to us is adequate to account for all the phenomena. In its origins Gnosticism is not Egyptian, nor is it Persian, nor is it Greek, although there are points of contact to be found in every case. The basic philosophy which underlies the Gnostic systems, for example, is that synthesis of Platonism and Stoicism, usually associated with the name of Posidonius, which formed the common background of contemporary thought. But a philosopher like Plotinus . . . found it necessary, despite the affinities of Neo-Platonism and Gnostic thought, to write a polemic against the Gnostics. Again, although Gnosticism in the narrower sense appears historically as a Christian heresy, it is fundamentally un-Christian. The refutations of its Christian opponents are sufficient proof of that.[365]

Gnosticism may well be the epitome of Hellenistic syncretism, drawing from and blending together philosophical ideas from Platonism and Stoicism and religious ideas from Jewish, Babylonian, Egyptian, and other Middle Eastern traditions. In addition to the heretical versions of the Christian Gnosticism that we know about from the church fathers, there seem to have been several non-Christian movements that some call Gnostic and others describe as semi-Gnostic.

The second-century Gnosticism described in patristic literature existed in at least three distinct schools. In Syria, Gnosticism was heavily influenced by the dualistic religion known as Zoroastrianism. Founded in Antioch by Menander, the Syrian school emphasized the sharp distinction between two gods—a good God of light and an evil power of darkness. A different Gnostic school developed in Alexandria, Egypt. Its two major thinkers were Basilides and Valentinus, who are both dated about the middle of the second century A.D. The third and last Gnostic school to be mentioned here was associated with Marcion, who is often thought to belong in a class by himself. Marcion added a third god to the good and evil deities of the dualists. This third god, the Demiurge, created the world. While paganism worshiped the evil god and Judaism followed the Demiurge (in Marcion's view), the Gnostic knew a higher deliverance from the power of both by means of a secret knowledge from the good god. Marcion rejected the Old Testament as a product of the inferior Demiurge. He taught a view called Docetism in which Christ only appeared to have a real physical body. Of all the apostles, only Paul possessed true authority.

Later Gnostic systems, with their various combinations of themes and ideas, dropped all pretense of being versions of Christianity. They presented themselves as competitors to Christianity—either superior (e.g., Manichaeanism) or simply antagonistic (e.g., Mandaeanism).

COMPETING DEFINITIONS OF GNOSTICISM

The conclusions most scholars reach about Gnosticism are a function of their initial definition. Much of the recent debate about Gnosticism is a conflict between advocates of a narrow definition versus proponents of a broader definition of the movement. Generally speaking, those who advance a narrow definition of the system conclude that no evidence for a pre-Christian Gnosticism exists. On the other hand, scholars who insist on a broad definition of the term tend to find Gnosticism all over the place; they even find it in the New Testament.[366]

One example of a broad definition of "Gnosticism" explains it as a religious movement in which salvation depends on knowledge. Anyone accepting this broad a definition will have no difficulty finding Gnosticism practically anywhere in the Hellenistic world. Advocates of a more narrow definition limit the essence of Gnosticism by pointing out that the system is basically dualistic, that it contains a myth of a descending and ascending Redeemer, and so on.

One real problem in any attempt to unravel the various threads of the Gnostic problem is the inability of scholars to agree on a definition.

While Bultmann and other advocates of a pre-Christian Gnosticism favor a broad definition, French New Testament scholar Simone Pétrement represents a position at the opposite extreme. She insists on defining Gnosticism so narrowly that she will not even allow the term to be applied to Gnostic tendencies. As she sees it, "Gnosticism does not consist merely of the use of the word 'gnōsis'; it is a teaching that is concerned with the relations of God, man, and the world, and this teaching is nowhere found, it seems, before Christianity."[367] Even scholars who doubt the existence of a legitimate candidate for the title of "Pre-Christian Gnosticism" think Pétrement's view is too extreme.

One attempt at a compromise came out of an important conference on "The Origins of Gnosticism" that was held in Messina, Sicily, in 1966. One suggestion that emerged from the congress was a recommendation that scholars adopt "pre-Gnostic" and "proto-Gnostic" as technical terms. Edwin Yamauchi explains:

> "Pre-Gnostic" would be used to designate elements in existence in pre-Christian times which were later incorporated into Gnosticism proper; "pre-Gnostic" elements do not constitute "Gnosticism" in the strict sense. On the other hand, "Proto-Gnostic" would designate the early or incipient forms of Gnosticism which preceded the fully developed Gnosticism of the second century.[368]

When we are dealing with isolated suggestions, beliefs, or other elements that just happened to be picked up by later Gnostics and incorporated in one of their systems, we get the sense of the term "pre-Gnostic." When we are examining an early, still undeveloped form of what would grow into Gnosticism, the term "proto-Gnostic" is appropriate. Although the Messina suggestion has obvious merit for the detailed work of scholars, it would probably help nonspecialists if a simpler distinction were used.

R. McL. Wilson has made a couple of suggestions along this line. One is that the label "Gnosticism" be reserved for the fully developed Gnostic systems and that all nonsystematic elements be treated as pre-Gnostic. Hence, on this view, we would have just two key terms: Gnostic and pre-Gnostic. The relevance of Wilson's terminology to the question of a pre-Christian Gnosticism should be obvious. The opponent of any pre-Christian Gnosticism (in the fully developed, systematic form) can readily acknowledge the pre-Christian existence of elements that would eventually become part of Gnostic systems.[369] In a later work, Wilson distinguished between Gnosticism and Gnosis: "By Gnosticism we mean the specifically Christian heresy of the second century A.D., by Gnosis, in a broader sense, the whole complex of ideas belonging to the Gnostic movement and related trends of thought."[370] Gnosis, then, could apply to the appearance of Gnostic ideas in other movements of the time that do not really qualify as Gnostic.* The point is that we should use the name "Gnosticism" very carefully; it should be applied exclusively to the fully developed Gnostic systems that extant evidence indicates existed after A.D. 100. We can find elements prior to Christianity that later would become incorporated in the Gnostic systems; these we can call pre-Gnostic. Alongside of even fully developed forms of Gnosticism there were movements that, while similar to it, should not be identified with it; call these Gnosis.

My own discussion of Gnosticism will follow

---

*For example, an idea that appears in the New Testament might, in Wilson's terminology, accurately be called Gnosis without entailing that the New Testament writer was influenced by Gnosticism proper or was even familiar with any pre-Gnostic elements. Similar ideas can appear in different literature independently.

Wilson's terminological suggestions. Like Wilson, I believe we must distinguish between Gnosticism as a developed movement and more general Gnostic tendencies, some of which may be present in pre-Christian times. Like Wilson, I think it is a mistake to take whatever pre-Gnostic elements we may find and try to turn them into Gnosticism proper. An important first step in resolving the Gnostic question is distinguishing between Gnostic tendencies and the later, more fully developed Gnostic systems.

THE GNOSTIC REDEEMER MYTH

Because speculation about the myth of a Gnostic Redeemer is so central in the thinking of those who maintain an early Christian dependence (in the strong sense) on Gnosticism, I begin my brief analysis of Gnostic beliefs with a description of the myth. My account of other major Gnostic beliefs will follow in the next section of this chapter.

Rudolf Bultmann claimed that he found traces of a pre-Christian Gnostic Redeemer myth in such New Testament books as the Fourth Gospel. One basic theme of the myth concerns the heavenly preexistence of human souls prior to their embodied existence in this world. Something happened in that heavenly world of light that caused each human soul to fall from its heavenly home and resulted in the soul being imprisoned in its body. But the good god, taking pity on these poor souls, sent to earth a Gnostic Redeemer who imparted a secret knowledge about their former state--a state that people had forgotten—and about how they might return to it. After giving this knowledge, the heavenly figure returned to the world of light. This is a general outline of the myth.

Examining the myth in more detail will fill in some of the obvious gaps from the above paragraph. For one thing, human souls are considered sparks of a heavenly Primal Man, a figure of light. Even before time began, the evil demonic forces of darkness conquered this heavenly figure of light, tearing him into pieces. The many particles of light that resulted from the Primal Man being torn apart were then used by the demons to create a world from the chaos of darkness. If the particles of light were ever removed from the material world, the world would return to its original chaotic state. For that reason, the demons guard the particles of light carefully to prevent the destruction of their world. The particles of light that are human souls became bound to material bodies. As part of their imprisonment, the demons cause these souls to forget their original heavenly state. The good god then sends the heavenly figure of light in bodily form to awaken the souls, remind them of their original home in the realm of light, and reveal how they may return. After imparting this secret knowledge (gnosis), the heavenly figure of light returns to heaven to prepare the way for his followers after their death. In this way, redeemed human souls become liberated from their bondage to an evil, material world.

As Bultmann sees it, the Christology of the New Testament is dependent on this myth. Accordingly, Jesus was the Primal Man, appearing in the form of a human being for the purpose of saving human souls; like the heavenly figure in the Gnostic myth, Jesus first descended, accomplished what he came to do, and then ascended. In addition to asserting that this myth is prominent in the Fourth Gospel, Bultmann also claimed to find traces of the myth in a number of Pauline passages (including 1 Cor. 2:8ff.; 2 Cor. 8:9; Eph. 4:8–10; Phil. 2:6–11; 1 Tim. 3:16). It should be apparent that if Bultmann were correct, Christianity would not simply be dependent on Gnosticism; in actuality, Christianity would be a major variety of Gnosticism.

The Gospel
and
The Greeks

Any attempt to identify the major Gnostic beliefs contains certain dangers, which are noted by G. W. MacRae:

> It must be understood . . . that it is impossible to sketch the contents of Gnostic teaching in such a way as to include all the pseudo-Christian forms, much less the later Christian and non-Christian forms. One can, however, detach from these many systems a series of assertions and attitudes that reflect the common atmosphere of Gnosticism. The scheme suits no one branch but is not completely foreign to any of them.[371]

One of the more obvious beliefs of Gnosticism is its fundamental dualism. In the myth of the Gnostic Redeemer, this dualism is apparent in the conflict between the two worlds (light and darkness), the two superhuman forces (the good god of light and the demons of darkness), and the two parts to human beings (a good soul imprisoned in an evil body). God, spirit, and light are diametrically opposed to demons, matter, and darkness. The idea of the inherent evil of matter has consequences for the entire Gnostic system. One of these involves the very existence of the material world. Given the good god's opposition to matter, it is impossible that he could have anything to do with bringing such a world into existence. Hence, the Gnostics reasoned, he did not. The material world must be the work either of evil demons (as noted in our account of the myth) or, in some versions, of a second and inferior god, akin to Plato's Demiurge, whom heretical Christian Gnostics viewed as the Yahweh of the Old Testament.

Human beings belong to both worlds—the spiritual world of the divine light and the material world of darkness. Human souls are sparks of the divine light that have become entrapped in matter. Unconscious of their divine origin and destiny but still impelled by a subconscious longing for the heavenly light from which they had fallen, these "pneumatics" (as they were called) were impelled to seek deliverance from their bondage to matter. The basic question of human existence is how to achieve deliverance from matter and finally return to the world of light and the god of that world.

Several things are necessary if human beings are to experience this redemption. For one thing, they need to be awakened from their slumber and reminded of their heavenly origin. The basic means by which humans attain salvation from the evil of matter is a special knowledge (gnosis) that they cannot attain themselves but only receive as a divine gift. This gnosis is not intellectual knowledge or philosophical speculation but a revelation from the good god. But it is not a knowledge that just anyone may obtain; it is a secret or esoteric knowledge made available only to those for whom it can be a means of salvation. "In some cases [*gnōsis*] is no more than a crude magical knowledge of spells and passwords, for to know the name of a god gives power over the owner of the name. In other cases, *gnōsis* meant an elevated mystical experience, a vision of the divine, a knowledge received by revelation from God Himself."[372] As explained by Gnostic specialist Hans Jonas,

> The goal of gnostic striving is the release of the "inner man" from the bonds of the world and his return to his native realm of light. The necessary condition for this is that he *know* about the transmundane God and about himself, that is, about his divine origin as well as his present situation, and accordingly also about the nature of the world which determines this situation.[373]

The Gnostics also believed in a huge host of intermediary beings who inhabit the regions between God and men. As noted in part 1, the postulation of intermediary beings between God and the world was prominent in the thought of Philo and the Middle Platonists. The Gnostics usually explained these intermediary beings (often called aeons) as emanations of the good god. The Gnostic picture of the various spheres or layers between this god and the material world often got quite complicated, as MacGregor and Purdy explain:

> The earth is separated from the upper realms of light by a series of intermediary spheres, usually seven in number, over each of which rules one of the planetary demons. . . . It is they who determine all that happens within their respective spheres, and through their domain that imprisoned divine spark which is the soul must find its way to the . . . transcendent world beyond all the seven spheres.[374]

These spheres symbolize the very real distance between man and god, as well as the difficulty awaiting the soul that wishes to return to the good god. The demon, or Archon (lord), that governs each sphere "bars the passage to the souls that seek to ascend after death, in order to prevent their escape from the world and their return to God."[375]

It is now possible to fit the Gnostic view of Jesus within this system. In the second-century Gnosticism described by the Fathers, Christ was one of the higher aeons, or intermediary beings, who descended to earth for the purpose of redeeming man. Christ came into the world, not in order to suffer and die, but in order to release the divine spark of light imprisoned in matter. The Gnostic Jesus was not a savior; he was a revealer. He came for the express purpose of communicating his secret gnosis. Central to almost all versions of the Christian forms of Gnosticism was the position known as Docetism. Docetism was a denial that Christ actually became a man with a real human body. Given the inherent evil of matter, the Gnostics regarded even the possibility of a genuine incarnation as unthinkable. Christ only *appeared* to have a human body. The Book of First John contains a number of allusions to a heresy that denied that

Christ had really come in the flesh (1 John 1:1– 2; 2:18ff.; 4:1ff.). Using Wilson's terminology noted earlier, we may regard John's knowledge of, and repudiation of, Docetism as an example of Gnosis (but not Gnosticism) in the New Testament. The Gnostic Jesus never became a man; he only appeared to become incarnate. Consequently, it was impossible for him really to die. Hence the Christian Gnostics had to explain away the sufferings and death of Jesus.

A legitimate area of concern regarding any theological movement is its system of ethics. Gnosticism's system was hardly one of its more commendable features. As Wilson points out, the Gnostic emphasis on the attainment of secret knowledge often led "to a considerable degree of spiritual pride and complacency among the more favoured members of the community, and to widely differing conclusions regarding the practical conduct of life. To some, the possession of gnosis made ethics irrelevant, whereas others held that it was necessary to mortify the flesh by ascetic practices in order to free the soul from its prison."[376] Thus the Gnostic system evidences a split personality. Because of its denigration of the body, some Gnostics were ascetics who avoided sex and marriage and sought liberation from their entrapment in the physical body. But since the Gnostic's salvation depended not on his conduct but on the attainment of secret knowledge, the movement often gave rise to immoral behavior.

One final Gnostic practice should be noted. A use of magic became very important in many later Gnostic sects. A number of inscriptions and drawings that have survived illustrate a Gnostic adoption of the practice of repeating magical names and formulas, some of which were pure gibberish. Astrology also was important. The Gnostics often proposed ways of escaping from man's bondage to the material world through a complex network of pseudoscientific theories about the world and the stars.

We are continuing our quest to answer the question of possible influences of Gnosticism on first-century Christianity. Now that we have reviewed the most important Gnostic beliefs, we can look to the major proponent of early Christian dependence on Gnosticism, Rudolf Bultmann.

chapter fourteen

Bultmann's Gnostic Thesis

Rudolf Bultmann's influence on the whole Gnostic question is introduced and a detailed evaluation presented.

Rudolf Bultmann's towering presence with respect to the Gnostic question makes a more detailed evaluation of his position mandatory. Three major claims constitute Bultmann's influential theory: (1) A Gnostic Redeemer myth (as described earlier) existed in pre-Christian times. (2) Important support for this claim, as well as information about the nature of this pre-Christian Gnosticism, can be gleaned from the writings of the Gnostic religion of Mandaeanism, remnants of which still survive in parts of contemporary Iraq and Iran. (3) Our knowledge of Gnosticism in general and the Redeemer myth in particular helps us recognize many stunning 225 parallels between them and such New Testament documents as the Fourth Gospel. According to Bultmann, these similarities force us to postulate a Gnostic source for these elements. This, in brief, is the theory that Bultmann constructed. However, I will argue, all Bultmann built was a house of cards that collapses once anyone begins to evaluate his evidence and inferences.

BULTMANN'S PRE-CHRISTIAN REDEEMER MYTH

For anyone unfamiliar with the skimpy historical foundation for Bultmann's speculation regarding the Redeemer myth, his claims can carry some clout. As the earlier description of the myth should have made clear, enough similarities exist between the myth and New Testament Christology that an unwary reader might conclude that perhaps such a story did influence Paul and John in the development of their views of Jesus. Yamauchi summarizes Bultmann's conclusions regarding John's Gospel:

> The Fourth Evangelist has demythologized and Christianized his Gnostic source. His former Gnosticism was an early oriental type of Gnosticism with a dualism of darkness and light, but without any complicated theories of emanation. The Evangelist both adopted and adapted the Gnostic Redeemer myth, while at the same time refuting it by reference to the earthly Jesus of Nazareth. In particular, the prologue shows that Christ was a cosmic figure, who was sent in the disguise of a man (Jn. 1:14).[377]

Unfortunately, there is one major snag in all of this: How do we know that the Gnostic Redeemer myth existed prior to, or contemporaneous with, first-century Christianity? In the words of New Testament scholar Stephen Neill:

> One question calls urgently for an answer. Where do we find the evidence for pre-Christian belief in a Redeemer, who descended into the world of darkness in order to redeem the sons of light? Where is the early evidence for the redeemed

Redeemer, who himself has to be delivered from death? The surprising answer is that there is precisely no evidence at all. The idea that such a belief existed in pre-Christian times is simply a hypothesis and rests on nothing more than highly precarious inference backwards from a number of documents which themselves are known to be of considerably later origin.[378]

Neill isolates one of the major problems with Bultmann's thesis. The rest of this section will explore his point in greater detail.

1. One of the more serious objections to Bultmann's view is the fact that there are absolutely no pre-Christian texts that support the existence of the Gnostic myth before the beginning of Christianity.[379] Bultmann reconstructs his picture of the allegedly pre-Christian myth from literature that is at least one hundred years after the Gospel of John! Although all of his textual support is clearly post-Christian, much of it (like the Mandaean literature) postdates the New Testament by several centuries.* Since the only first-century document that Bultmann quotes is the New Testament itself, his theory lacks any extrabiblical evidence from the first century A.D. or before. If any borrowing took place, then, it is far more likely that this later Gnostic literature borrowed from the New Testament.

Even German scholar Walter Schmithals, a strong proponent of Christianity's dependence on a pre-Christian Gnosticism, admits that it is impossible to find traces of a pure version of the Redeemer myth dating before the end of the first Christian century. Recognition of this fact suggests that the hypothesis of a pre-Christian Gnostic Redeemer is nothing more than a fabrication.[380]

According to Martin Hengel, "There really should be an end to presenting Manichaean texts

---

*Examples of Bultmann's source material include the Hermetic writings, writings from the religion known as Manichaeanism, and literature from Mandaeanism.

of the third century like the 'Song of the Pearl' in the *Acts of Thomas* as evidence of supposedly pre-Christian gnosticism and dating it back to the first century B.C. In reality there is no gnostic redeemer myth in the sources which can be demonstrated chronologically to be pre-Christian."[381] Andrew Helmbold sides with those who object to Bultmann's game-playing with the historical evidence:

> Therefore, all extant manuscripts with Redeemer Hymns in the Gnostic mold are from A.D. 140 or later—while the hymns of Philippians and 1 Timothy can be dated no later than the first century A.D. Obviously, then, the written source of the Redeemer Hymn genre used by the early Christians cannot be any of the Gnostic works mentioned. In fact, the presupposition would be the reverse. Aside from this weighty chronological consideration, however, there are major differences in content between the Christian and the Gnostic hymns.[382]

British New Testament scholar James D. G. Dunn concurs:

> Since the publication of Bultmann's *Theology* it has become increasingly evident that his formulation of the myth is an abstraction from later sources. There is nothing of any substance to indicate that a gnostic redeemer myth was already current at the time of Paul. On the contrary all the indications are that it was a *post*-Christian (second century) development using Christian beliefs about Jesus as one of its building blocks.[383]

Therefore, the evidence available to us indicates that there was no Gnostic Redeemer before Jesus. As Robert M. Grant notes, "The most obvious explanation of the origin of the Gnostic Redeemer is that he was modeled after the Christian conception of Jesus. It seems significant that there is no redeemer before Jesus, while we encounter other redeemers (Simon Magus, Menander) immediately after his time."[384] I conclude, then, that the Gnostic Redeemer is not a pre-Christian myth functioning as one source for the New Testament picture of Christ but is instead a post-Christian effect that is itself dependent on the historical Christ.[385]

2. British scholar Alan Richardson, among others, has shown us a second objection to Bultmann's position: The Pauline and Johannine teachings about the Son of Man are extensions of what Jesus himself had already taught.[386] Even if Jesus' teachings are considered from a purely human perspective, they could have resulted from reflection about similar themes in the Old Testament. According to Carsten Colpe,

> The Johannine Son of Man is primarily rooted in the Jewish apocalyptic tradition, which also remains recognizable in the Synoptics. And the Fourth Gospel's identification of Jesus with the Son of Man does not have its basis in the fact that the Evangelist wanted Jesus to suppress or temporalize a Gnostic redeemer-figure. Instead, the identification is based on the fact that the early Christian community took Jesus to be the Son of Man, and apparently this is precisely because of Jesus' own words prior to Easter.[387]

The fact that the New Testament teaching about the Son of Man can thus be explained without resorting to Bultmann's unsupported speculations provides an additional reason for rejecting his hypothesis.

3. But what if new evidence should come to light that finally establishes that there was indeed a Gnostic Redeemer myth in pre-Christian times? Would such a discovery prove Bultmann's thesis? Even if this were to happen, Bultmann's conclusions would not follow. It is completely within reason to suppose that an evangelist like John or a missionary like Paul would recognize the wisdom of communicating the Christian message through language and ideas with which the audience could identify.*

---

*As we saw in part 1, this was certainly true in the case of the writer of the Epistle to the Hebrews.

Communicators have always used not only analogies, or illustrations, but also cultural metaphors. We must not confuse a simple usage of Hellenistic language and thought-forms with the quite separate matter of claiming that the New Testament contains a syncretistic adulteration of the Christian message with pagan ideas.

4. Additional support for the claims made under point three emerge from the truly major differences between the New Testament Redeemer and the heavenly figure of the Gnostic myth. Herman Ridderbos draws attention to at least three such dissimilarities. First, "The Redemption in Christ proclaimed by Paul has a clearly demonstrable and datable *historical* character. The gnostic myth speaks of an inconceivable primeval period and has no relation to a single historical figure."[388] Second, Ridderbos maintains, "The Redeemer whom Paul preaches was born as a man and was a man in the full sense of the word. . . . The Gnostic Redeemer . . . is a mythical hero from a primeval period, who conducts a cosmic war against unspeakable mythical powers, in order to ascend again to the world of light, but he is in no single respect a man among men, nor does he share in their destiny (birth, suffering, and death)."[389] As our discussion of Philo in part 1 made clear, radical dualists who disparage matter and the body as evil simply cannot tolerate a genuine Incarnation. In his third point, Ridderbos contrasts the Gnostic hero, who has powers against the demonic forces of evil, with Paul's Redeemer who "sets aside his glory, humiliates himself, and takes on the figure of a servant, and becomes poor (2 Cor. 8:9; Phil. 2:7)."[390] Ridderbos's conclusion to this three-point comparison is instructive:

> The only thing which presents itself for comparison here is the very general idea of the descent of the preexistent Son of God, as Paul in Philippians 2 and in other places describes the coming of Christ, and

as in the gnostic myth, the coming of the pretempo-
ral, mythical figure of the hero. . . . No one would
dare to affirm, however, that Paul and John (or their
predecessors) only arrived at the idea of the
preexistence of Christ and of his coming out of the
heavens with the aid of this cosmological gnostic
myth.[391]

But, it might be countered, the attacks on the
flimsy historical foundation of Bultmann's hypothesis are outdated by the discovery, translation, and publication of new texts that may
provide the evidence admittedly absent from his
own argument. In the next section of this
chapter, we will examine in more detail Bultmann's appeal to the literature of the Mandaean
religion. In the following chapters, we will
analyze the extent to which possible support for
his position may be present in other literature,
such as the Nag Hammadi texts or the Hermetic
writings.

BULTMANN'S USE OF MANDAEANISM

Like Reitzenstein before him, Bultmann appealed to the small Middle Eastern religion of
Mandaeanism in support of his belief in a pre-
Christian Gnosticism.[392] Mandaeanism is basically a variety of Gnosticism, though it differs in
several ways from the traditional Gnosticism
described earlier. It borrows from Iranian,
Babylonian, Egyptian, Jewish, and even Christian sources. As C. H. Dodd describes the
literature of the cult:

> The Mandaean writings are an extraordinary farra-
> go of theology, myth, fairy-tale, ethical instruction,
> ritual ordinances, and what purports to be history.
> There is no unity or consistency, and it is not
> possible to give a succinct summary of their
> teaching. It is neither consistently monotheistic nor
> consistently dualistic. But in its main intention it is
> based upon a dualism not unlike that of the
> Manichees.[393]

The Mandaean sect, which still survives in parts of Iraq and Iran, is claimed by some to have existed in or around Palestine in pre-Christian times. Further, this allegedly pre-Christian Mandaeanism is linked to John the Baptist. "The circle of John [the Baptist], out of which Jesus also came forth, would thus be the nursery of a very early Gnosis, which freely mixed Babylonian, Persian, and Syrian elements with basic Jewish ideas, grouped around the old Iranian myth of the primal man who descended from the heavens. It is here that the origin of the New Testament Christology is thought to lie."[394] Bultmann believed that the baptismal sect started by John the Baptist was the major source of the Mandaean religion. Dodd explains Bultmann's supposed Mandaean link back to John the Baptist:

> First it is argued that the kernel of Mandaeanism is a myth connected with the ancient Iranian mystery of redemption. The myth and mystery are pre-Christian, and underlie the formation of Christian doctrine, especially in its Johannine and Gnostic forms. Secondly, it is argued that the Mandaean ritual and myth were actually formulated by John the Baptist, and that the Mandaeans of the eighth and following centuries are the successors of that Baptist sect to which allusions are found in Acts xviii.24–xix.7. Christianity arose out of this Baptist sect. Its members were called Nazoreans, a name by which the Mandaeans call themselves in their Scriptures. Jesus the Nazorean, a disciple of John, took the name over with him into the new sect which he founded.[395]

Bultmann's elaborate Mandaean hypothesis has been criticized on a number of grounds. Some of his critics have objected to the lack of proof for the existence of a Mandaean or pre-Mandaean sect in pre-Christian times. There is certainly no proof that any pre-Christian Gnosis—Mandaean or otherwise—had any direct influence on the New Testament. Attempts to link Mandaeanism with John the Baptist are both unpersuasive and unnecessary. Dodd points out that there is "no need to have recourse to any individual founder to explain the Mandaean baptismal rite. Frequent ritual lustrations [washings] were common in most ancient religions, including Judaism. The distinctive thing about Christian baptism, as to all appearance about its prototype, Johannine baptism, is its solitariness as a rite of initiation performed once for all."[396] We have already seen the lack of any evidence supporting the existence of the Redeemer Myth in pre-Christian times.

Critics of Bultmann's Mandaean thesis stress particularly the chronological problems his theory raises. Given the late date of the Mandaean literature (compiled not much before A.D. 700), English scholars have been very hesitant to allow the origin of Mandaeanism to be dated early enough for it to have had any direct influence on first-century Christianity. Attempts to use Mandaeanism in arguing for a pre-Christian Gnosticism clearly rest on very shaky historical ground. Referring to this point, Yamauchi asserts: "As a historian, I find it more than a little ironic that a scholar like Bultmann, who is so extremely skeptical of such first-century A.D. sources as the canonical gospels, is at the same time uncritically credulous in using late post-Islamic texts if they suit his purpose."[397]

Although C. H. Dodd wrote his words as a criticism of Reitzenstein's earlier attempt to use Mandaeanism as evidence for a pre-Christian Gnosticism, they apply with equal force to Bultmann. Dodd states that the "whole process of reconstruction is a masterpiece of characteristic ingenuity, but it depends on too many arbitrary assumptions."[398] "The reconstruction," he continues, "is too speculative to provide any trustworthy source of historical information."[399] We have pointed out that Bultmann discusses several points foundational to his reconstruction of the Gnostic myth. The major difficulty, however, is determining the date at which these ideas first become apparent in the specific synthesis so necessary for his reconstruction. As Dodd continues:

> Too often the documents cited are of quite uncertain date, and we wander in a world almost as timeless as the world of the myth itself. When some more precise chronology is possible, it always, or almost always, turns out either that the document in question belongs to the fourth century or later, or that it belongs to an environment in which the influence of Christian or at least of Jewish thought is probable, so that it is hazardous to use the document to establish a pre-Christian, non-Jewish mystery.[400]

Because of the late date of the historical evidence, Dodd concludes that appeals to the Mandaean writings exaggerate greatly the significance of these works for our understanding of John's Gospel. To be specific, "alleged parallels drawn from this medieval body of literature have no value for the study of the Fourth Gospel unless they can be supported by earlier evidence."[401] Even though some Mandaean studies after Dodd's book have led a number of scholars to conclude that the origin of Mandaeanism may be earlier than some have supposed, the evidence still leaves us short of the first century A.D.[402] Many scholars even maintain that the Mandaean notion of redemption and of a Redeemer (who appears but once in its literature) evidence a Christian influence.[403]

All in all, then, the Mandaean hypothesis is a remarkable example of the lengths to which a rich imagination can lead some theologians. But historians are not supposed to earn high grades for the fancifulness of their theories but rather for their success in establishing their hypotheses on a solid historical foundation. Based on the evidence presently available, Bultmann's Mandaean hypothesis fails.

While few pages of the New Testament have escaped completely the taint of allegations of Hellenistic influence, proponents of early Christian syncretism have tended to focus their attention on the Fourth Gospel and the Pauline Epistles. Thus, Bultmann and other proponents of a Christian dependence on Gnosticism give John's Gospel a central place in their argument.

Bultmann's
Gnostic Thesis

Viewed superficially, the text of the Gospel may appear to support this line of thinking. Consider several sample texts:

The Evidence of Parallels

> In him [the Logos] was life, and that life was the light of men. The light shines in the darkness, but the darkness has not understood it. (John 1:4–5)

> This is the verdict: Light has come into the world, but men loved darkness instead of light because their deeds were evil. Everyone who does evil hates the light, and will not come into the light for fear that his deeds will be exposed. (John 3:19–20)

> When Jesus spoke again to the people, he said, "I am the light of the world. Whoever follows me will never walk in darkness, but will have the light of life." (John 8:12)

> I have come into the world as a light, so that no one who believes in me should stay in darkness. (John 12:46)*

If one is familiar with the basic details of the Gnostic Redeemer myth and the other major tenets of Gnosticism, it is easy to see how texts like these could be compared with various tenets of Gnosticism—namely, the Gnostic dualism between light and darkness, the belief that God and the heavenly Redeemer belong to the realm of light, and the injunction to embodied souls to turn away from the darkness and seek the light.

*The emphasis on light as opposed to darkness is also prominent in the First Epistle of John (1 John 1:5, 7; 2:8–10).

Other alleged Gnostic themes that are supposed to appear in John's Gospel include the contrast between spirit and flesh, an emphasis on knowledge,* and the doctrine of a descending and ascending Redeemer (John 3:13; 6:62). Earlier, I criticized Bultmann's speculations about a pre-Christian Gnostic Redeemer myth and rejected it for lack of evidence. Then I examined his elaborate hypothesis about Christianity arising out of a Gnostic sect fathered by John the Baptist, a sect with specific ties to the surviving remnants of Mandaeanism. This hypothesis also lacks sufficient historical evidence to commend it to open-minded scholars. But even without any evidence for his other theories, the fact remains that the Gospel of John does contain terms, images, and themes that can be made to appear Gnostic.† What then can be said about these apparent parallels between the Fourth Gospel and Gnosticism?

The Explanation of Parallels

First, whatever similarities in language and ideas may appear in John's Gospel and the Gnostic systems, the Johannine teaching about light, spirit, and knowledge is, if anything, anti-Gnostic! Any attempt to read John's Gospel through Gnostic spectacles produces a message diametrically opposed to what the church has always understood the Gospel to be saying. For example, John repeatedly stresses the fact that the Logos really became a human being. There is no room anywhere in John's Gospel for the Docetic doctrine that the descending Redeemer only assumed the form of a human being. John tells us that he became flesh (John 1:14; 6:51).

This anti-Docetism is even more apparent in 1 John, where Docetism is associated with the spirit of Antichrist. As John states in the first

---

*While John often uses forms of the verb "to know," it is interesting to note that he never once uses the noun *gnōsis*.

†After all, the Gospel of John was the favorite book of the second-century Gnostic heretics.

verse of the epistle: "That which was from the beginning, which we have heard, which we have seen with our eyes, which we have looked at and *our hands have touched*—this we proclaim concerning the Word of life" (1 John 1:1, my emphasis). In fact, the major sin repeatedly condemned throughout 1 John includes two components: a denial of Christ's full humanity (Docetism) and a denial of Jesus' messiahship.

It is certainly true that John depicts Christ as the eternal and divine Logos who descends to earth to accomplish the redemption of sinful men and then ascends to return to the Father. But as New Testament scholar George Ladd notes, "There is certainly no need to look to a Hellenistic background for the descent-ascent motif; this is at home on Jewish soil."[404] There are some remarkable parallels between the the Dead Sea Scrolls (the literature of the Essene community at Qumran) and John's Gospel. Although scholars generally agree that these similarities are not strong enough to prove any direct dependence, and although there are enough major differences to suggest no direct dependence in either direction,[405] we know that many ideas hitherto thought to be Hellenistic appear to have risen independently in first-century Palestine. As Ladd further states:

> Even if direct dependence cannot be established between John and the Qumran writings, the similarities have proven that the idiom and thought patterns of the Fourth Gospel could have arisen in Palestine in the mid-first century A.D.—a position few critical scholars of a generation ago would have dared to support. . . . Many contemporary scholars now recognize a solid Johannine tradition independent of the Synoptics, stemming from Palestine and dating from A.D. 30–66, and attribute to the Fourth Gospel a degree of historical worth hardly dreamed of a generation ago except by the most conservative scholars.[406]

This new information from the Dead Sea Scrolls considerably weakens the attempts of scholars like Bultmann to trace the sources of Johannine teaching about light and a heavenly Redeemer to Hellenistic movements like Gnosticism. As the Dead Sea Scrolls show, such themes were already prominent in a non-Hellenistic, Palestinian package in the first Christian century.

But suppose, in spite of this new information from Qumran, we meet Bultmann halfway and acknowledge some awareness of Gnostic tendencies (what R. McL. Wilson earlier called "Gnosis") in the writings of John. Would even this admission support Bultmann's theory about a Gnostic influence? Once again, I must answer in the negative. In part 1, we noted that the writer of Hebrews was clearly familiar with the language and concepts of Alexandrian philosophy and theology. The presence of this material in Hebrews does no more to prove dependence on Platonism than a presence of "Gnosis" in the Fourth Gospel would prove dependence in its case. Regarding these elements of Gnosis in John's writing, Ladd has suggested a theory similar to my own suggestion about the Book of Hebrews:

> The similarities between John and popular Hellenistic thought can hardly be accidental, in spite of the similarities to Qumran. The best solution seems to be that John was written, as patristic tradition suggests, late in the first century to refute a gnostic tendency in the church.* . . . If the Gospel, like the First Epistle, was written to refute an incipient gnosticism, the reason for its particular idiom and message becomes clear. John makes use of words and ideas familiar in gnostic circles to refute these very gnostic tendencies. The base of this idiom

---

*I want neither Ladd nor myself misunderstood at this point. Earlier, I stressed the difference between Gnosticism and Gnostic tendencies. The existence of what R. McL. Wilson calls Gnosis, as opposed to Gnosticism, seems well-established. All that Ladd is admitting is that John's writings show an awareness that there were Gnostic tendencies in the beliefs of a few, not that Gnosticism was an essential feature of Christianity.

goes back to Palestine, and undoubtedly to Jesus himself. But John chose to formulate his entire Gospel in language that probably was used by our Lord only in intimate dialogue with his disciples or in theological argument with learned scribes in order to bring out the full meaning of the eternal Word that became flesh (Jn. 1:14) in the historical event of Jesus Christ.[407]

So what does Bultmann's case for an early Christian dependence on Gnosticism amount to? Not much. It is pure speculation from start to finish, aided no doubt by Bultmann's own personal aversion to the message that the Christian church has always read in the Fourth Gospel. Even if Bultmann were correct in his claim that Gnostic overtones appear throughout John's writings, it is because John (like Paul in his own attacks on similar errors) is contrasting the revealed truth of the Christian gospel with the dangerous errors present in a pre-Gnostic collection of ideas.

chapter fifteen

The Hermetic Writings and Paul

*The Hermetic writings constitute another represen-
tation of non-Christian Gnostic thought. Claims of
alleged Pauline dependence on these writings are
examined in light of external historical sources and
(internally) Paul's use of the term* gnōsis.

In this chapter, we will explore the possibility
that the form of Gnosticism that appears in the
so-called Hermetica, or Hermetic writings,
influenced early Christianity. As a subdivision of
this topic, the chapter will also consider Paul's
alleged dependence on the Hermetica in particular and on Gnosticism in general.

THE HERMETICA

The Hermetic literature is a diverse collection
of tracts written in Egypt in the second and third
centuries A.D., tracts that represent a speculative, non-Christian form of Gnosticism.[408]   241

Reconstruction of the writings is based on manuscripts written in Greek that date from the fourteenth century and after. Largely because of theories developed by Richard Reitzenstein, the Hermetica began to be used early in this century as evidence for a pre-Christian Gnosticism. The writings purport to be revelations of Thoth, an Egyptian god otherwise known as Hermes Trismegistus.*

The Hermetic writings are an odd mixture of Egyptian, Greek, and Jewish ideas, with some influence from the Orient. The writings are Gnostic. For example, they evidence the traditional Gnostic dualism. The human soul is trapped in a body, but through the medium of gnosis it can be freed from the influence of matter and make its way back to God. The Greeks regarded Hermes as the messenger of the gods. During the Hellenistic age, Hermes came to be regarded as the special god of wisdom. This helps explain his adoption by certain Gnostics, since the Hermetic literature depicts Hermes as the revealer of secret knowledge, often in dialogue form, about such things as God, creation, and salvation.[409]

Different accounts refer to varying numbers of tracts in the Hermetic literature, ranging from fourteen to nineteen. The entire collection of writings is often given the title *Poimandres*, though this label more accurately describes the first tractate only. For our purposes, the two most important tracts are the first and thirteenth, since they evidence the clearest parallels to portions of the New Testament.[410]

---

*Hermes was one of the Greek deities. During the Hellenization of Egypt, Hermes came to be identified with the Egyptian god Thoth. The title "Trismegistus" appears to be Greek rendering of an Egyptian title that meant "very great" (literally "thrice great"). Hermes is also known under the names Poimander and Asklepios.

Richard Reitzenstein argued that Paul had been influenced by the Gnosticism of the Hermetic writings. The major support for his position was the presence of what Reitzenstein claimed were Gnostic concepts and language in Paul's writings—e.g., *gnōsis* ("knowledge"), *phōs* ("light"), *phōtizō* ("to bring to light"), and *metamorphoomai* ("to be transformed or changed").[411] Of course, these were also common words in ordinary Greek usage, but it helps to ignore this fact when one is attempting to prove that Paul was influenced by Gnosticism. While Paul, in Reitzenstein's view, may not have been the first Gnostic, he was certainly the greatest Gnostic.

In arguing that Paul derived important elements of his theology from the Hermetic writings, Reitzenstein maintained that significant portions of the Hermetica were written prior to the Pauline Epistles. Such an early date for the Hermetica is today almost universally rejected, a fact that makes claims of a Hermetic influence on Christian theology extremely implausible. Several scholars suggest A.D. 200 or 300 as the earliest date for the literature.[412] According to philosopher Gordon Clark, an authority on Hellenistic thought,

> None of the tractates was written before the Christian era and they were not collected into a single group much before A.D. 300. . . . Without sufficient evidence to warrant greater exactitude the safest thing to do is to consider the tractates as having been produced sometime during the second and third centuries.[413]

Edwin Yamauchi places them in the second century A.D. or later.[414] Without question, the Hermetic literature was written after the death of Paul, suggesting that if Christian elements appear in the writings, they were borrowed from Christianity.[415]

The First Tractate

The first of the Hermetic tracts, entitled *Poimandres*, is clearly the most significant in the entire collection. It is thought that the title comes from the Egyptian language and suggests "the knowledge of God." The root of the Egyptian word is altered by its Greek usage and is used to refer to the one who mediates the revelation. Hence Poimander is the name of the revealing god who communicates the revealed message. *Poimandres* uses a number of different mythological traditions to explain the origin of the world, the beginnings of man, and the redemption that can free the human race from its bodily prison. Therefore, we find in *Poimandres* a convenient outline of Gnostic cosmology, anthropology, and soteriology. In the tract, the god Poimander reveals the way of salvation to his prophet and then charges him to preach the message to the world. The claim of syncretists like Reitzenstein is that the New Testament contains significant similarities to the general theme of *Poimandres* and its message of salvation. But, of course, unless the tract can be dated early enough, any genuine parallels (if they exist) would suggest that Christianity influenced it, not vice versa.

Reitzenstein developed a rather ingenious argument as his defense for an early date of *Poimandres*. The *Shepherd of Hermas* is a Christian writing from the middle of the second century A.D. According to Reitzenstein, this Christian work was based on an earlier version of *Poimandres*. But of course no evidence actually attesting the existence of this early version has ever been uncovered. As Machen observes, Reitzenstein's "argument has not obtained any general consent. It is impossible to push the material of the Poimandres back into

into the first century—certainly impossible by any treatment of literary relationships."[416]

Equally serious problems arise once we notice the significant differences between the soteriology set forth in *Poimandres* and the salvation described by Paul and the other New Testament writers. Addressing this point, Gordon Clark argues that the salvation offered by Poimander in the first tractate "is deification procured by a cosmological revelation; but for Paul salvation is not deification and the message by which salvation is mediated, instead of being cosmological, is an account of recent historical facts—the death and resurrection of Jesus Christ."[417] Clark reiterates this point in his history of philosophy text, *Thales to Dewey:* "The salvation they [The Hermetica] talk about is a deification and is more closely allied with the dualism mentioned above than with the Pauline doctrine of redemption from sin. The method as well as the nature of salvation is different. In the New Testament the death of Christ saves; in Hermes one is saved by learning cosmology."[418]

Machen has also drawn attention to the important differences between Paul and Poimander:

> There could be no sharper contrast than that between the fantastic speculations of the Poimandres and the historical gospel of Paul. Both the Poimandres and Paul have some notion of a transformation that a man experienced through a divine revelation. But the transformation, according to Paul, comes through an account of what had happened but a few years before. Nothing could possibly be more utterly foreign to Hermes. On the other hand, the result of the transformation in Hermes is deification. . . . Paul could never have used such language. For, according to Paul, the relation between the believer and the Christ who has transformed him is a personal relation of love.[419]

Other significant differences could likewise be noted. For example, there is no place in Paul's thought for the pantheism that is so prominent throughout the Hermetica. For reasons like these, therefore, Reitzenstein's sweeping generalizations have long since been rejected.

The Thirteenth Tractate

Those who maintain a Hermetic influence on first-century Christianity have frequently claimed that the thirteenth tractate conveys the idea that salvation depends on being born again. As Eduard Lohse explains this idea:

> The process of rebirth, which signifies deification, cannot be perceived with the physical eyes, but takes place as a total transformation in a mystical and ecstatic vision. The transformation is so thorough that the reborn person can say that he is someone different. One enters upon the way to regeneration by a deliberate decision, by putting aside the passions which one bears within oneself. . . . Where gnosis is attained, unrighteousness is put to flight and man becomes righteous.[420]

Writing almost fifty years before Lohse and under the apparent influence of Reitzenstein, Harold R. Willoughby thought there was little doubt but that the Hermetic religion stressed a personal experience of regeneration.[421]

But most of the earlier arguments against Hermeticism as a source of New Testament doctrine serve equally well to disqualify appeals to the thirteenth tractate. Once again, the nature of the transformation described by the writer of the thirteenth tractate is qualitatively different from New Testament transformation; it is still deification.[422] Since most scholars date Corpus Hermeticum 13 at the end of the third century A.D., it is difficult to see how it could have influenced early Christianity. It is entirely possible that the differences between Tractate 13 and the rest of the Hermetic literature may result from a Christian influence. Claims about a possible Christian influence on this tractate are discussed by William C. Grese in a book titled *Corpus Hermeticum XIII and Early Christian*

Literature.[423] While Grese's discussion leaves the matter undecided,* many scholars think the case for a possible Christian influence on Tractate 13 is plausible. [424] After all, as Machen suggests, we know

that pagan teachers of the second century (the Gnostics) should have been so ready to adopt Christian elements and so anxious to give their systems a Christian appearance. Why should a similar procedure be denied in the case, for example, of Hermes Trismegistus? If second-century paganism, without at all modifying its essential character, could sometimes actually adopt the name of Christ, why should it be thought incredible that the compiler of the Hermetic literature, who did not go quite so far, should yet have permitted Christian elements to creep into his syncretistic work? Why should similarity of language between Hermes and Paul, supposing that it exists, be regarded as providing dependence of Paul upon a type of paganism like that of Hermes, rather than dependence of Hermes upon Paul?[425]

Of course, it is also possible that the parallels between the New Testament and the thirteenth tractate may not reflect causal influence in either direction but only result from both sharing a common milieu.

PAUL'S USE OF *GNŌSIS*

The noun *gnōsis* appears twenty-three times in the Pauline epistles. While the prominence of the term in Paul's writings is usually discussed in the broader context of Paul's alleged relation to Gnosticism in general and not simply to the Hermetic literature, this is a convenient point at which to show how flimsy any case based on Paul's use of *gnōsis* really is. Consider just a few of these verses and how a truly committed Gnostic might read them:†

---

*Grese himself thinks the Hermetic regeneration mentioned in Tractate 13 may be derived from elements of earlier Egyptian religion; see page 58 in his book.

†I use the New International Version but substitute *gnōsis* for "knowledge."

I myself am convinced, my brothers, that you yourselves are full of goodness, complete in *gnōsis* and competent to instruct one another. (Rom. 15:14)

For God, who said, "Let light shine out of darkness," made his light shine in our hearts to give us the light of the *gnōsis* of the glory of God in the face of Christ. (2 Cor. 4:6)

What is more, I consider everything a loss compared to the surpassing greatness of the *gnōsis* of Christ Jesus my Lord, for whose sake I have lost all things. (Phil. 3:8)

The mere fact that such statements can be read in a Gnostic light does not mean the words contain in any sense a Gnostic message. Many years ago a popular American song contained the line, "Two different worlds—we live in two different worlds." Had this love song been available in the first century and had Paul by chance alluded to it, I can imagine some syncretists using it as proof of Paul's commitment to the Platonic belief in two worlds. Meaning arises out of the entire context in which words are used, and Paul's context makes clear the non-Gnostic and occasionally anti-Gnostic emphasis in his thought. It is interesting to see how the proponents of a Gnostic influence on Paul seldom refer to the times when he denigrated *gnōsis,* something that no Gnostic would ever do. For example, Paul notes how useless *gnōsis* would be if he lacked love (1 Cor. 13:1–2). He goes on to speak of the time when *gnōsis* will pass away (1 Cor. 13:8).

"Gnosis" in the early church (including Paul) . . . is not a technical term; it is no more a technical term than is, for example, "wisdom." In 1 Cor. xii. 8 it appears, not by itself, but along with many other spiritual gifts of widely diverse nature. Gnosis, therefore, does not stand in that position of prominence which it ought to occupy if Reitzenstein's theory were correct. It is, indeed, according to Paul, important; and it is a direct gift from God. But what reason is there to have recourse to

Hellenistic mystery religions [or Gnosticism] in order to explain either its importance or its nature? Another explanation is found much nearer at hand—namely, in the Old Testament. The possibility of Old Testament influence in Paul does not have to be established by an elaborate argument, and is not opposed by his own testimony. On the contrary, he appeals to the Old Testament again and again in his Epistles.[426]

The gnosis encountered in the Hermetic writings is, as Machen explains, a mystical and immediate revelation from one's god. " 'Gnosis' was not regarded as an achievement of the intellect; it was an experience granted by divine favor. The man who had received such favor was exalted far above ordinary humanity; indeed he was already deified."[427] But Paul downplayed the importance of mystical visions. It was enough for Paul's converts "to receive the historical account of Christ's redeeming work, through the testimony of Paul and of the other witnesses. That account, transmitted by ordinary word of mouth, is a sufficient basis for faith; and through faith comes the new life."[428] The mystical vision was central in the Hellenistic religions.

> But according to Paul, the mighty change was produced by the acceptance of a simple story, an account of what had happened only a few years before, when Jesus died and rose again. From the acceptance of that story there proceeds a new knowledge, a gnosis. But this higher gnosis in Paul is not the means of salvation, as it is in the mystery religions [and Gnosticism]; it is only one of the effects of salvation. This difference is no mere matter of detail. On the contrary, it involves a contrast between two entirely different worlds of thought and life.[429]

Therefore, not even Paul's frequent use of *gnōsis* establishes that his thinking depended in any way on Gnosticism.

Our study of the Hermetic writings and their alleged role as a source of Paul's religion reveals some additional serious problems that are passed over by advocates of syncretism. To cite Machen once more:

> Two reservations, therefore, are necessary before the investigator can enter upon an actual comparison of the Pauline Epistles with Hermes Trismegistus and other similar sources. In the first place, it has not been proved that the type of religion attested by these sources existed at all in the time of Paul; and in the second place, it is difficult to see how any pagan influence could have entered into Paul's life.* But if despite these difficulties the comparison be instituted, it will show, as a matter of fact, not agreement, but a most striking divergence both of language and of spirit.[430]

To reiterate just one of these differences, the mysticism of the Hermetica is pantheistic. Even if mysticism can be found in Paul, it is never pantheistic. Paul is always careful to distinguish between the individual believer and the indwelling Christ. Therefore, we must conclude, both chronology and content preclude any possibility of a Hermetic influence on Paul.

---

*See my earlier discussion in chapters 10 and 11.

chapter sixteen

Pre-Christian Gnosticism?

Two remaining potential sources of pre-Christian Gnosticism are examined: the Nag Hammadi writings and Jewish Gnosticism. The author then draws final conclusions regarding alleged early Christian dependence on Gnosticism.

This chapter will consider several remaining questions arising from the supposed influence of Gnosticism on early Christianity. The last section of the chapter will also serve as my conclusion to part 3 by reviewing the major problems of seeking to derive early Christian beliefs from an alleged pre-Christian Gnosticism.

THE NAG HAMMADI WRITINGS

I have already mentioned the 1945 discovery of the Coptic Gnostic codices near Nag Hammadi, Egypt.[431] Given the line-up of arguments we have already examined, it is not surprising to

251

learn that these codices have been appealed to in defense of the thesis that a pre-Christian Gnosticism exerted a formative influence on primitive Christianity. The key inference in such arguments runs something like this:

1. Writing A (some specific work found at Nag Hammadi) is an example of non-Christian Gnosticism.

2. *Therefore*, writing A is an example of pre-Christian Gnosticism.

Obviously, inferring a pre-Christian Gnosticism from non-Christian Gnosticism is fallacious.

Jewish Writings at Nag Hammadi?

Ignoring for the moment the invalidity of such reasoning, what do the Nag Hammadi writings tell us about the presence of any non-Christian Gnosticism in the codices? It is often alleged that the Nag Hammadi writings contain two basic kinds of non-Christian Gnostic texts: pagan and Jewish. Claims about a Jewish Gnosticism in these writings involve some tricky reasoning. The Jewishness of certain Coptic texts is alleged on two grounds: (1) they contain no references to Christianity and (2) they contain references to Judaism. However, the references to Judaism raise a problem, since they turn out to be critical, even hostile. The so-called Jewish Gnostic texts from Nag Hammadi present Judaism as a religion replete with problems. Obviously, then, attempts to read such codices as Jewish works appear a bit odd. But even if we ignore this fact and grant that there were Jewish Gnostics (whether or not their views are represented in the Nag Hammadi writings), this in itself would not prove that the Jewish Gnostics were also pre-Christian Gnostics. The evidence needed to support this additional inference is still missing. Furthermore, even if we grant the existence of a pre-Christian Jewish Gnosticism, evidence of its influence on first-century Christianity is also absent.

The search for a non-Christian and supposedly pre-Christian Gnosticism in the Coptic texts usually centers on two writings—*The Apocalypse of Adam* and *The Paraphrase of Shem.* When Edwin Yamauchi published his important book *Pre-Christian Gnosticism* in 1973, he was cautiously skeptical about the possibility that Nag Hammadi would provide any significant support for the existence of a pre-Christian Gnosticism. But of course in 1973, two-thirds of the writings from Nag Hammadi had not yet been translated, leaving open the possibility that new information might appear that would invalidate some of his conclusions.

In a 1978 article, written after all of the Nag Hammadi texts had become available in translation, Yamauchi returned to the subject.

> Now that the entire Nag Hammadi corpus has been translated, we can be assured that there are no unexploded bombshells. That is, the vast majority of the fifty-two tractates are Christian Gnostic compositions from the second and third centuries. The case for pre-Christian Gnosticism can be argued from only a handful of the "non-Christian-tractates" which had been known before, the most important of which are *The Apocalypse of Adam* and *The Paraphrase of Shem.*[432]

Yamauchi's article examines these two writings in detail. He maintains that *The Apocalypse of Adam* should be dated in the middle of the third century A.D., making it post-Christian.[433] He also offers arguments in support of a post-Christian dating for *The Paraphrase of Shem.* Yamauchi concludes that these two texts are probably non-Christian. However he adds, "What seems quite probable is that these texts do not antedate the second century A.D. and do not therefore establish a case for a pre-Christian Gnosticism."[434]

In his 1980 book *Christology in the Making,* James D. G. Dunn refers to efforts to defend Bultmann's thesis about a Gnostic influence on Christianity by appealing to such Nag Hammadi writings as *The Apocalypse of Adam* and *The Paraphrase of Shem*.[435] He finds these more recent efforts no more convincing than Bultmann's earlier speculations:

> These [the two Coptic works already cited] are typical of second-century Gnostic (particularly Sethian) writings with their multiplicity of aeons and angels or powers. . . . There are fairly clear allusions to Christian teaching about Jesus in the former (*Apoc. Ad.* V.77–9) and the polemic against (Christian) baptism in the latter [*Paraphrase of Shem*] probably alludes to the Christian account of Jesus' baptism and anointing by the Spirit at Jordan.[436]

Nor is Dunn impressed by the fact that the works in question are devoid of more clear allusions to Christian faith and practice. In his words:

> The argument that absence of more explicit allusions to Christianity points to a pre-Christian origin is an odd one. Since various strange sects today make only passing or garbled reference to Christian teaching, it would hardly be surprising if the same was true in the second century. After all at that period Christianity was still only one (rather variegated) element in the much larger melting pot of religious-philosophical speculation in the eastern Mediterranean, so it would hardly constitute an indispensable component in every flight of religious fancy then or later.[437]

It may be concluded, therefore, that although it is possible that a very few of the writings uncovered at Nag Hammadi might be examples of a non-Christian Gnosticism, the vast majority of them belong to varieties of Christian Gnosticism. Surprisingly, even the best examples of supposedly non-Christian Gnostic texts at Nag Hammadi appear to contain some allusions to Christianity. What seems clear is that none of the Nag Hammadi writings appears to be an example of pre-Christian Gnosticism.

As other theories about the origins of Gnosticism fade in the sunset, one can hear—with
increasing frequency—scholars proposing the
possibility of a Jewish background for Gnosticism. Among the evidence supporting this possibility is the fact that allusions to, and quotations
from, the Old Testament regularly appear in
Gnostic writings. This is especially true of the
Gnostic texts found at Nag Hammadi. But
Yamauchi issues this important warning: "As in
the case of the Mandaeans, however, it is
necessary to take a closer look at the particular
portions of the Old Testament which were used
by the Gnostics and the manner in which they
were used before jumping to the conclusion that
Old Testament citations are necessarily a proof
of Jewish origins."[438] As we have already noticed, the fact that there were Jewish Gnostics
hardly constitutes proof that pre-Christian Gnosticism originated in Judaism.[439] And even if early
Gnostics used the Old Testament or other
Jewish material, how could this fact by itself
justify the inference to a Jewish origin of
Gnosticism?[440]

Earlier, I mentioned the critical and sometimes hostile way the allegedly Jewish Gnostic
texts from Nag Hammadi refer to the Old
Testament and to Judaism. In addition, Yamauchi observes that "for the most part the Gnostics' knowledge of the Old Testament seems
very truncated and limited generally to the
opening chapters of Genesis. . . . Then, too,
most of the OT materials are used in quite a
perverse way. In the first place, the God of the
OT is frequently degraded into an inferior,
obtuse demiurge."[441] Yamauchi thinks it possible
that the Old Testament knowledge reflected in
Gnostic writings may be second-hand in the
sense that it was derived from Israel's pagan
neighbors living in Transjordan.[442]

The weakness of any Nag Hammadi evidence

for a Jewish source of Gnosticism has led to a reliance on other, and in some cases older, arguments. For example, some have suggested that the personification of Wisdom in pre-Christian Judaism might be the model of the Gnostic Redeemer.[443] But G. W. MacRae, a proponent of a Jewish source for Gnosticism, expresses his reservations about any appeal to one exclusive prototype: "No single form of Jewish tradition can account for the precosmic fall, nor indeed can any single line of non-Jewish thought account for it."[444]

Some scholars appeal to Philo's speculation about Sophia (Wisdom) as another possible source of a pre-Christian Jewish Gnosticism.[445] But this is countered by other scholars, who point out that some elements of Gnosticism that appear Jewish cannot be found in Philo. Still others argue that Philo is out of step with Gnosticism because of his clear respect for the Old Testament. Moreover, Philo never advocated the kind of radical dualism* that characterizes Gnosticism.[446] Although R. McL. Wilson denies that Philo was Gnostic in the narrow sense of the term, he does admit that Philo marks "one of the preliminary stages, showing contemporary trends and tendencies, but he belongs at most to Gnosis, not to Gnosticism."[447]

The Dead Sea Scrolls are also cited as proof of a pre-Christian Gnosticism. R. M. Grant suggested that Gnosticism grew out of Qumran disappointment over their unfulfilled eschatological hopes.[448] But this would seem to place such a development in the first century A.D. Wilson thinks that Grant's hypothesis may be right, but only to a degree.

> I should prefer to say that *some* Gnostics may have formerly been Qumran sectarians, as others may have been former proselytes, both reacting in utter

---

*By radical dualism, I mean one in which the evil principle is equal to the good.

revulsion to the Fall of Jerusalem and the collapse of their hopes and expectations, and therefore degrading the God of Israel to the status of an inferior Demiurge. . . . Others might have been pagans, mocking at the Jews from whom they derived so much.[449]

But Wilson stresses that theories like this only mark out possibilities; they do not tell the whole story.[450]

Yamauchi concludes that the evidence adduced to support a full-fledged Jewish Gnosticism is "either ambiguous or late, or both. For example, such early sources as the Apocrypha, Philo, the Dead Sea Scrolls, and the New Testament itself do not reveal clear-cut cases of Gnosticism." So while a Gnosticism tinged with Jewish elements may be possible, we still lack proof for "a full-fledged pre-Christian Jewish Gnosticism."[451] Recognizing that Judaism may have been important in the evolution of Gnosticism is one thing. But this is entirely different from claiming that Gnosticism developed out of movements within pre-Christian Judaism.

SUMMARY AND CONCLUSIONS

In this final section, we will review several of the major objections that have been raised to theories of a Christian dependence on Gnosticism.[452]

1. Advocates of a Gnostic source for early Christianity are faulted first of all for their uncritical use of late sources. As Wilson phrases this point,

> Sometimes it would appear that scholars have formulated a synthesis on the basis of second or third century sources, and have then proceeded to force the New Testament writings into the resultant mold, on the assumption that the hypothetical pre-Christian Gnosis which they postulate was identical with their reconstruction from the later documents.[453]

The use of late Mandaean and Manichaean writings as the basis for speculative reconstructions of a supposed pre-Christian Gnosticism makes question-begging an inherent part of the proponent's methodology: "The assumption that the full development of later Gnosticism is already present in pre-Christian Gnosis obviously involves a begging of the question, a reading of first-century texts with second-century spectacles, and this amply justifies the reluctance of some scholars . . . to admit any widespread 'Gnostic influence' in the formation stages of early Christianity."[454] A. D. Nock was correct when he declared: "Certainly it is an unsound proceeding to take Manichaean and other texts, full of echoes of the New Testament, and reconstruct from them something supposedly lying back of the New Testament."[455]

2. Edwin Yamauchi and others criticize proponents of a Gnostic source of early Christianity for their uncritical assumption that Gnosticism remained a unified movement throughout the centuries. Once this question is begged, it is a simple matter to take a few key words, elevate them to a status of technical terms, and then conclude that the mere presence of such words marks an appearance of a fully developed Gnosticism.[456]

3. Alan Richardson objects to the frequency with which proponents of the dependence theory appeal to ambiguous New Testament texts. In his words, "when scholars like Bultmann describe a Gnostic doctrine they take their first-century 'evidence' from the New Testament itself. But this is a question-begging proceeding, since the New Testament is susceptible of a very different interpretation."[457] Yamauchi points out that Bultmann first assumes that the Gospel of John is heavily dependent on Gnosticism and then uses the Gospel as the major source of information for his reconstruction of the pre-Christian Gnosticism that supposedly influenced

John in the first place.[458] Is this reasoning in a circle or is it reasoning in a circle?

4. Another questionable feature of the methodology of those who see early Christianity as dependent on Gnosticism is their tendency to transform parallels into instances of dependence. Consider, for example, Reitzenstein's treatment of the supposed parallel between Christian and Mandaean baptism. He specifically ruled out any possibility of independent development and concluded that Christian baptism must have been dependent on an earlier Gnostic rite. Walter Schmithals did the same thing for the apostolic office in the early church.[459] Wilson contests this reasoning:

> When we are studying the phenomena we have to note the similarities, the typical features, but these similarities do not necessarily guarantee any historical continuity, a point that has not always been borne in mind. From the phenomenological point of view it may be perfectly legitimate to group religious movements together on the basis of their common elements; but this does not necessarily mean that these movements stand in any genetic relationship, or that there is any direct connection between the earlier and the later.[460]

The practice of treating parallels as instances of dependence effectively makes the fallacy of false cause an inherent part of the syncretist's methodology.

5. Finally, the case for a Christian dependence on Gnosticism requires that the scholar ignore the many and weighty dissimilarities between Paul and the Gnostics. For example, Paul's gospel contains implications that never occurred to the Gnostics. Paul not only elevated love "above all mysteries and all knowledge," he also, "in contrast to the proud and self-reliant Gnostic, sure in his gift of *gnōsis* . . . urges consideration for those less strong in the faith, on the ground that they too are brethren for whom Christ died."[461] Yet, in spite of apparent

similarities between the language of Paul and that of the Gnostics, the concepts conveyed by each are distinct.[462] R. McL. Wilson argues that

> whereas *gnōsis* delivers its possessor from this evil world of matter, to Paul the evil consists in sin, from which Christ by His death has set men free. The difference is significant. . . . To Paul, the alienation of man from God is not due to his creatureliness, but to his disobedience, his failure to comply with the demands of a righteous God. Thus the forgiveness of sins marks off Christianity from all its competitors. The Gnostics transformed forgiveness of sins into release from Fate, from the bondage of the flesh, from matter; in a word, they changed the distinctively Christian view into the current Hellenistic conception.[463]

Wilson further puts his finger on perhaps the central issue raised by apparent similarities of thought or language:

> The vital question is not whether a particular word or idea can be paralleled in the later Gnostic theories, or even whether its "Gnostic" meaning can be read into its use in Paul or Philo, but whether this Gnostic meaning was in the mind of the author when he wrote. In point of fact, it would seem more accurate to suggest that the Gnostics derived their language and ideas from Paul.[464]

R. P. Casey's conclusion to his essay on Gnosticism is a fitting way to end any investigation of the subject:

> The New Testament and Gnosticism occupy narrow strips of common ground but this is partly to be explained by their joint heritage of Greek philosophical ideas, partly by the indebtedness of the Gnostic theologians to the New Testament. The remarkable thing about the earliest Christian literature is not what it perpetuated but what it created. It was not a creation *ex nihilo* but old materials were miraculously transformed.[465]

We still await the discovery of evidence that will conclusively demonstrate the existence of a fully developed pre-Christian Gnosticism that could serve as the source of first-century Christian beliefs. But as noted earlier, even if such evidence some day appears, we would still lack a causal link between such a pre-Christian Gnosticism and primitive Christianity.

chapter seventeen

Conclusion

Final conclusions regarding early Christian syncretism are drawn. The author offers a definitive checklist of questions by which the student may carefully examine claims of syncretism and thus better perceive the motives behind, as well as the conclusions drawn from, those claims.

CLAIMS AND PRESUPPOSITIONS

We have covered a bewildering variety of theories and countertheories offered by dozens of scholars representing several different nations and fields of learning. For many, another reading or two may be necessary to grasp the lay of the land and put everything into perspective. Our subject has involved the complex of often interlocking claims that the canonical writings produced by the first-century church were not, and indeed could not be, divinely revealed truth. On the contrary, as the claims go, the writers of the New Testament were children of their time. 263

Instead of the New Testament being a true, inspired, and normative set of writings (as the Christian church has traditionally held it to be), it is said to be a document heavily influenced at many key points by various movements in the Hellenistic world.

The three parts of this book correspond to the general chronological order in which the claims of dependence have been historically set forth. Generally speaking, as the nineteenth century progressed, there was an increasing emphasis on alleged philosophical dependence in the New Testament. After many leading scholars saw the weakness of this approach, attention turned to the pagan mystery religions. And when that trend became untrendy, certain scholars shifted their attention to Gnosticism. Considering the weakness of the Gnostic thesis, it is interesting to speculate what gambit will be tried next.

An interesting corollary of all this is what the academic community perceives as creative scholarship. I do not wish to deny that some proponents of the now-discarded theories we have examined have helped draw our attention to many important features of the early Christian milieu. To a great extent these observations have helped us better understand early Christianity and the biblical text. But there is another side to all this. What is regarded by many segments of the academic community as exclusively creative scholarship rests, by their definition, on one or more central presuppositions.

One of the most important of these is the assumption of a naturalistic world view. Even if there is a God, on this view, the world is a closed system of mechanical laws. Because it is closed even to the Creator, it is impossible that He should be active in the world. The nice thing about making this a presupposition is that the scholars who build on this foundation never feel obliged either to defend it or to make it explicit. Obviously, that makes their task that much easier. Once naturalism is assumed in this way, it follows by definition that miracles are impossible. Therefore, one way in which this kind of creative scholarship can attract attention is by discovering some new way to explain away the miraculous content of the New Testament. If miracles are impossible, then neither the Incarnation nor the Resurrection is possible. So the creative scholar can play around with alternative explanations of these beliefs as well as seek sources for them in the pagan culture of the early Christians.[466] And if naturalism is true, the traditional picture of the New Testament as the product of divine revelation must also go out the window so creative scholarship can entertain itself exploring interpretations of "revelation" that are consistent with its naturalism.*

But how many serious blunders does a scholar have to make before his reputation is tarnished? If a scientist or even a historian made as many fanciful suggestions in his field that were as devoid of support as some of the theologians we have noticed, or if he begged as many crucial questions, his reputation would surely suffer. But sometimes in theology, it appears, the reverse often holds. I am not sure that this speaks well for theology and biblical studies as intellectual disciplines.

Equally disturbing is the fact that a number of scholars in such other fields as history and philosophy uncharacteristically fail to critically examine the claims of certain authorities in theology and biblical studies and thus continue to perpetuate errors that most specialists in these latter disciplines abandoned years before. In this way, many half-truths, errors, and even myths continue to circulate among the masses long after scholars have abandoned them in favor of some new theory.

---

*Bultmann is a good example of this. See Ronald Nash, *Christian Faith and Historical Understanding* (Grand Rapids: Zondervan, 1983).

What should the reader of this book do the next time he or she encounters either a new theory of Christian dependence or one of the older views revived because of allegedly new evidence? Let me suggest that this reader approach all such claims by asking a series of questions, making sure that, beginning with the first, each question is satisfactorily answered before moving on.

1. The first question to ask is, What is the evidence for the claim? If our study has revealed anything, it is that even recognized authorities can blunder and make unsupported claims. Do not be put off with generalizations. Ask for "chapter and verse" of the evidence that supports the theory.

2. What are the dates for the evidence? Is the evidence pre- or post-Christian? How was the alleged date determined? Do any scholars disagree with the dating?

3. What literature pro and con has already been published about this theory? Usually, new claims and theories are discussed in journals first. In good libraries, the indexes to scholarly journals point the reader to what is being written concerning the view.

4. Is the language used to describe the evidence faithful to the original source material, or does it include interpretive material such as Christian language, themes, or imagery? As we have seen, it is a lot easier to prove the dependence of some Christian belief on a Hellenistic source if the pagan practice or belief is described in Christian language.

5. Are the alleged parallels really similar, or are the likenesses a result of either exaggeration, oversimplification, inattention to detail, or— once again—the use of Christian language in the description? We saw many examples of such in our discussion of the mystery religions.

6. In the case of any genuine parallel, is the

point of analogy significant? Does it relate to an essential Christian belief or practice? Or does it refer to something incidental, such as the late Christian adoption of December 25 as the date of Christ's birth?

7. Is the parallel the sort of thing that could have arisen independently in several different movements? For example, could it have arisen from common language? We saw the relevance of this point in our discussion of alleged parallels regarding the notion of rebirth.

8. Is the claim consistent with the historical information we have about the first-century church? We know, for example, that the Christian church began in the first half of the first century in the face of tremendous obstacles. We know that the early church believed that Jesus was God, that He became incarnate, that His death was a sacrifice for human sins, that He rose and ascended, and that He would return. Whether segments of twentieth-century scholarship refuse to believe some or all of these things is irrelevant. The fact is that the early church did; and the relevant question is, Why? What set of circumstances and conditions is sufficient to explain the origin of the church and its beliefs? One of the more ironic inconsistencies present in some of the theories we have examined is this: if those theories were true, there would never have been a Christian church. Other examples in this area include the exclusivism of the early church and its leaders (like Paul), as well as the dramatic conversion of Paul. Many of the theories about Paul's alleged dependence stumble over their inability to come to grips with the radical change produced by Paul's conversion. Many of them are inconsistent with what we know to be the early church's repudiation of pagan inclusivism.

9. Even when we discover prior to, or contemporaneous with, early Christianity a significant parallel to an essential Christian belief, there is one final question to ask: Does the fact that

some New Testament writer knew of a pagan belief or term prove that what he knew had a formative or genetic influence on his own essential beliefs? Chapter 6 dealt extensively with this question as it relates to the Book of Hebrews. The appropriate answer to this question may well reveal what can be termed *the missionary motive*.[467] People who are witnessing to pagans often find it helpful to present their message in ways that will get the attention of their audience and then communicate with them in language that they will understand. In Hebrews, the presence of ideas and language from Alexandrian Judaism can be explained as a function of the writer, who himself was converted out of that movement, communicating with similar converts who were being tempted to return to their earlier convictions. The language fits the situation. If there is an element of Gnosis (not Gnosticism) present in John's Gospel, it may well reflect the writer's purpose to counteract Gnostic tendencies (not yet Gnosticism) in his day. In other words, when Paul and John appear to approach the subject of Gnosis, they are clearly anti-Gnosis. When Hebrews alludes to Alexandrian Judaism, the author is clearly anti-Alexandrian as he argues for the clear superiority of Christianity and its mediator, Jesus Christ.

T. W. MANSON'S OBSERVATIONS

British scholar T. W. Manson has made several observations that are worth noting at this point. He begins his work *On Paul and John* by explaining that the early church did not first develop its doctrine of Christ and then look around for some historical events to which it could be pegged. On the contrary, what the early Christians came to believe about Christ's deity, incarnation, atonement, and resurrection had its start in their own experience—in other words, in their own *history*.

A great deal of what passes for up-to-date critical method on the Continent and in America—happily not in this country [Britain]—proceeds on these lines. The dogmas of the early Church are supposed to be derived from all kinds of sources—pagan mystery cults, late Greek philosophy, Alexandrian Hellenistic Judaism, Iranian redemption mysteries, and so on. The early Church having selected one or other of these theories, then fitted Jesus into it, or if we take account of more radical formulations of this scientific theory, created the Jesus of the Gospels out of a few fragments of tradition and its own vivid imagination playing on its own life-situations, problems, social needs, behaviour patterns, and I know not what besides.[468]

By now the reader of this book is fairly familiar with the kinds of speculation Manson describes. He continues:

On this theory and on all theories of this sort I think it is sufficient to say that they explain fairly successfully almost everything except how there came to be a Church to perform these theological feats, and why the Church pitched upon Jesus of Nazareth as the hero of its age. If you can get over these two little difficulties there is no reason why you should not be perfectly at home with the extreme Form-critics or the Chicago School—or anywhere else *except* in the ministry of the Gospel.[469]

Manson suggests we do two things: first, assume that whatever else may be the case, the New Testament at the very least gives us evidence about what the early church believed and did; second, read the New Testament "with ordinary common sense" and not through the spectacles of naturalistic unbelief or fanciful speculation. If we do this, Manson argues, we will find good reason to believe

that the Church began with the picture and tried to find a frame for it rather than that the Church first built an elaborate frame and then painted the portrait to suit. In other words that the first Christians were Christians in the sense that they knew in their hearts that they owed their life to Christ, that he had done for them something that they could not do for themselves and something that no other man, no institution, could do for them.[470]

Therefore, Manson concludes, we should be done with these flights of fancy and begin with the recognition that "the Church is built on the *fact* and not on a theory. The theories that we meet in the New Testament and in later doctrines are attempts to explain the fact. The fact is not an invention to suit the theories."[471]

Because that which divides scholars on this issue of Christian origins and originality is basically a difference in presuppositions—especially presuppositions that are subjectively oriented—evidence and arguments are seldom sufficient to settle the matter. How that problem should be addressed is a subject for another book. The question that this book has dealt with is this: Was early Christianity a syncretistic faith? Did it borrow any of its essential beliefs and practices either from Hellenistic philosophy or religion or from Gnosticism? The evidence requires that this question be answered in the negative.[472]

References

References

[1] For example, in a 1956 essay H. Riesenfeld of the University of Uppsala (Sweden) called the appeal to the mystery religions outdated. See his "Mythological Background of New Testament Christology" in *The Background of the New Testament and Its Eschatology,* ed. W. D. Davies and D. Daube (Cambridge: Cambridge University Press, 1956), pp. 81–95 (esp. p. 81).

[2] Edwin A. Burtt, *Types of Religious Philosophy,* rev. ed. (New York: Harper, 1951), p. 35.

[3] Ibid., p. 36.

[4] See W. T. Jones, *The Medieval Mind* (New York: Harcourt, Brace and World, 1969).

[5] Thomas W. Africa, *The Ancient World* (Boston: Houghton Mifflin, 1969). See also Africa's later work, *The Immense Majesty: A History of Rome and the Roman Empire* (New York: Crowell, 1974), pp. 340–42.

[6] Ibid. See chapter 18.

[7] I examine some of the issues raised by this claim in my book *The Word of God and the Mind of Man* (Grand Rapids: Zondervan, 1982).

[8] Gordon H. Clark, *Thales to Dewey* (Boston: Houghton Mifflin, 1957), p. 195.

[9] Ibid.

[10] J. Gresham Machen, *The Origin of Paul's Religion* (New York: Macmillan, 1925), p. 222.

[11] Samuel Angus, *The Environment of Early Christianity* (New York: Scribner, 1915), pp. 222–23. The reader should know that Angus was an early supporter of Christianity's dependence (in the strong sense) on its pagan milieu. But in spite of some overstatement, his paragraph is essentially correct.

[12] G. H. C. MacGregor and A. C. Purdy, *Jew and Greek: Tutors Unto Christ* (London: Nicholson & Watson, 1937), p. 236. Once again a warning is in order: MacGregor and Purdy held a much looser view of Christianity's relationship to its intellectual environment than the evidence warrants. My quotes from their book have value in drawing

attention to the importance of salvation in the Hellenistic world. It would be a mistake to make any hasty inferences from their terminology as to any supposed parallels with the Christian message.

13 Ibid.

14 Ibid., p. 237.

15 More complete introductions to these systems are available in the following books: A. H. Armstrong, *An Introduction to Ancient Philosophy* (Boston: Beacon, 1963) and Frederick Copleston, *A History of Philosophy* (Westminster, Md.: Newman, 1960), vol. 1, *Greece and Rome.* Armstrong's book is the best short introduction available. It is made even more helpful because of the author's frequent practice of relating the philosophical ideas he discusses to early Christianity.

16 Armstrong, *Ancient Philosophy,* pp. 64–65.

17 This question arises in connection with what many people regard as Plato's most difficult writing, the *Parmenides.*

18 *The Republic of Plato,* trans. F. M. Cornford (New York: Oxford, 1945), p. 215. The standard pagination for this passage is *Republic* 505a. Subsequent references to Plato's writings will give the standard pagination.

19 Ibid., 509b.

20 I have discussed the possible influence of Plato's view on the thought of St. Augustine (A.D. 354–430) in my article "Some Philosophical Sources of Augustine's Illumination Theory," *Augustinian Studies* 2 (1971): 47–66. See also Ronald Nash, *The Light of the Mind: St. Augustine's Theory of Knowledge* (Lexington: University of Kentucky Press, 1969).

21 Plato *Timaeus* 28b.

22 Ibid., 28c.

23 See Plato's *Symposium* 202e.

24 See Gordon H. Clark, *Selections from Hellenistic Philosophy* (New York: Appleton-Century-Crofts, 1940), p. 206.

25 See Nash, *Light of the Mind.* For a contemporary restatement of Augustine's position, see Nash, *Word of God.*

26 See Plato's *Parmenides* 134c–e. Gordon Clark provides an excellent introduction to the problems generated by this dialogue in his *Thales to Dewey,* pp. 85ff.

[27]Heb. 1:1–2. See also Romans 1:18–20 and John 1:18. The objections that advocates of an early Christian syncretism have with texts like these will be examined later in this book. For a discussion of how the Christian philosopher Augustine resolved Plato's problem, see Nash, *Light of the Mind*. In another book, *Word of God,* I present and defend a contemporary restatement of Augustine's position.

[28]See Nash, *Word of God,* where I explain and defend a more moderate form of rationalism than Plato's.

[29]The relevant text here, Aristotle's *De Anima* 430a 10–25, is one of the most perplexing and most frequently debated passages in all of Aristotle's writings. See my discussion in "Augustine's Illumination Theory," pp. 61ff.

[30]See Copleston, *Greece and Rome,* pp. 330–31.

[31]Given the limitations of this book, the topic is too complex to pursue further. The more materialistic interpretation of Aristotle can be examined in John Herman Randall's *Aristotle* (New York: Columbia University Press, 1960). The interpretation I accept is available in Henry B. Veatch's *Aristotle, A Contemporary Appreciation* (Bloomington: Indiana University Press, 1974).

[32]I have elsewhere discussed some apparent but misleading affinities of Aristotle's doctrine to the Christian belief in divine immutability. See Ronald Nash, *The Concept of God* (Grand Rapids: Zondervan, 1983).

[33]Armstrong, *Ancient Philosophy,* p. 149.

[34]However, at least one of the Middle Platonists, Atticus, opposed Aristotelianism.

[35]Armstrong, *Ancient Philosophy,* p. 154.

[36]Ibid., p. 148.

[37]William Fairweather, *Jesus and the Greeks* (Edinburgh: T. & T. Clark, 1924). Sample passages appear on pp. 290ff.

[38]As an example, see MacGregor and Purdy, *Jew and Greek,* pp. 335ff.

[39]Frederick C. Grant, *Roman Hellenism and the New Testament* (New York: Scribner, 1962), p. 94.

[40]W. T. Jones, *Medieval Mind,* pp. 41ff.

[41]George Holley Gilbert, *Greek Thought in the New Testament* (New York: Macmillan, 1928).

[42]Ibid., p. 85.

[43]See Fairweather, *Jesus and the Greeks,* p. 290.

[44]Clark, *Thales to Dewey,* p. 192.

[45]Machen, *Origin of Paul's Religion,* pp. 275–76.

[46]Ibid., p. 276.

[47]See Machen, *Origin of Paul's Religion,* p. 276. For a more detailed discussion of Paul's concept of the body, see Robert H. Gundry, *Sōma in Biblical Theology* (New York: Cambridge University Press, 1976). For a detailed analysis of *sarx,* see the article on the term in Gerhard Friedrich, ed., *Theological Dictionary of the New Testament,* trans. and ed. by Geoffrey W. Bromiley (Grand Rapids: Eerdmans, 1971), 7:98–151. For more on Paul's teaching in Romans 7, see J. Dunn, "Rom. 7:14–25 in the Theology of Paul," *Theologische Zeitschrift* 31 (1975); Robert H. Gundry, "The Moral Frustration of Paul Before His Conversion: Sexual Lust in Romans 7:7–25," in *Pauline Studies: Essays Presented to F. F. Bruce,* ed. Donald A. Hagner and Murray J. Harris (Grand Rapids: Eerdmans, 1980), pp. 228–45.

[48]A. H. Armstrong and R. A. Markus, *Christian Faith and Greek Philosophy* (New York: Sheed and Ward, 1960), p. 47.

[49]Ibid., p. 49.

[50]Gilbert, *Greek Thought,* p. 86.

[51]Ibid., p. 87.

[52]Clark, *Thales to Dewey,* p. 193.

[53]For some recent literature on Paul's attitude toward women and marriage, see R. Jewett, "The Sexual Liberation of the Apostle Paul," *Journal of the American Academy of Religion* 47 (1979): 55–87; J. K. Howard, " 'Neither Male nor Female': An Examination of the Status of Women in the New Testament," *Evangelical Quarterly* 55 (1983): 31–42; J. C. Laney, "Paul and the Permanence of Marriage in 1 Cor. 7," *Journal of the Evangelical Theological Society* 25 (1982): 283–94; J. Murphy-O'Connor, "Sex and Logic in 1 Corinthians 11:2–16," *Catholic Biblical Quarterly* 42 (1980): 482–500; E. Pagels, "Paul and Women," *Journal of the American Academy of Religion* 42 (1974): 538–49; R. Scroggs, "Paul and the Eschatological Woman," *Journal of the American Academy of Religion* 40 (1972): 283–303; and Don Williams, *The Apostle Paul and Women in the Church* (Glendale, Calif.: Regal, 1977).

[54]Robert H. Gundry, *A Survey of the New Testament* (Grand Rapids: Zondervan, 1981), p. 265.

[55]Herman Ridderbos, *Paul: An Outline of His Theology* (Grand Rapids: Eerdmans, 1975), p. 312. Ridderbos's entire discussion (pp. 306–14) should be consulted.

[56]They include Epictetus's *Enchiridion*, his *Discourses*, and Marcus Aurelius's *Meditations*. All are reprinted in Whitney J. Oates, ed., *The Stoic and Epicurean Philosophers* (New York: Modern Library, 1940).

[57]Armstrong, *Ancient Philosophy*, pp. 128–29.

[58]Ibid., p. 143.

[59]Ibid., p. 145.

[60]See J. B. Lightfoot, "St. Paul and Seneca," in J. B. Lightfoot, *St. Paul's Epistle to the Philippians* (1913; reprint, Grand Rapids: Zondervan, 1953), p. 304.

[61]See John Herman Randall, Jr., *Hellenistic Ways of Deliverance and the Making of the Christian Synthesis* (New York: Columbia University Press, 1970), p. 155.

[62]Fairweather, *Jesus and the Greeks*, p. 296.

[63]Lightfoot's essay "St. Paul and Seneca" (Lightfoot, *Philippians*, pp. 270–333) is an example of the importance once attributed to such views.

[64]Albert Schweitzer, *Paul and His Interpreters* (1912; reprint, New York: Macmillan, 1951), p. 96.

[65]Ibid.

[66]For examples, see Lightfoot, "St. Paul and Seneca," p. 295.

[67]Fairweather, *Jesus and the Greeks*, pp. 300–301.

[68]Lightfoot, "St. Paul and Seneca," p. 295.

[69]Ibid., p. 296.

[70]Machen, *Origin of Paul's Religion*, p. 226. See also Albert Schweitzer, *The Mysticism of Paul the Apostle* (1913; reprint, New York: Macmillan, 1955), pp. 10–11.

[71]Lightfoot, "St. Paul and Seneca," p. 308. Lightfoot found little reason to believe that Seneca and Paul ever met. See his discussion on pp. 300–302.

[72]Gilbert, *Greek Thought*, pp. 148–49. Similar sentiments are expressed by MacGregor and Purdy, *Jew and Greek*, p. 334, and by Fairweather, *Jesus and the Greeks*, p. 284.

[73]Gordon Clark, *Thales to Dewey*, p. 191.

[74]Ibid.

[75]For an example, see Fairweather, *Jesus and the Greeks,* p. 283.

[76]For more on chapters 3 and 4, see B. Gärtner, *The Areopagus Speech and Natural Revelation* (Lund, 1955); H. Koester, *Introduction to the New Testament,* 2 vols. (Philadelphia: Fortress, 1982); A.P.F. Sell, "Platonists and the Gospel," *Irish Theological Quarterly* 44 (1977): 153–74; and J. Sevenster, *Paul and Seneca* (Leiden: Brill, 1961).

[77]There is a considerable body of material on the Johannine Prologue, including A. W. Argyle, "Philo and the Fourth Gospel," *Expository Times* 63 (1951): 385–86; P. Borgen, "Logos Was the True Light," *Novum Testamentum* 14 (1972): 115–30; idem, "Observations on the Targumic Character of the Prologue of John," *New Testament Studies* 16 (1969): 288–95; R. B. Brown, "The Prologue of the Gospel of John," *Review and Expositor* 62 (1965): 426–39; P. J. Cahill, "The Johannine *Logos* as Center," *Catholic Biblical Quarterly* 38 (1976): 54–72; D. G. Deeks, "The Prologue of St. John's Gospel," *Biblical Theology Bulletin* 6 (1976): 62–71; C. H. Dodd, "The Prologue to the Fourth Gospel," in *Studies in the Fourth Gospel,* ed. F. L. Cross (London, 1957); E. J. Epp, "Wisdom, Torah, Word: The Johannine Prologue and the Purpose of the Fourth Gospel," in *Current Issues in Biblical and Patristic Interpretation,* ed. G. Hawthorne (Grand Rapids: Eerdmans, 1975), pp. 128–46; D. A. Hagner, "The Vision of God in Philo and John," *Journal of the Evangelical Theological Society* 14 (1971): 81–94; R. Kysar, "The Background of the Prologue of the Fourth Gospel," *Canadian Journal of Theology* 16 (1970): 250–55; E. Lovelady, "The Logos Concept of Jo 1,1," *Grace Theological Journal* 4 (1963): 15–24; J. C. O'Neill, "The Prologue to St. John's Gospel," *The Journal of Theological Studies* 20 (1969): 41–52; T. Pollard, "Cosmology and the Prologue of the Fourth Gospel," *Vigiliae Christianae* 12 (1958): 147–53; H. Ridderbos, "The Structure and Scope of the Prologue to the Gospel of John," *Novum Testamentum* 8 (1966): 180–201; J. Robinson, "The Relation of the Prologue to the Gospel of St. John," *New Testament Studies* 9 (1962–63): 120–29; R. McL. Wilson, "Philo and the Fourth

Gospel," *Expository Times* 65 (1953–54): 47–49; E. Yamauchi, "Jewish Gnosticism?: The Prologue of John, Mandaean Parallels, and the Trimorphic Protennoia," *Studies in Gnosticism and Hellenistic Religions,* ed. R. Van Den Broek and M. J. Vermaseren (Leiden: Brill, 1981), 467–97. Yamauchi's essay contains helpful bibliographic data on all the topics mentioned in the title of his article.

[78]Typical of these older works is MacGregor and Purdy, *Jew and Greek,* pp. 337ff. They also claimed to find echoes of Philo in some of Paul's writings, e.g., Phil. 2:6 and Col. 1:16.

[79]Randall, *Hellenistic Ways of Deliverance,* p. 157.

[80]Jones, *Medieval Mind,* p. 52.

[81]T. W. Manson, *On Paul and John* (London: SCM, 1963), p. 141.

[82]James D. G. Dunn, *Christology in the Making* (Philadelphia: Westminster, 1980), p. 215. See also Oscar Cullmann, *The Christology of the New Testament,* rev. ed. (Philadelphia: Westminster, 1963), p. 257.

[83]Dunn, *Christology in the Making,* p. 218.

[84]Manson, *Paul and John,* p. 149.

[85]Dunn, *Christology in the Making,* p. 249. The emphasis is Dunn's.

[86]L. W. Bard, *Justin Martyr* (New York: Cambridge University Press, 1967), p. 87.

[87]Justin Martyr, *I Apol.* 5.46.

[88]See Nash, *Word of God,* p. 68, as well as Nash, *Light of the Mind.*

[89]Ronald Nash, "The Notion of Mediator in Alexandrian Judaism and the Epistle to the Hebrews," *Westminster Theological Journal* 40 (1977): 89–115. Portions of this chapter are drawn from that article and are used with permission.

[90]George Barker Stevens does not hesitate to affirm that the writer of Hebrews "was a literary Hellenist, who was familiar with the philosophical ideas which were current at Alexandria and practised in the argumentative use of the Septuagint. . . . The author of the Epistle to the Hebrews was strongly imbued with Platonic and Alexandrian thought." *The Theology of the New Testament* (1899; reprint, Edinburgh: T. & T. Clark, 1968), pp. 484, 488. Note Steven's elaboration on pp. 488–89.

[91]Ronald Williamson cites most of the important sources on both sides of the question in the first chapter of his *Philo and the Epistle to the Hebrews* (Leiden: Brill, 1970). Contemporary evangelicals like F. F. Bruce have not been reluctant to point out the apparent familiarity of the writer of Hebrews with some teachings of Plato. See F. F. Bruce, *The Epistle to the Hebrews* (Grand Rapids: Eerdmans, 1964), p. lxix and passim, as well as Bruce's commentary on Hebrews in Peake's *Commentary on the Bible,* ed. M. Black and H. H. Rowley, rev. ed. (New York: Nelson, 1962), p. 1008.

[92]Ceslans Spicq, *L'Epître aux Hébreux, 2 vols.* (Paris: Gabalda, 1952).

[93]Williamson, *Philo and Hebrews,* p. 579. The positions of Spicq and Williamson (and those on the continuum between them) are not the only options, of course. Some, like Oscar Cullmann, have sought the background of Hebrews in Palestinian Hellenism (see his *Christology,* p. 304). Others prefer searching within the literature of the Qumran community. See Y. Yadin, "The Dead Sea Scrolls and the Epistle to the Hebrews," *Scripta Hierosolymitana 4* (1958): 36ff. and K. Kosmala, *Hebraer-Essener-Christen* (Leiden: Brill, 1959).

[94]Williamson, *Philo and Hebrews,* p. 493. Williamson (p. 492) also recognizes a more moderate statement of Spicq's thesis: "Spicq concedes that the ideas of Hebrews are not exactly those of Philo, that they had been developed and enriched in the light of the writer's Christian faith, but he has no doubt whatever that it is the thought of Philo that lies behind the thought of the epistle." Williamson rejects this position too.

[95]Earlier in his book, Williamson suggested something more moderate than his final conclusion: If the writer was a Philonist before he became a Christian, then "by the time he wrote his Epistle only vestigial traces of Philonism remained in his outlook" (ibid., p. 92; see also p. 78).

[96]Hebrews avoids the term because it had already been filled with a specific content. The avoidance of the term and the appropriation of the predicates of Wisdom, permitted the writer to fill the conception with his own, distinctively Christian, understanding of Jesus.

[97] Hugh Montefiore is only one of many commentators impressed by the parallels between Hebrews 1:1–4 and the Alexandrian writings of Philo and The Wisdom of Solomon. See his *Epistle to the Hebrews* (New York: Harper Row, 1964), p. 36. See also William L. Lane, "Detecting Divine Wisdom Christology in Hebrews 1:1–4," *The New Testament Student* (1982), 150–158.

[98] Ronald Williamson is one of the most cautious commentators on this subject. Therefore, even his most reluctant admissions are worth noting. He grants that the linguistic parallels between Hebrews 1:3 and *Wisdom* 7:26 are close enough to suggest a direct influence from The Wisdom of Solomon. "This fact alone is perhaps sufficient to prove that the Writer of Hebrews, when he came to develop and expound his view of the Person and Work of Christ, applied to Christ titles and appellations applied in the Wisdom literature of Judaism, of which in his pre-Christian days he would seem to have been a devoted student, to Wisdom personified. . . . If the Writer was doing no more than transposing from the hypostatized Wisdom of Alexandrian speculation to Christ this function of world government, he was not alone among the writers of the N.T. Col. 1:17 represents a similar transposition." Williamson, *Philo and Hebrews,* p. 97.

[99] Spicq, *L'Epître aux Hébreux,* 2:70, argues that the Logos-Christology of Hebrews is dependent on Philo's Logos doctrine.

[100] Philo uses Logos, Sophia, and Nous interchangeably. See Harry A. Wolfson, *Philo,* 2 vols. (Cambridge: Harvard University Press, 1962), 1:258.

[101] Philo *Who Is the Heir of Divine Things?* 205–6. Oepke discusses the nuances of Philo's use of *mesitēs* in *Theological Dictionary of the New Testament,* ed. Gerhard Friedrich, trans. and ed. Geoffrey W. Bromiley (Grand Rapids: Eerdmans, 1971), 4:602.

[102] Philo *On the Special Laws* 1.81; *On the Sacrifices of Abel and Cain* 8; *On the Migration of Abraham* 6; *On the Unchangeableness of God* 57.

[103] Philo *On Flight and Finding* 101; *On Dreams* 2.45; *Special Laws* 1.81.

[104] Philo *Heir of Divine Things* 205–6.

[105] Philo *Special Laws* 3.62.

[106] Philo *On the Confusion of Tongues* 146; *Dreams* 1.215; *Unchangeableness of God* 31; *On Husbandry* 51.

[107] Philo *Flight and Finding* 101.

[108] Philo *Dreams* 1.75. Williamson (*Philo and Hebrews,* pp. 38ff.) points out that although Philo frequently speaks of the Logos as "light" (*phōs*), he never uses the term *apaugasma* of the Logos as the author of Hebrews does of the Son (Heb. 1:3).

[109] Philo *Special Laws* 3.31.

[110] Williamson, *Philo and Hebrews,* p. 410.

[111] Both functions discussed in this section are also found in the prologue to John's Gospel. Cullmann notes that "Hebrews actually belongs to the Johannine environment," though he identifies that environment as the Palestinian Hellenism found in Acts (Cullmann, *Christology,* p. 304). Robert McL. Wilson adds that Paul, John, and the author of Hebrews all "move in the same circle of ideas as does Philo, although Paul is much less influenced than the other two" (*The Gnostic Problem* [London: A. R. Mowbray, 1958], p. 35).

[112] Philo appears to have accepted the Platonic doctrine of the eternity of matter and the evil nature of matter. In Philo's words, "When out of that confused matter God produced all things, he did not do so with his own handiwork, since his nature, happy and blessed as it was, forbade that he should touch the limitless chaotic matter. Instead he made full use of the incorporeal potencies well denoted by their name of Forms to enable each kind to take its appropriate shape." (Philo *Special Laws* 1.329, Loeb trans. [Cambridge: Harvard University Press, 1958]). Philo clearly states that since God could not come in contact with matter, He used intermediaries to create the world out of preexistent matter. See also Clark, *Hellenistic Philosophy,* p. 156. In spite of passages like this, H. A. Wolfson (*Philo,* 1:281–82, 289, 301–6) claims that Philo taught that God could still act directly on the material world. Disagreeing with interpreters like Drummond and Brehier, Wolfson insists that Philo viewed matter as created by God. Wolfson's handling of Philo must be seen in the light of his strained exaggeration of Philo's importance in the history of philosophy. A more temperate view is expressed by Gordon Clark: "Although it is com-

pletely inconsistent with the Hebrew background, Philo asserts the eternity of matter. Then, as God forms the world out of matter, it is discovered that even if matter is not positively evil or wicked, it is none the less too imperfect and recalcitrant to receive the perfect goodness and order God wishes to bestow" (*Hellenistic Philosophy*, p. 155). Compare also The Wisdom of Solomon 11:7; in this passage the world is described as having been created "out of formless matter." For other evidence of Platonism and Stoicism in The Wisdom of Solomon, see William L. Lane, "Apocrypha" in *The Encyclopedia of Christianity*, ed. Edwin H. Palmer (Wilmington, Del.: National Foundation for Christian Education, 1964), 1:323.

[113]In some systems, these two questions merge into one. For example, it might be argued that man cannot attain any knowledge of God except that which God himself reveals. In such a system, only one question would exist. For someone like Aquinas who maintained the existence of human knowledge about God independent of special revelation, both questions would remain.

[114]Philo *Dreams* 2.249.

[115]Williamson, *Philo and Hebrews*, p. 428.

[116]The notion of soteriological mediation does appear in Philo's *Confusion of Tongues* 149. See also The Wisdom of Solomon 7:27 and 10:1–11:1. A soteriological mediator (called Sophia, but different from the Alexandrian Sophia) can be found in late Gnosticism; but this is a post-Christian usage.

[117]Philo *Dreams* 1.215.

[118]Philo *Heir of Divine Things* 75.

[119]Found in books 6 and 7 of Plato's *Republic*.

[120]Philo *Confusion of Tongues* 190; *Dreams* 1.185–88; *Questions and Answers on Exodus* 2.90; *On the Life of Moses* 2.188–91. A. M. Hunter finds Hebrews 8:1–5 decisive evidence that the writer of Hebrews had an Alexandrian education. See his *Introducing New Testament Theology* (Philadelphia: Westminster, 1957), p. 120.

[121]James Moffatt, *A Critical and Exegetical Commentary on the Epistle to the Hebrews* (New York: Scribner, 1924), p. xxxiv.

[122]Some other articles and monographs that pursue the theme of Alexandrianism in Hebrews are S. G. Sowers, *The Hermeneutics of Philo and Hebrews*

(Richmond, Va.: John Knox, 1965), pp. 64ff.; R. Williamson, "Platonism and Hebrews," *Scottish Journal of Theology* 16 (1963): 415–24; J. H. Burtness, "Plato, Philo, and the Author of Hebrews," *Lutheran Quarterly* 10 (1958): 54–64; L. Dey, *The Intermediary World and Patterns of Perfection in Philo and Hebrews* (Missoula: Scholars, 1975).

[123]Throughout his book, Williamson notes practically every difference that could be cited between Philo and Hebrews. He cites these differences as evidence to minimize the influence of Philo on Hebrews. But these differences also serve as evidence for my thesis that the author of Hebrews intended explicitly to contradict the Alexandrian views at these points.

[124]The sober judgment of William Manson is worth noting: "But while it is right to see in the Alexandrian Jewish theology the background against which the conception of the Two Worlds in the Epistle to the Hebrews is elaborated, it has to be carefully observed that the interests of the writer to the Hebrews are not in cosmology but in redemption, and that his exposition of the heavenly sanctuary is put into entire subservience to his exposition of the sacrifice and atoning work of Jesus within the veil. The element of Alexandrianism does not enter into the Epistle until this point is reached, and it is not continued after this point is passed" (William Manson, *The Epistle to the Hebrews* [London: Hodder and Stoughton, 1951], pp. 124–25). See also C. K. Barrett, "The Eschatology of Hebrews" in *The Background of the New Testament and Its Eschatology*, ed. W. D. Davies and D. Daube (Cambridge: Cambridge University Press, 1964), pp. 363–93.

[125]Williamson, *Philo and Hebrews*, p. 158.

[126]See the discussion in Grace E. Cairns, *Philosophies of History* (New York: Citadel, 1962), ch. 10. Compare Ronald H. Nash, *Ideas of History, 2 vols.* (New York: Dutton, 1969), 1:3ff.

[127]Philo *Allegorical Interpretation* 3.25; *On the Creation* 60. See the discussion in Williamson, *Philo and Hebrews*, pp. 148ff.

[128]Williamson, *Philo and Hebrews*, p. 148.

[129] A. H. Armstrong, *Ancient Philosophy*, p. 162. Armstrong adds, therefore, that Philo's Logos "differs entirely from the Logos of St. John's Prologue, an actual historical Person who is also Divine . . ." (ibid.). Gordon Clark has a helpful insight: "Obviously Philo personifies the Logos, but this personification is entirely metaphorical. Philo also says that Laughter is a Son of God, God is the husband of Wisdom, Wisdom is the daughter of God, Wisdom is the mother of the Logos, and, even, Wisdom is the father of instruction. Such metaphors cancel each other out" (*Thales to Dewey*, p. 202).

[130] A related contrast that should not be overlooked at this point is the doubtfulness about any orthodox Jewish Messianic expectation in the thought of Philo. Although Philo did speak of the Logos in kingly terms and did relate Melchizedek to the Logos, he apparently did not consider the Logos to be the Messiah.

[131] Copleston, *Greece and Rome*, 1:459.

[132] Philo *The Worse Attacks the Better* 82–83. Cf. The Wisdom of Solomon 9:15.

[133] Philo, *Migration of Abraham* 9; *On Giants* 61.

[134] Philo *Special Laws* 4. 188.

[135] Copleston, *Greece and Rome*, 1:461.

[136] Philo *On the Posterity and Exile of Cain* 1.

[137] Philo *Sacrifices of Abel and Cain* 95ff.

[138] Philo *Unchangeableness of God* 53; *Confusion of Tongues* 98; *Sacrifices of Abel and Cain* 94; *Dreams* 1.237.

[139] Cullmann, *Christology*, p. 96. Williamson adds: "The manhood of Jesus, according to Hebrews, was real manhood, full, authentic and unimpaired. And such a genuine manhood was an indispensable qualification for His successful priesthood" (*Philo and Hebrews*, p. 153).

[140] This phrase is borrowed from Williamson, *Philo and Hebrews*, pp. 138–39. It should be noted that Williamson goes on to reject this possibility. I have already indicated my differences with him.

[141] According to Thomas Hewitt, *metriopathein* (used of Jesus in Heb. 5:2) "is a philosophical term which expresses the feeling of moderation which lies between apathy, or 'lack of feeling,' and undue excitement. There should be no lack of feeling on the part of the high priest for those who have fallen

into error and sin, nor should he be unduly disturbed, otherwise he may fail to bear gently with them" (Thomas Hewitt, *The Epistle to the Hebrews, an Introduction and Commentary* [Grand Rapids: Eerdmans, 1960], p. 95). E. K. Simpson's comment on *metriopatheō* is most helpful: "This striking expression traces its genesis to the Peripatetic philosophy, in contradistinction from the Stoic's affectation of a marble apathy of demeanour. Within the bounds of self-respect it advocates a tolerant or sympathetic posture of mind in respect of provocations from others or misfortunes that may have overtaken them. . . . Such a blend of forbearance and condolence was ideally requisite in God's high priest under the old dispensation, both in his sacerdotal and judicial functions. But human infirmity marred the fair vision, till the Eternal Priest, Perfection's real Counterpart, trod the scene. For (and this renders the word almost untranslatable) *metriopatheia* is the golden mean between indifference and mawkish sentimentality" (E. K. Simpson, "The Vocabulary of the Epistle to the Hebrews," *Evangelical Quarterly* 18 [1946]: 36–37).

[142] Philo *Special Laws* 1.115 (Loeb trans.).

[143] Ibid., 1.113.

[144] Williamson, *Philo and Hebrews*, pp. 89–90.

[145] 1 Corinthians 1:23.

[146] The complex question of a pre-Christian source for the biblical Logos and the Alexandrian Logos will be touched on in part 3 of this book. See also Cullmann's discussion and critique in his *Christology*, pp. 252–53.

[147] Cf. Alexander Nairne, *The Epistle of Priesthood: Studies in the Epistle to the Hebrews* (Edinburgh: T. & T. Clark, 1913), p. cxxxi. Nairne notes that the Book of Hebrews seems "to correct Philo at least as much as it takes from him." While E. F. Scott admits affinities between Philo and Hebrews, he warns: "So far, then, from merely reproducing the thought of Philo, our Epistle breaks away from it at precisely the most vital points" (E. F. Scott, *The Epistle to the Hebrews: Its Doctrine and Significance* [Edinburgh: T. & T. Clark, 1922], p. 57).

[148] See the summary of several of these theories in Montefiore, *Epistle to the Hebrews*, pp. 39ff.

149 Williamson, *Philo and Hebrews*, p. 194.

150 Philo *Special Laws* 3.177ff.; *Husbandry* 51; *On the Cherubim* 3. See James Drummond, *Philo Judaeus*, 2 vols. (Edinburgh: Williams and Norgate, 1888), 2:239.

151 Philo *Giants* 16.

152 Philo *Dreams* 1.141–42.

153 Hebrews 2:2 is not an exception to this. The writer, like Paul in Galatians 3:19, was referring to a current Jewish belief that the angels had played a role when the Mosaic Law was given (see Acts 7:53). There is no reason to believe either writer was necessarily endorsing this belief, which appears to lack any Old Testament support. The argument in both Hebrews 2:2 and Galatians 3:19 can be viewed as hypothetical. That is, even if angels did play a role in the mediation of the Law, consider how much greater is the Gospel and *its* Mediator, Jesus Christ.

154 Drummond (*Philo Judaeus*, 2:239–73) examines the Philonic texts in which "Logos" is applied to angels.

155 The description of Christ as Mediator at this early point in the epistle does not depend on the actual use of *mesitēs* but on the prior statements in 1:1–4.

156 These quotations are used to make three main points: (1) Christ is God the Son, whom the angels must worship (1:5–6); (2) Christ is God the King, whom the angels must obey (1:7–9); and (3) Christ is God the Creator, whom the angels must serve (1:10–12). Therefore, Jesus is "better." Hebrews 2:5 adds a footnote to the superiority of Christ: the world to come will be ruled, not by angels, but by Christ.

157 Cf. Philippians 2:11. It should be noted that Hebrews 2:10 declares that God's action in providing Jesus as Savior was entirely appropriate; it was a "fitting" thing for God to do. Because of his sin, man was precluded from attaining the perfection for which God created him. The temporary humiliation of Jesus was part of God's plan to provide a new and effectual means for attaining the goal of perfection.

158 Philo *Dreams* 1.143.

159 Williamson, *Philo and Hebrews*, p. 454. Williamson's entire discussion of this point can be consulted with profit.

[160]Philo *Dreams* 1.214–15, 219; 2.183; *Migration of Abraham* 102; *Flight and Finding* 108ff. While Philo refers to the Logos as High Priest, The Wisdom of Solomon does not. Since the argument earlier in this chapter supported the contention that the writer of Hebrews was familiar with The Wisdom of Solomon, Philo's use of Logos in this way may suggest that the writer of Hebrews knew and used both sources. This fact does not constitute proof, however, since it is also possible that the writer was familiar with a tradition frozen in both and did not necessarily know both sources.

[161]Philo *Dreams* 2.188–89; 2.213–14.

[162]Philo *Special Laws* 1, 116.

[163]*Ibid.*, 1.230, 242–43; 3.134; 1.113; *Flight and Finding* 108ff.

[164]See F. F. Bruce's elaboration of these temporal dimensions of Christ's work in connection with Hebrews 13:8 (*Epistle to the Hebrews*, pp. 396–97).

[165]Hebrews 7:22 marks the only occurrence of *enguos* in the New Testament.

[166]F. F. Bruce, *Hebrews*, p. 151, n. 70.

[167]For additional references relevant to the material in this chapter, see B. Demarest, *A History of the Interpretation of Hebrews 7, 1–10* (Tübingen: J. C. B. Mohr, 1976); R. A. Horsley, "Wisdom of Word and Words of Wisdom in Corinth," *Catholic Biblical Quarterly* 39 (1977) pp. 224–39; F. L. Horton, *The Melchizedek Tradition* (Cambridge: Cambridge University Press, 1976); G. Hughes, *Hebrews and Hermeneutics* (Cambridge: Cambridge University Press, 1979); G. Johnston, "Christ as Archegos," *New Testament Studies* 27 (1981): 381–84; P. Owen, "The 'States of Ascent' in Hebrews v.11–vi.3," *New Testament Studies* 3 (1956–57): 243–53; M. Silva, "Perfection and Eschatology in Hebrews," *Westminster Theological Journal* 39 (1976): 60–71; A. F. Staples, "The Book of Hebrews in Its Relationship to the Writings of Philo Judaeus," doctoral dissertation, Southern Baptist Theological Seminary, 1951; James W. Thompson, *The Beginnings of Christian Philosophy: The Epistle to the Hebrews* (Washington, D.C.: Catholic Biblical Association of America, 1982); A. Wedderburn, "Philo's 'Heavenly Man,'" *Novum Testamentum* 15 (1973): 301–26;

Robert McL. Wilson, " 'Jewish Gnosis' and Gnostic Origins," *Hebrew Union College Annual* 45 (1974): 177–89.

[168] For the development between Reitzenstein's earlier Iranian and later Mandaean theories, see his books *Das iranische Erlösungmysterium* (Leipzig, 1921) and *Die Vorgeschichte der chrislichen Taufe* (Leipzig, 1929).

[169] See Richard Reitzenstein, *Die hellenistischen Mysterienreligionen* (Leipzig, 1927), p. 86. Reitzenstein's book is now available in English under the title *The Hellenistic Mystery-Religions*, trans. John E. Steely (Pittsburgh: Pickwick, 1978). Allegations of a Gnostic source of early Christian beliefs will be examined in part 3 of this book.

[170] Bousset's book was first published in 1913. After going through several German editions, it was translated into English in 1970 as *Kyrios Christos: A History of the Belief in Christ from the Beginnings of Christianity to Irenaeus* (Nashville: Abingdon, 1970). Bousset's theories will be examined in more detail in a later chapter.

[171] See Alfred Loisy, *Les Mystères payens et le mystère chrétien* (Paris, 1930).

[172] See Samuel Angus, *The Mystery Religions and Christianity* (1925; reprint, New Hyde Park, N.Y.: University Books, 1967). Two related books by Angus are his *Environment of Early Christianity* (see note 11) and *The Religious Quests of the Graeco-Roman World* (New York: Scribner, 1929).

[173] Edwin Hatch, *The Influence of Greek Ideas and Usages Upon the Christian Church* (London, 1890; reprint, Harper & Row, 1957); Percy Gardner, *The Origin of the Lord's Supper* (London, 1893); idem, *The Growth of Christianity* (London, 1907); idem, *The Religious Experience of St. Paul* (London, 1911); John Glasse, *The Mysteries and Christianity* (Edinburgh: 1921); Arthur Weigall, *The Paganism in our Christianity* (London, 1928); Shirley Jackson Case, *The Origins of Christian Supernaturalism* (Chicago: University of Chicago Press, 1946); idem, *Experience With the Supernatural in Early Christian Times* (New York: Century, 1929); Walter Hyde, *Paganism to Christianity in the Roman Empire* (Philadelphia: University of Pennsylvania, 1946); idem, *Greek Religion and Its Survivals* (New York: Cooper Square, 1963); and William Vassall,

The Origin of Christianity (New York: Exposition, 1952). Strictly speaking, these authors did not belong to the History of Religions School.

[174]For an English translation of one work, see Carl Clemen, *Primitive Christianity and Its Non-Jewish Sources* (Edinburgh: T. & T. Clark, 1912). More relevant to my comment is Clemen's *Der Einfluss der Mysterienreligionen auf das altest Christentum* (Giessen, 1913).

[175]Adolf von Harnack, *Wissenschaft und Leben,* (Giessen, 1911), 2:191.

[176]Samuel Cheetham, *The Mysteries, Pagan and Christian* (London, 1897); H. A. A. Kennedy, *St. Paul and the Mystery Religions* (London: Hodder and Stoughton, 1913); A. D. Nock, "Early Gentile Christianity and Its Hellenistic Background" in *Essays on the Trinity and the Incarnation,* ed. A. E. J. Rawlinson (London: Longmans, Green, 1928). Machen's book *The Origin of Paul's Religion,* first published in 1925, has already been cited. For an extensive listing of foreign and English sources on both sides of the question, see "Methodology in the Study of the Mystery Religions and Early Christianity," in Bruce M. Metzger, *Historical and Literary Studies* (Grand Rapids: Eerdmans, 1968), pp. 1–24. Metzger's essay is required reading for any student of this subject.

[177]Burtt, *Types of Religious Philosophy,* p. 36.

[178]Joscelyn Godwin, *Mystery Religions in the Ancient World* (New York: Harper & Row, 1981).

[179]Hyam Maccoby, *The Sacred Executioner* (New York: Thames & Hudson, 1982), p. 116.

[180]Randall, *Hellenistic Ways of Deliverance,* p. 105. See also page 154, where Randall states, "Christianity, at the hands of Paul, became a mystical system of redemption, much like the cult of Isis, and the other sacramental or mystery religions of the day."

[181]Jones, *Medieval Mind,* p. 39.

[182]Ibid., pp. 47–48.

[183]Clark, *Thales to Dewey,* p. 194.

[184]Hugo Rahner, "The Christian Mystery and the Pagan Mysteries," in *Pagan and Christian Mysteries,* ed. Joseph Campbell (New York: Harper & Row, 1955), p. 152. Rahner's essay (pp. 146–210) is also required reading for this topic.

[185]Ibid., p. 159.

[186] Angus, *Mystery Religions and Christianity,* p. 53.

[187] Ibid., pp. 58–59.

[188] Ibid., p. 58.

[189] Ibid., p. 61.

[190] Ibid., p. 59.

[191] Preserved in Synesius *Dion,* 7.

[192] Angus, *Mystery Religions and Christianity,* pp. 50, 52.

[193] Rudolf Bultmann, *Primitive Christianity in Its Contemporary Setting* (New York: World, 1956), p. 158.

[194] See Joseph B. Tyson, *A Study of Early Christianity* (New York: Macmillan, 1973), especially pp. 77–86.

[195] Godwin, *Mystery Religions,* p. 111. On the taurobolium, see R. Duthoy, *The Taurobolium: Its Evolution and Terminology* (Leiden: Brill, 1969). On alleged parallels to Christ's resurrection, see Edwin Yamauchi, "Easter—Myth, Hallucination, or History?" *Christianity Today* 18 (1973–74): 660–63.

[196] Compare Bultmann's statement that "the initiate is 'born again' . . ." (*Primitive Christianity,* p. 159).

[197] See Rahner, "Christian Mystery."

[198] Ibid., p. 157.

[199] Clemen, *Der Einfluss,* pp. 81ff., cited and trans. by Rahner, "Christian Mystery," p. 162.

[200] The terminology is Rahner's, "Christian Mystery," p. 158.

[201] See ibid., p. 163.

[202] Ibid.

[203] George Emmanuel Mylonas, "Mystery Religions of Greece," in *Ancient Religions,* ed. Vergilius T. A. Ferm (New York: Philosophical Library, 1950), p. 176.

[204] On Isis, see J. G. Griffiths, *Apuleius: The Isis Book* (Leiden: Brill, 1975); F. Solmsen, *Isis Among the Greeks and Romans* (Cambridge: Harvard University Press, 1980); R. E. Witt, *Isis in the Greco-Roman World* (Ithaca: Cornell University Press, 1971).

[205] On Serapis, see W. Horbostel, *Sarapis* (Leiden: Brill, 1973); John E. Stambaugh, *Sarapis Under the Early Ptolemies* (Leiden: Brill, 1972); R. Stiehl, "The Origin of the Cult of Sarapis," *History of Religions* 3 (1963): 21–23.

[206]Joseph Klausner, *From Jesus to Paul* (New York: Macmillan, 1943), p. 104.

[207]See Yamauchi, "Easter," pp. 660–63.

[208]"Osiris knew no resurrection, but was resuscitated to be a ruler of the Nether world" (Günter Wagner, *Pauline Baptism and the Pagan Mysteries* [Edinburgh: Oliver and Boyd, 1967], p. 261).

[209]Ibid., pp. 260ff.

[210]Ibid., p. 233. The initiation rite is described by Apuleius (mid-second century A.D.). Wagner's evaluation agrees with Machen. See Wagner, *Pauline Baptism*, p. 260.

[211]On Cybele and Attis, see F. Cumont, *Oriental Religions in Roman Paganism* (1911; reprint, New York: Dover, 1956); E. and J. Harris, *The Oriental Cults in Roman Britain* (Leiden: Brill, 1965); J. Ferguson, *The Religions of the Roman Empire* (Ithaca: Cornell, 1970); Grant Showerman, *The Great Mother of the Gods* (Chicago: Argonaut, 1969); Maarten J. Vermaseren, *The Legend of Attis in Greek and Roman Art* (Leiden: Brill, 1966); idem, *Cybele and Attis: The Myth and the Cult* (London: Thames and Hudson, 1977).

[212]Machen, *Origin of Paul's Religion*, p. 228.

[213]Once again, see Yamauchi, "Easter," pp. 660–63.

[214]Angus, *Mystery Religions and Christianity*, p. 60.

[215]Wagner, *Pauline Baptism*, p. 265.

[216]Firmicus Maternus *Error* 3:1.

[217]See Wagner, *Pauline Baptism*, p. 265.

[218]Gordon J. Laing, *Survivals of Roman Religion* (New York: Cooper Square, 1963), p. 125.

[219]Ibid.

[220]Godwin, *Mystery Religions*, p. 111.

[221]On Mithraism, see H. Betz, "The Mithras Inscriptions of Santa Prisca and the New Testament," *Novum Testamentum* 10 (1968): 52–80; U. Bianchi, *Mysteria Mithrae* (Leiden: Brill, 1979); S. Brandon, "Mithraism and Its Challenge to Christianity," *Hibbert Journal* 53 (1955): 107–14; L. Campbell, *Mithraic Iconography and Ideology* (Leiden: Brill, 1968); J. Ferguson, "More About Mithras," *Hibbert Journal* 53 (1955): 319–26; R. L. Gordon, "Mithraism and Roman Society," *Religion* 2 (1972): 92–121; G. Halsberghe, *The Cult of Sol Invictus* (Leiden: Brill, 1972); J. Hinnells, ed., *Mithraic Studies*, 2 vols. (Manchester: Manchester University Press, 1975); J. Hinnells, "Zo-

roastrian Saviour Imagery and Its Influence on the New Testament," *Numen* 16 (1969): 161–85; S. Laeuchli, *Mithraism in Ostia* (Chicago: University of Chicago Press, 1967); idem, "Urban Mithraism," *Biblical Archaeologist* 31 (1968): 73–99; A. D. Nock, "The Genius of Mithraism," *Journal of Religious Studies* 27 (1937): 108–13; M. Meyer, *The "Mithras Liturgy"* (Missoula: Scholars, 1976); J. Rutter, "The Three Phases of the Taurobolium," *Phoenix* 22 (1968): 226–49; Michael P. Speidel, *Mithras: Orion, Greek Hero and Roman Army God* (Leiden: Brill, 1980); J. Toynbee, "Still More About Mithras," *Hibbert Journal* 54 (1956): 109–14.

[222]Irach J. S. Taraporewala, "Mithraism," in *Ancient Religions*, ed. Vergilius T. A. Ferm (New York: Philosophical Library, 1950), p. 213.

[223]Ibid.

[224]Justin Martyr *Apol.* 66.

[225]See M. J. Vermaseren, *Mithras: The Secret God* (London: Chatto & Windus, 1963), pp. 129–53.

[226]See Franz Cumont, *The Mysteries of Mithra* (Chicago: Open Court, 1903), pp. 87ff.; Schweitzer, *Paul and His Interpreters*, p. 192.

[227]George Widengren, "The Mithraic Mysteries in the Greco-Roman World With Special Regard to Their Iranian Background," *Academia Nazionale dei Lincei* (1966), p. 452.

[228]M. J. Vermaseren, *Corpus Inscriptionum et Monumentorum Religionis Mithriacae* (1956), p. 57.

[229]Vermaseren, *Mithras: The Secret God*, p. 29.

[230]See Edwin Yamauchi, *Pre-Christian Gnosticism* (Grand Rapids: Eerdmans, 1973), pp. 121–22; idem, "*The Apocalypse of Adam*, Mithraism, and Pre-Christian Gnosticism," in *Textes et Mémoires*, IV, *Études Mithraiques Act Iranica*, ed. J. Duchesne-Guillemin (Téhéran-Liège: Bibliotheque Pahlavi, 1978), pp. 537–63 (esp. pp. 553ff.).

[231]Yamauchi, *Pre-Christian Gnosticism*, p. 112.

[232]The names of several lesser-known and less important Middle Eastern cults sometimes appear in discussions of supposed Christian syncretism. Yet, pointing to these cults as evidence of Christian syncretism has involved the same exaggerations and oversimplifications already noted in connection with the major mystery religions. Perhaps the most frequently cited of these lesser cults is that of

Adonis, a religion that originated in Syria; Adonis is sometimes identified by later writers with Tammuz of Babylonian religion. With respect to the cult of Adonis, Wagner states, "In no sense at all is Adonis to be claimed as a dying-god, and there is no evidence that the worshipper of Adonis believed in a personal resurrection" (Wagner, *Pauline Baptism,* p. 264). The religion lacks all of the essential ingredients of a mystery religion. Wagner also notes, "That Tammuz is at once a 'god of resurrection' . . . and a 'God of salvation' is hardly perceptible. His death does not signify a sacrifice for sin, nor has it anything to do with eschatology. The fate of the dead . . . is not in his hands . . . his own death does not enable the god to give succour; but only when he is enjoying abundant life himself is it possible for Tammuz—like any god!—to bring deliverance from sin and condemnation" (ibid., p. 157). The important common element in the cults of Adonis and Tammuz is a story about the god's death and his worshipers' commemorative mourning of that legendary event. See Edwin Yamauchi, "Descent of Ishtar," *The Biblical World,* ed. Charles F. Pfeiffer (Grand Rapids: Baker, 1966), pp. 196–200; idem, "Tammuz," in *Wycliffe Bible Encyclopedia,* ed. Charles F. Pfeiffer (Chicago: Moody, 1975), p. 707; idem, "Easter," pp. 660–63. Yamauchi argues that the identification of Adonis and Tammuz is mistaken. Tammuz never rose from the dead. The texts used to support a resurrection of Adonis date between the second and fourth centuries A.D. See also T. Jacobsen, *Toward the Image of Tammuz* (Cambridge: Harvard University Press, 1970); S. N. Kraemer, *The Sacred Marriage Rite* (Bloomington: Indiana University Press, 1969).

[233]Machen, *Origin of Paul's Religion,* p. 280. Machen's entire treatment of this issue is still worth consulting.

[234]Metzger, "Methodology," p. 14.

[235]Machen, *Origin of Paul's Religion,* pp. 282–83. See the rest of Machen's discussion.

[236]Metzger, "Methodology," p. 14. This is Paul's teaching in 1 Corinthians 10. A. D. Nock discusses this question in "Baptism and the Eucharist as 'Dona Data' " in his *Early Gentile Christianity and*

Its Hellenistic Background (New York: Harper & 295
Row, 1964), pp. 109–45.

References

[237] For a lengthy refutation of the high sacramentarianism this view is forced to ascribe to Paul, see Machen, *Origin of Paul's Religion*, pp. 284ff.

[238] Older German scholars who argued for such a connection include H. Gunkel and J. Weiss.

[239] Fairweather, *Jesus and the Greeks*, p. 283.

[240] Ibid.

[241] Wagner, *Pauline Baptism*, p. 266.

[242] Duthoy, *Taurobolium*, p. 108.

[243] Wagner, *Pauline Baptism*, p. 266.

[244] See Duthoy, *Taurobolium*, pp. 116ff. Duthoy (pp. 111ff.) provides a list of scholars on each side of the question of whether the taurobolium underwent evolution or whether it was always the ceremony of consecration that I have described.

[245] Ibid., pp. 120–21. Duthoy is not dogmatic about this, however. He identifies several scholars who explain the later features of the taurobolium as a result of Christian influence; see ibid., p. 113.

[246] Ibid., p. 121.

[247] Ibid.

[248] Ibid., p. 116.

[249] Some of Duthoy's conclusions are based on an analysis of terminology that some have challenged. M. J. Vermaseren supplies bibliographical help on this debate. See his *Cybele and Attis*, p. 107.

[250] Alfred Loisy, "The Christian Mystery," *Hibbert Journal* 10 (1911): 51–52.

[251] Bultmann, *Theology of the New Testament*, 1:140. Günter Wagner, in his *Pauline Baptism*, pp. 276ff., has criticized this hypothesis concerning Romans 6.

[252] Wagner, *Pauline Baptism*, p. 268.

[253] Ridderbos, *Paul*, p. 24.

[254] Mircea Eliade, *Rites and Symbols of Initiation* (New York: Harper & Row, 1958), p. 116. According to Eliade, after the third century A.D., the Christian church added to its symbolism of baptism some language and imagery that could have been borrowed from the mystery cults. But, he insists, these borrowings did not occur in early Christianity; see p. 116.

[255] Ibid., pp. 115–16. No Christian writer related the word *mysterion* to either baptism or the Lord's Supper until after A.D. 100. See E. Glenn Hinson,

The Evangelization of the Roman Empire (Macon, Ga.: Mercer University Press, 1981), p. 179. Justin Martyr objected to referring to Christian sacraments as "mysteries" (1 *Apol.* 66). Tertullian refused to call pagan ceremonies "sacraments." Both Justin and Tertullian thought of the pagan rites as satanically inspired counterfeits or imitations. By the third century, however, Christian writers were illustrating the terminological looseness abhorred by Justin and Tertullian; see Origen, *Contra Celsum* 3:59ff., where he actually referred to Christians being initiated into the mysteries of the faith.

[256]See Wagner, *Pauline Baptism*, p. 284.

[257]Schweitzer, *Paul and His Interpreters*, p. 195.

[258]Ibid., p. 197.

[259]See Ridderbos, *Paul*, p. 24.

[260]Metzger, "Methodology," p. 17.

[261]For additional helpful material on the mysteries relevant to both chapters 9 and 10, see A. Athnassakis, *The Orphic Hymns* (Missoula: Scholars, 1977); U. Bianchi, *The Greek Mysteries* (Leiden: Brill, 1976); R. Brown, "The Semitic Background of the NT *Mysterion*," *Biblica* 39 (1958): 426–48 and 40 (1959): 70–87; S. Cole, "New Evidence for the Mysteries of Dionysus," *Greek, Roman, and Byzantine Studies* 21 (1980): 223–38; K. Dowden, "Grades in the Eleusinian Mysteries," *Revue de l'Historie des Religions* 197 (1980): 409–28; F. Dunand and P. Lévèque, *Les syncrétismes and les religions de l'antiquité* (Leiden: Brill, 1975); R. Gordon, "Reality, Evocation and Boundary in the Mysteries," *Journal of Mithraic Studies* 3 (1980): 19–99; A. Harvey, "The Use of Mystery Language in the Bible," *Journal of Theological Studies* 31 (1980): 320–36; J. Hinnells, "Christianity and the Mystery Cults," *Theology* 71 (1968): 20–25; Samuel H. Hooke, "Christianity and the Mystery Religions," in *Judaism and Christianity*, ed. William O. E. Oesterley, 3 vols. (London, 1937), 1:235–50; M. Nilsson, *The Dionysiac Mysteries of the Hellenistic and Roman Age* (Lund, 1957); A. D. Nock, "Hellenistic Mysteries and Christian Sacraments," *Mnemosyne*, 4th ser., 5 (1952): 177–213; R. Oden, "Method in the Study of Near Eastern Myths," *Religion* 9 (1979): 182–96; R. Ribichini, *Adonis* (Rome, 1981); M. Smith, "On

the Wine God in Palestine," *Salo Wittmayer Baron Jubilee Volume* (Jerusalem, 1975), pp. 815–29; J. Teixidor, *The Pagan God* (Princeton: Princeton University Press, 1977); M. J. Vermaseren, *Studies in Hellenistic Religions* (Leiden: Brill, 1979); R. Wasson et al., *The Road to Eleusis* (New York: Harcourt Brace Jovanovich, 1978); H. Willoughby, *Pagan Regeneration* (Chicago: University of Chicago Press, 1929).

[262] John W. Drane, "The Religious Background," in *New Testament Interpretation*, ed. I. Howard Marshall (Grand Rapids: Eerdmans, 1977), p. 120. The reader should know that Drane himself is a critic of Bousset's thesis.

[263] See Bultmann, *Theology of the New Testament*, 1:52–53, 121ff.

[264] Critical discussions of Bousset's views may be found in Vincent Taylor, *The Names of Jesus* (New York: St. Martin's, 1953), pp. 38–51; Martin Hengel, *The Son of God* (Philadelphia: Fortress, 1976), pp. 70–71; Oscar Cullmann, *Christology*, pp. 196ff.; Herman Ridderbos, *Paul and Jesus* (Philadelphia: Presbyterian and Reformed, 1958), pp. 52–53; and Machen, *Origin of Paul's Religion*, pp. 293–317.

[265] See Hengel, *Son of God*, p. 77.

[266] Cullmann, *Christology*, pp. 214–15.

[267] Ibid., p. 202.

[268] See Machen, *Origin of Paul's Religion*, p. 258ff.

[269] Ibid., p. 259.

[270] Ridderbos, *Paul and Jesus*, p. 52.

[271] Machen, *Origin of Paul's Religion*, p. 259.

[272] Ibid., pp. 259–60.

[273] A. D. Nock, "Early Gentile Christianity," p. 85.

[274] Machen, *Origin of Paul's Religion*, p. 306.

[275] Ibid., p. 307.

[276] The reasons why the Greek translators of the Septuagint selected *Kyrios* for this purpose are not especially relevant here. But Machen's suggestions are interesting, nonetheless. See ibid., pp. 307–8.

[277] Loisy, "Christian Mystery," p. 51.

[278] Gilbert, *Greek Thought*, pp. 71–72.

[279] Burtt, *Types of Religious Philosophy*, p. 36.

[280] Jones, *Medieval Mind*, p. 41.

[281] See Hengel, *Son of God*, p. 26.

[282] Wagner, *Pauline Baptism*, p. 284.

[283] See W.K.C. Guthrie, *Orpheus and Greek Religion*, 2nd ed. (London: Methuen, 1952), p. 268.

[284] Machen, *Origin of Paul's Religion*, p. 315. See also Metzger, "Methodology," p. 18.

[285] See Nock, *Early Gentile Christianity*, p. 106.

[286] See Metzger, "Methodology," p. 20. For more on the alleged resurrections of the mystery gods, see also Yamauchi, "Easter," pp. 660–63.

[287] Metzger, "Methodology," p. 21.

[288] Ibid.

[289] See Machen, *Origin of Paul's Religion*, pp. 234–35.

[290] André Boulanger, *Orphée: Rapports de l'orphisme et du christianisme* (Paris, 1925), p. 102.

[291] See Nock, *Early Gentile Christianity*, pp. 80–81; Dunn, *Christology in the Making*, p. 251. For an older rejection of such attempts, see Schweitzer, *Paul and His Interpreters*, p. 193. Further documentation along this line is provided by Wagner, *Pauline Baptism*, p. 269.

[292] Wagner, *Pauline Baptism*, p. 269.

[293] Worth consulting in connection with this topic is William Mounce, "The Origin of the New Testament Metaphor of Rebirth" (Ph.D. dissertation, University of Aberdeen, Scotland, 1981).

[294] Angus, *Mystery-Religions and Christianity*, pp. 95–96.

[295] Wilfred L. Knox, *Some Hellenistic Elements in Primitive Christianity* (London: British Academy, 1944), p. 90.

[296] Bultmann, *Primitive Christianity*, p. 159.

[297] See W.K.C. Guthrie, *The Greeks and Their Gods* (Boston: Beacon, 1955), p. 288. Many scholars doubt that Tertullian's statement is even relevant to this problem. His terminology obviously has a Christian source, and he does not really refer to the Eleusinian mysteries.

[298] See Apuleius, *Metamorphoses*, ch. 11; Plutarch, *On Isis and Osiris* (Loeb edition) 5.7–191.

[299] See H. Betz, "The Mithras Inscriptions of Santa Prisca and the New Testament," *Novum Testamentum* 10 (1968): 52–80.

[300] See Vermaseren, *Cybele and Attis*, p. 106.

[301] Machen, *Origin of Paul's Religion*, pp. 240–41.

[302] Grant, p. 78.

[303]It is also possible that the defenders of Christian syncretism may be reading a Christian meaning into the Latin word *renatus*. Since one meaning of the term is simply a new beginning or fresh start, it may never have been intended to connect the taurobolium with a quasi-Christian notion of rebirth.

[304]Wagner, *Pauline Baptism*, pp. 270–71.

[305]See W. F. Flemington, *The New Testament Doctrine of Baptism* (London: SPCK, 1948), pp. 76–81.

[306]MacGregor and Purdy, *Jew and Greek*, pp. 339–40. The entire passage is an excellent example of what Hugo Rahner calls the "ruinous mania for painting the [mystery religions] in Christian colors." Rahner, "Christian Mystery," p. 170.

[307]Machen, *Origin of Paul's Religion*, p. 274.

[308]See Rahner, "Christian Mystery," p. 170.

[309]Richard Reitzenstein, *Poimandres* (Leipzig, 1904), p. 180, n. 1.

[310]Machen, *Origin of Paul's Religion*, pp. 277–78. See also Ridderbos, *Paul and Jesus*, p. 11.

[311]See Ridderbos, *Paul and Jesus*, pp. 11–12.

[312]Rahner, "Christian Mystery," pp. 169–70. The lack of an ethic in pagan cults is also discussed by Guthrie, *Orpheus and Greek Religion*, p. 269. See also Machen's comments (*Origin of Paul's Religion*, p. 276).

[313]Rahner, "Christian Mystery," p. 163.

[314]For an interesting statement along this line from a surprising source, see Norman Perrin and Dennis C. Duling, *The New Testament: An Introduction*, 2nd ed. (New York: Harcourt, Brace, Jovanovich, 1982), p. 12.

[315]MacGregor and Purdy, *Jew and Greek*, p. 289.

[316]Hengel, *Son of God*, p. 28.

[317]Schweitzer, *Paul and His Interpreters*, p. 238.

[318]Hinson, *Evangelization of the Roman Empire*, p. 181. For an older statement of this view, see G. H. Box, *Early Christianity and Its Rivals* (New York: McBride, 1925), p. 75.

[319]Nock, *Early Gentile Christianity*, p. 183. In a 1952 article, Nock added: "Any idea that what we call the Christian sacraments were in their origin indebted to pagan mysteries or even to the metaphorical concepts based upon them shatters on the rock of linguistic evidence. . . . It is the more

surprising to see how slow and slight was the adaptation before the fourth century of anything like mystery terminology and even of its metaphorical application as seen in Greek philosophers and in Philo, let alone of any effective approximation or reinterpretation of any feeling that a serious analogy to Christian practice existed in the world around." ("Hellenistic Mysteries," pp. 200, 202).

320Wagner, *Pauline Baptism,* pp. 274–75. Wagner provides a detailed list of such technical terms on p. 274.

321Metzger, "Methodology," p. 12, provides a list.

322Ibid.

323See Machen, *Origin of Paul's Religion,* p. 273.

324Ibid.

325See Rahner, "Christian Mystery," pp. 165–66; Hinson, *Evangelization of the Roman Empire,* p. 181.

326Eliade, *Rites and Symbols of Initiation,* p. 118.

327Rahner, "Christian Mystery," p. 172, explores some additional aspects of this problem. He points out that many concepts and terms that appear both in Christianity and in the Hellenistic world could have developed in common language. His remarks should be consulted.

328That this view still has its advocates is evident from a 1982 book—Maccoby, *The Sacred Executioner.*

329Schweitzer, *Paul and His Interpreters,* p. 87.

330Machen, *Origin of Paul's Religion,* p. 256.

331Ibid., p. 257.

332Ibid.

333Machen critiques other attempts to rescue a theory of Pauline dependence (ibid., pp. 260ff.).

334See W. C. Van Unnik, *Tarsus or Jerusalem,* trans. George Ogg (London: Epworth, 1962).

335Seyoon Kim, *The Origin of Paul's Gospel* (Grand Rapids: Eerdmans, 1982), p. 38. See Kim's entire discussion of Paul's early training (pp. 32ff.).

336Ibid., pp. 332, 335 (emphasis his).

337Ibid., pp. 333–34.

338Ibid., pp. 334–35.

339E. Earle Ellis, *Paul and His Recent Interpreters* (Grand Rapids: Eerdmans, 1961), p. 29.

340Edwyn Bevan, *The History of Christianity in the Light of Modern Knowledge* (Glasgow, 1929), p. 105.

[341] Machen, *Origin of Paul's Religion*, p. 237.

[342] Ibid., p. 241.

[343] Ibid. See also Metzger, "Methodology," pp. 6–7.

[344] Metzger points out that there is very little evidence of any Mystery presence in first-century Palestine. He writes, "In estimating the degree of opportunity afforded the early Palestinian Church of being influenced by the Mysteries, it is certainly a significant fact that, unlike other countries bordering the Mediterranean Sea, Palestine has been extremely barren in yielding archaeological remains of the paraphernalia and places of worship connected with the Mysteries." Metzger, "Methodology," p. 8.

[345] Ibid., p. 7. See also R. E. O. White, *The Biblical Doctrine of Initiation* (Grand Rapids: Eerdmans, 1960), p. 218 n. 3.

[346] Rahner, "Christian Mystery," p. 168.

[347] Machen, *Origin of Paul's Religion*, p. 9. Later in his book (p. 238) Machen adds, "It must be remembered that the paganism of the Hellenistic age had elevated syncretism to a system; it had absolutely no objection of principle against receiving elements from every source. In the Christian Church, on the other hand, there was a strong objection to such procedure; Christianity from the beginning was like Judaism in being exclusive. It regarded with the utmost abhorrence anything that was tainted by a pagan origin. The abhorrence, at least in the early period, more than overbalanced the fact that the Christians for the most part had formerly been pagans, so that it might be thought natural for them to retain something of pagan belief. Conversion involved a passionate renunciation of former beliefs."

[348] Metzger, "Methodology," p. 13

[349] Ridderbos, *Paul and Jesus*, p. 11. See also Rahner, "Christian Mystery," p. 168.

[350] Metzger, "Methodology," p. 11. The possible parallels in view here would naturally be dated late, after A.D. 200 for the most part.

[351] Ibid.

[352] Africa, *Ancient World*, p. 460.

[353] The greatest of the patristic anti-Gnostic writings was *Adversus Haereses* by Irenaeus (late second century A.D.). For the patristic sources, see R. M.

Grant,. "The Earliest Christian Gnosticism," *Church History* 22 (1953): 81–98.

[354]Simone Pétrement stands almost alone, however, in the high degree of credibility she attaches to the patristic information about Gnosticism. See S. Pétrement, "Le Colloque de Messine et le problème du gnosticisme," *Revue de Métaphysique et de Morale* 72 (1967): 344–73 (esp. p. 361).

[355]See J. Doresse, *The Secret Books of the Egyptian Gnostics* (New York: Viking, 1960), pp. 249–50.

[356]Bousset, *Kyrios Christos*, p. 245.

[357]Bultmann, *Primitive Christianity*, p. 162.

[358]See E. Percy, *Untersuchungen über den Ursprung der johanneischen Theologie* (1939); C. H. Dodd, *The Interpretation of the Fourth Gospel* (New York: Cambridge University Press, 1965); W. F. Albright, *New Horizons in Biblical Research* (New York: Oxford University Press, 1956); R. P. Casey, "Gnosis, Gnosticism and the New Testament," in *The Background of the New Testament and Its Eschatology*, ed. W. D. Davies and D. Daube (New York: Cambridge University Press, 1956), pp. 52–80. I do not mean to say that these authors accepted every feature of the patristic teaching.

[359]Casey, "Gnosis, Gnosticism," p. 54.

[360]Dodd, *Fourth Gospel*, p. 115. On the same page, Dodd notes that the oldest literary reference to the Mandaean sect can be dated A.D. 792.

[361]For these Coptic sources see Doresse, *Secret Books;* A. Helmbold, *The Nag Hammadi Gnostic Texts and the Bible* (Grand Rapids: Baker, 1967). See also D. M. Scholer, *A Classified Bibliography of the Coptic Gnostic Library and of Gnostic Studies 1948–1969* (Leiden: Brill, 1971). Subsequent updates appear in *Novum Testamentum* in 1971 and following years.

[362]James M. Robinson and H. Koester, *Trajectories Through Early Christianity* (Philadelphia: Fortress, 1971), p. 234 n. 4. See also James M. Robinson, "The Coptic Gnostic Library Today," *New Testament Studies* 14 (1968): 356–401.

[363]Yamauchi (*Pre-Christian Gnosticism,* p. 103) quotes this passage in his own translation from the German.

364 Yamauchi, *Pre-Christian Gnosticism*, is required reading for anyone desiring more complete information about this issue. See also Yamauchi, "Pre-Christian Gnosticism in the Nag Hammadi Texts?" *Church History* 48 (1978): 129–41.

365 Robert McL. Wilson, "Gnostic Origins," *Vigilae Christianae* 9 (1955): 208.

366 Yamauchi (*Pre-Christian Gnosticism*, pp. 26–27) provides a list of the major scholars who hold positions on the question of a pre-Christian Gnosticism.

367 Pétrement, "Le Colloque de Messine," p. 371.

368 Yamauchi, *Pre-Christian Gnosticism*, p. 18.

369 See Wilson, "Gnostic Origins," pp. 203, 208.

370 Robert McL. Wilson, *Gnosis and the New Testament* (Philadelphia: Fortress, 1968), p. 9.

371 G. W. MacRae, "Gnosticism," *New Catholic Encyclopedia, 17 vols.* (New York: McGraw-Hill, 1967), 6:525.

372 Wilson, *Gnostic Problem*, 70.

373 Hans Jonas, *The Gnostic Religion*, 2nd ed. (Boston: Beacon, 1963), p. 44.

374 MacGregor and Purdy, *Jew and Greek*, p. 313.

375 Jonas, *Gnostic Religion*, p. 43.

376 Wilson, *Gnostic Problem*, p. 70.

377 Yamauchi, *Pre-Christian Gnosticism*, p. 31. For a critical analysis of Bultmann's notion of demythologization, see Ronald Nash, *Christian Faith and Historical Understanding* (Grand Rapids: Zondervan, 1983).

378 Stephen Neill, *The Interpretation of the New Testament, 1861–1961* (New York: Oxford University Press, 1964), pp. 179–80.

379 See Yamauchi, *Pre-Christian Gnosticism*, pp. 163–69; Carsten Colpe, "New Testament and Gnostic Christology," in *Religions in Antiquity*, ed. Jacob Neusner (Leiden: Brill, 1968), p. 235.

380 See Robert McL. Wilson, "Some Recent Studies in Gnosticism," *New Testament Studies* 6 (1959–60): 43.

381 Hengel, *Son of God*, p. 33.

382 Andrew K. Helmbold, "Redeemer Hymns—Gnostic and Christian," in *New Dimensions in New Testament Study*, ed. Richard N. Longenecker and Merrill C. Tenney (Grand Rapids: Zondervan, 1974), p. 73.

[383]Dunn, *Christology in the Making*, p. 99. See also Robert M. Grant, *A Historical Introduction to the New Testament* (New York: Harper & Row, 1963), p. 203.

[384]Robert M. Grant, ed., *Gnosticism, A Source Book of Heretical Writings From the Early Christian Period* (New York: Harper & Row, 1961), p. 18.

[385]See Carl Kraeling, "The Fourth Gospel and Contemporary Religious Thought," *Journal of Biblical Literature* 49 (1930): 146–47.

[386]Alan Richardson, *An Introduction to the Theology of the New Testament* (New York: Harper & Row, 1958), pp. 138ff.

[387]Colpe, "New Testament and Gnostic Christology," p. 235.

[388]Ridderbos, *Paul and Jesus*, p. 111.

[389]Ibid.

[390]Ibid.

[391]Ibid., p. 112.

[392]See the helpful discussion of this subject in Yamauchi, *Pre-Christian Gnosticism*, pp. 117–42.

[393]Dodd, *Fourth Gospel*, pp. 115–16. Dodd (pp. 115–30) provides an excellent outline of the sect.

[394]Ridderbos, *Paul and Jesus*, p. 107.

[395]Dodd, *Fourth Gospel*, pp. 120–21.

[396]Ibid., p. 124.

[397]Edwin Yamauchi, "Some Alleged Evidences for Pre-Christian Gnosticism," in *New Dimensions in New Testament Study*, ed. Richard N. Longenecker and Merrill C. Tenney (Grand Rapids: Zondervan, 1974), p. 68.

[398]Dodd, *Fourth Gospel*, p. 121.

[399]Ibid., p. 122.

[400]Ibid., p. 128.

[401]Ibid., p. 130.

[402]See Yamauchi's discussion of this point in his *Pre-Christian Gnosticism*, pp. 121ff.

[403]See Dodd, *Fourth Gospel*, p. 127, and Ridderbos, *Paul and Jesus*, p. 108.

[404]George Eldon Ladd, *A Theology of the New Testament* (Grand Rapids: Eerdmans, 1974), p. 246. See also Richard Longenecker, *The Christology of Early Jewish Christianity* (London: SCM, 1970), pp. 58–62.

[405]Leon Morris sees "a tremendous gap" between the Dead Sea Scrolls and John's Gospel. While there are many parallels in language and thought, direct

dependence is ruled out. Morris suggests that John may have been partly concerned to oppose the Essenes. Certainly the content of John's thought is far removed from that of the Essenes. See "The Dead Sea Scrolls and St. John's Gospel," in Leon Morris, *Studies in the Fourth Gospel* (Grand Rapids: Eerdmans, 1969), pp. 321–58. Morris agrees that whatever affinities exist between John and the Scrolls, they support a Palestinian, not a Hellenistic, environment for the Fourth Gospel.

[406]Ladd, *Theology of the New Testament*, pp. 219–20. Worth consulting is Ladd's entire discussion (pp. 219–36).

[407]Ibid., p. 222.

[408]For more information, see Edwin Yamauchi, "Hermetic Literature," in *The Interpreter's Dictionary of the Bible, Supplementary Volume*, ed. Keith R. Crim et al. (Nashville: Abingdon, 1976), p. 408.

[409]The Hermetic writings have an apparent connection with Neo-Pythagoreanism mentioned in chapter 6. According to Copleston (*Greece and Rome*, pp. 448–49), the literature "owes its main contents to earlier Greek philosophy, and seems to have been indebted particularly to Posidonius. The fundamental notion expressed in this literature is that of *salvation through knowledge of god . . .* a notion that played a great role in 'Gnosticism.'"

[410]Selections from the Hermetic writings may be found in Clark, *Selections From Hellenistic Philosophy;* Hans Jonas, *The Gnostic Problem*, 2nd rev. ed. (Boston: Beacon, 1963); C. K. Barrett, *The New Testament Background: Selected Documents* (London: SPCK, 1958).

[411]See Richard Reitzenstein, *Die hellenistischen Mysterienreligionen*, 2nd ed. (1920), p. 65.

[412]See Machen, *Origin of Paul's Religion*, p. 242.

[413]Clark, *Selections from Hellenistic Philosophy*, p. 185.

[414]Yamauchi, *Pre-Christian Gnosticism*, p. 71.

[415]It is generally agreed that the Hermetic literature is a product of several writers, a fact that helps explain the many inconsistencies.

[416]Machen, *Origin of Paul's Religion*, p. 242.

[417]Clark, *Selections*, p. 186

[418]Clark, *Thales to Dewey*, p. 193. Clark (*Selections*, pp. 189–90) also points out that any possible connection between *Poimander* and the Prologue of the Fourth Gospel "is not one of dependence, in either direction, but of opposition. For Poimander the Logos was not in the beginning, as John asserts; for John, 'all things were made by him and without him was not anything made that was made,' and this Poimander denies. . . . the nature of the [Hermetic] system and the conception of salvation by a cosmological gnosis, tacitly excludes the Christian idea of an historical Incarnation according to which 'the Logos became flesh and dwelt among us.' "

[419]Machen, *Origin of Paul's Religion*, p. 245.

[420]Eduard Lohse, *The New Testament Environment* (Nashville: Abingdon, 1976), p. 276.

[421]See Willoughby, *Pagan Regeneration*, pp. 207ff.

[422]Oddly enough, even Willoughby (ibid., pp. 219ff.) recognizes this without seeing how the differences undercut his claims of dependence.

[423]William C. Grese, *Corpus Hermeticum XIII and Early Christian Literature* (Leiden: Brill, 1979), esp. pp. 55ff.

[424]See the discussions in Clark, *Selections*, p. 186; Machen, *Origin of Paul's Religion*, p. 243.

[425]Machen, *Origin of Paul's Religion*, p. 248.

[426]Ibid., pp. 263–64.

[427]Ibid., p. 263.

[428]Ibid., p. 264.

[429]Ibid., p. 265. It is equally important to notice the significant differences between the Hermetic writings and any alleged mysticism in the Johannine writings. As Ladd (*Theology*, p. 278) states, "This 'Johannine mysticism' is very different from the mysticism of Hellenistic religions as represented by the Hermetica where the worshipper becomes one with God in the sense of being deified. In John there is no merging of personalities or loss of human identity. There is no evidence that the Johannine mysticism involves ecstasy. Rather, it is mysticism of personal and ethical fellowship involving the will rather than the emotions."

[430]Machen, *Origin of Paul's Religion*, p. 261.

[431]See James M. Robinson, ed., *The Nag Hammadi Library in English* (San Francisco: Harper & Row, 1977).

[432] Yamauchi, "Pre-Christian Gnosticism," p. 130.

[433] Ibid., p. 135.

[434] Ibid., p. 141. See also Yamauchi, *"The Apocalypse of Adam*, Mithraism, and Pre-Christian Gnosticism" (esp. pp. 545, 562). See also Wilson, *Gnosis and the New Testament*, p. 139.

[435] See for example, Robinson, "Coptic Gnostic Library," pp. 377–80.

[436] Dunn, *Christology in the Making*, p. 99.

[437] Ibid.

[438] Yamauchi, *Pre-Christian Gnosticism*, p. 143.

[439] Ibid., pp. 148–49. Yamauchi devotes chapter 9 of his book to the question of Jewish Gnosticism.

[440] A Jewish source for Gnosticism is argued by G. W. MacRae in his article "The Jewish Background of the Gnostic Sophia Myth," *Novum Testamentum* 12 (1970): 86–101.

[441] Yamauchi, *Pre-Christian Gnosticism*, pp. 144–45.

[442] Ibid.

[443] This view is proposed by Walter Schmithals, *The Office of Apostle in the Early Church* (Nashville: Abingdon, 1969), p. 126.

[444] MacRae, "Jewish Background," p. 98.

[445] See L. Cerfaux, "Gnose préchrétienne et biblique," *Dictionnaire de la Bible, Supplément III* (1938), cols. 659–701. Bultmann found Gnosticism in Philo; see his *Primitive Christianity*, p. 163.

[446] See Yamauchi, *Pre-Christian Gnosticism*, p. 147.

[447] Robert McL. Wilson, "Philo of Alexandria and Gnosticism," *Kairos* 14 (1972): 213–19. The quote is from p. 215. See also Wilson, "Gnostic Origins," p. 210.

[448] See Grant, *Gnosticism and Early Christianity*.

[449] Wilson, *Gnosis and the New Testament*, p. 27.

[450] An example of still another theory developed to support a Jewish pre-Christian Gnosticism is the appeal to Jewish apocalypticism. See Yamauchi's evaluation of this in his *Pre-Christian Gnosticism*, pp. 156ff.

[451] Ibid., p. 162.

[452] For the general order of this section, I am indebted to several of Yamauchi's published discussions on the subject.

[453] Wilson, *Gnosis and the New Testament*, p. 9.

[454] Ibid., p. 24.

[455] A. D. Nock, "Gnosticism," *Harvard Theological Review* 57 (1964): 278. See also Casey, "Gnosis, Gnosticism," pp. 52–80 (esp. pp. 79–80).

[456] Compare Neill (*Interpretation,* p. 177): "There is a tendency to suppose that when any Gnostic word or phrase occurs in any document that is available to us, the whole of the Gnostic myth must have been present in the mind of the writer whoever he may have been. Clearly, this is an assumption which is more readily made than proved."

[457] Richardson, *Theology,* p. 41.

[458] Yamauchi, *Pre-Christian Gnosticism,* p. 173.

[459] See Schmithals, *Office of Apostle,* p. 229.

[460] Wilson, *Gnosis and the New Testament,* p. 7.

[461] Ibid., p. 77.

[462] See also Robert McL. Wilson, "Nag Hammadi and the New Testament," *New Testament Studies* 28 (1982): 289–302.

[463] Wilson, *Gnosis and the New Testament,* p. 76.

[464] Ibid., p. 71.

[465] Casey, "Gnosis, Gnosticism," p. 80.

[466] To view the possibility of miracles from the perspective of scholars who believe in an open universe, see C. S. Lewis, *Miracles: A Preliminary Study* (New York: Macmillan, 1951); Norman Geisler, *Miracles and Modern Thought* (Grand Rapids: Zondervan/Probe, 1982).

[467] See Nock, "Early Gentile Christianity," p. 83.

[468] Manson, *On Paul and John,* p. 136.

[469] Ibid.

[470] Ibid., pp. 136–37.

[471] Ibid.

[472] It is a pleasure to acknowledge with appreciation several scholars who were kind enough to comment on an early draft of this book. They include Edwin Yamauchi, Gordon Clark, William Lane, and Joseph Trafton. These men may not agree with every judgment expressed in this book, but their advice, when taken, improved the work immeasurably.

For Further Reading

It is not the purpose of this brief bibliography to cite all the relevant books and articles on this subject. That information can be gleaned from the extensive notes to the book. Rather, this list is given to direct the reader to works that support the position of the book.

Armstrong, A. H. **An Introduction to Ancient Philosophy.** Boston: Beacon, 1963.

Armstrong's book is the clearest and best-written introduction to ancient and Hellenistic philosophy available.

Clark, Gordon H. **Selections from Hellenistic Philosophy.** New York: Appleton-Century-Crofts, 1940.

Clark not only supplies lengthy selections from major Hellenistic thinkers but also provides helpful introductions that often relate the subject to Christianity.

Cullmann, Oscar. **The Christology of the New Testament.** Rev. ed. Philadelphia: Westminster, 1963.

Cullmann's account includes important criticisms of Bousset and others who argued that early Christianity's picture of Jesus was influenced by paganism.

Davies, W. D. and Daube, D., eds. **The Background of the New Testament and Its Eschatology.** Cambridge: Cambridge University Press, 1956.

This collection of scholarly essays contains a number of chapters that deal with questions raised in this book.

Kim, Seyoon. **The Origin of Paul's Gospel.** Grand Rapids: Eerdmans, 1982.

A Korean scholar updates the argument of Machen's Origin of Paul's Religion.

309

Machen, J. Gresham. **The Origin of Paul's Religion.** New York: Macmillan, 1925.

Still a classic in spite of its age, Machen's work is outdated for the most part only in its treatment of Gnosticism.

Marshall, I. Howard, ed. **New Testament Interpretation.** Grand Rapids: Eerdmans, 1977.

Another collection of essays, many of which are relevant to the concerns of this book.

Metzger, Bruce M. "Methodology in the Study of the Mystery Religions and Early Christianity." Chapter 1 in **Historical and Literary Studies: Pagan, Jewish, and Christian.** Grand Rapids: Eerdmans, 1968.

Required reading on the relationship between Christianity and the mystery religions.

Nock, A. D. "Early Gentile Christianity and Its Hellenistic Background." In **Essays on the Trinity and the Incarnation,** edited by A.E.J. Rawlinson. London: Longmans, Green, 1928.

As old as it is, Nock's essay is still relevant to the debate.

Rahner, Hugo. "The Christian Mystery and the Pagan Mysteries." In **Pagan and Christian Mysteries,** edited by Joseph Campbell. New York: Harper & Row, 1955.

Another indispensable source, this time by a Roman Catholic scholar.

Wagner, Günter. **Pauline Baptism and the Pagan Mysteries.** Edinburgh: Oliver and Boyd, 1967.

An extremely important book dealing with more than just baptism. It is full of much helpful material on Christianity's alleged dependence on the mystery religions.

Wilson, Robert McL. **Gnosis and the New Testament.** Philadelphia: Fortress, 1968.

One of many books and articles by a prominent British scholar on Christianity's alleged dependence on Gnosticism.

Yamauchi, Edwin. **Pre-Christian Gnosticism.** Grand Rapids: Eerdmans, 1973.

This is the first book anyone should read on the subject of Christianity and Gnosticism.

Index of Persons

312

Index of Subjects